Lewis Carroll: A Celebration

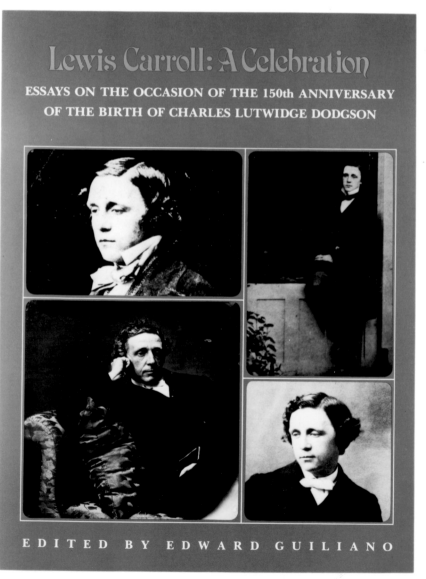

Lewis Carroll: A Celebration

ESSAYS ON THE OCCASION OF THE 150th ANNIVERSARY OF THE BIRTH OF CHARLES LUTWIDGE DODGSON

E D I T E D   B Y   E D W A R D   G U I L I A N O

Jacket design for LEWIS CARROLL: A Celebration edited by Edward Guiliano, published by Clarkson N. Potter.

Photographs of C. L. Dodgson through the years. *(Courtesy Graham Ovenden; Parrish Collection, Princeton University; Gernsheim Collection, University of Texas* (bottom)*)*

Lewis Carroll: A Celebration

ESSAYS ON THE OCCASION OF THE 150th ANNIVERSARY OF THE BIRTH OF CHARLES LUTWIDGE DODGSON

EDITED BY EDWARD GUILIANO

Clarkson N. Potter, Inc./Publishers   New York

DISTRIBUTED BY CROWN PUBLISHERS, INC.

Inquiries should be addressed to Clarkson N. Potter, Inc., One Park Avenue, New York, New York 10016

Printed in the United States of America

Published simultaneously in Canada by General Publishing Company Limited

Library of Congress Cataloging in Publication Data

Main entry under title:

Lewis Carroll, a celebration.

    Includes index.
    1. Carroll, Lewis, 1832-1898—Addresses, essays, lectures.   2.   Authors, English—19th century—Biography—Addresses, essays, lectures.   I. Guiliano, Edward.

PR4612.L453   1981   828'.809   81-8655

ISBN: 0-517-545578   AACR2

10 9 8 7 6 5 4 3 2 1

First Edition

Contents

Preface

Lewis Carroll survives, furthermore he flourishes, and that is the ultimate tribute to his genius. On the 150th anniversary of his birth, there is little doubt that Carroll has earned a place in the distinguished tradition of Shakespeare and Dickens. Like them, Lewis Carroll is a popular author of permanent value. His *Alice* books are classics, and like all great works of literature they repay readers with fresh insights and aesthetic rewards.

Charles Lutwidge Dodgson was born on January 27, 1832, in Daresbury, Cheshire, and resided the whole of his adult life at Christ Church, Oxford, where as the Reverend Charles L. Dodgson he served as a mathematics don, and as Lewis Carroll he wrote the children's books that have also appealed to adults since their publication. During his lifetime there would have been little reason to mention Carroll's name in the same breath as Shakespeare's or Dickens's. But the existence of this sesquicentennial collection of new essays on Carroll's life and art attests to his endurance, and by extension, to his place in the world of Shakespeare and Dickens. Today Carroll's impact on the popular culture is extensive, like that of England's two preeminent writers. All three continue to attract the attention of filmmakers, TV producers, stage directors, and not insignificantly, advertising directors. Also, they remain popular with armchair, student, and professional readers alike. And like that of Shakespeare and Dickens, Carroll's following is international. His works are widely translated and part of the cultural heritage of many non-English-speaking nations. The first translation of *Alice in Wonderland,* for example, was issued just four years after the book appeared in print, and now *Alice* has been translated into fifty-five languages.

But the profound impact of Carroll's art, like Shakespeare's and Dickens's, is especially noticeable in the areas of language and character. It is often said that after Shakespeare, Lewis Carroll is the most frequently quoted, or misquoted, author in the English language. Today journalists and politicians, logicians and literary critics, teachers and executives, have found an extraordinary number of contexts in which to quote Lewis Carroll. It is all, as Alice said, "curiouser and curiouser." " 'The time has come,' the Walrus said, 'To talk of many things: Of shoes—and ships—and sealing-wax—Of cabbages and kings.' " " 'Contrariwise,' continued Tweedledee, 'if it was so, it might be; and if it were so, it would be; but as it isn't, it ain't. That's logic.' "

And, apparently, today's world is remarkably ripe for Carroll's brand of logic. His metaphors and startling images are proving more applicable each day. "Faster! Faster," the White Queen tells Alice. "Here, you see, it takes all the running you can do, to keep in the same place." "You may call it 'nonsense' if you like, but I've heard nonsense, compared with which that would be as sensible as a dictionary!" Several of Carroll's words have, in fact, found their way into dictionaries—for example, chortle, galumph, and most recently boojum. And more than one of Carroll's humorous insights into the nature of language have been taken up in earnest by linguists. In Humpty Dumpty we have a forefather of modern linguistics, a specialist in semantics. " 'When I use a word,' Humpty Dumpty said, in a rather scornful tone, 'it means just what I choose it to mean—neither more nor less.' "

Humpty Dumpty, the White Rabbit, the Cheshire Cat, the Caterpillar, the Duchess, the Mad Hatter, the White Knight—like the list of quotable passages, the list of unforgettable characters Carroll shaped can go on and on. As Dickens did so many times, Carroll gave birth to characters who have since lived lives of their own, and with Alice in Wonderland, he created a character whose fame far exceeds that of her author—the staid and proper Victorian, the Oxford don and clergyman, the puzzle-loving and child-loving conformist, the teacher and mathematician, the photographer and letter writer, the paradoxical and whimsical bachelor at home in the world of children.

The Carroll/Dodgson duality continues to fascinate readers. How does one reconcile Carroll's mirth, whimsy, and nonsense with Dodgson's seriousness, dedication, and relentless logic? From what deep inner springs of imagination did Carroll's creations flow? The contributors to this anthology have attempted to understand and explain many facets of Carroll's enigmatic life and his extraordinary art. He was, after all, not only an enormously popular and imaginative writer but the most outstanding children's photographer of the nineteenth century, an unparalleled letter writer, an inspired though unskilled illustrator, and a gifted logician. In this volume Carroll's relationships with Ellen Terry and with John Tenniel, his obsession with order, his life in fin-de-siècle England, are all unfolded in new essays. The full scope of his literary output is explored in various essays ranging from commentaries on "the most inexhaustible tale in the world"—the *Alice* books—to *The Hunting of the Snark*, to the *Sylvie and Bruno* books, and to his brilliant but neglected mathematical/political pamphlets. His drawings and photographs are exhibited. Also, there are full studies of Carroll and the surrealists, of Carroll and Joyce, and assessments of his work in the traditions of the folktale, fairy tale, and modern novel.

The true sign of genius, according to Goethe, is posthumous productivity. I hope that this ranging anthology will be a fitting posthumous birthday tribute to Lewis Carroll and that readers everywhere will find much in it to enrich their appreciation of Carroll's life and art.

E.G.

The Actress and the Don: Ellen Terry and Lewis Carroll

MORTON N. COHEN

The Ellen Terry-Lewis Carroll relationship has vexed biographers since Carroll's death, more than eighty years ago. What, they all seek to know, was the basis of the friendship that lasted for thirty-five years? What was the attraction between the glittering beauty of the London stage and the shy Oxford don? Carroll's biographer Derek Hudson, after examining the evidence, came to this cautious conclusion: "That Lewis Carroll may at one period have been in some sense in love with her is a suggestion that cannot be disproved." [1] Phyllis Greenacre, in her psychoanalytical study of Carroll, suggests that his friendship with Miss Terry may have been a "shadowy" love affair. Such shadowy love affairs, she tells us, "are the frequent concomitants of unresolved oedipal attachments." [2] And Anne Clark, in her recent life of Carroll, takes the sympathetic, understanding view: "If Dodgson was a little in love with her," she writes, "he could surely be forgiven." [3]

Actually members of the Dodgson family were the first to plant the seeds of doubt about the relationship. Perhaps they themselves wanted to think that their Uncle Charles was capable of falling in love with a mature woman, a famous and accomplished actress at that. Perhaps they thought that by suggesting a love for Ellen Terry, they would take the spotlight off Dodgson's attachment to prepubescent girls. In any event, Stuart Collingwood, in writing the official life of his uncle, perpetuated the family myth that "a shadow of some disappointment lay over Lewis Carroll's life." [4] When the nephew was pressed, in later years, to explain what he meant by this statement, he answered that he remembered one of Dodgson's sisters telling him "that it was the family's opinion that Uncle Charles had had a disappointment in love, and that they thought . . . the lady in question was Ellen Terry." The nephew's explanation continues: "When Ellen Terry was just growing up—about 17—she was lovely beyond description . . . and it is highly probable that he fell in love with her; he may even have proposed to her." [5]

Langford Reed, who published his biography of Dodgson in 1932, got at least a glimpse of the carefully guarded Dodgson diaries before some of the volumes disappeared, and in his life of Dodgson he quotes a passage from those diaries that had not before seen the light of day and that does not appear in the diary volumes that survive. After a visit backstage to see Miss Terry, Dodgson thought about her life, it seems, and then reflecting on the subject of the actress's dresser, he mused: "I can imagine no more delightful occupation than brushing Ellen Terry's hair!" [6]

But in spite of that passage—and we have to rely on Langford Reed's assurance that it was there and on his care in transcribing it—we must question seriously whether Dodgson was in fact in love with Miss Terry. Was he even capable of loving her? The evidence that has emerged from the letters that Dodgson wrote to the actress (sixteen, at least, have survived, covering the years 1880 to 1894), the availability of the unpublished portions of the Dodgson diaries, and the numerous allusions to Miss Terry in letters that Dodgson wrote to others—all these help us to answer the questions raised above.[7]

We are so well acquainted with the outline of Dodgson's life that we need not repeat it here. But perhaps it will help to review the essentials of Ellen Terry's life. She was born in 1847, fifteen years after Dodgson, into a family of actors, and she grew up in the theater. She herself first acted at the age of nine, and by the time she was thirty-four, she was the highest-paid woman in Victorian England. She was an actress by nature and left an indelible mark on all the roles she portrayed, from Shakespearean heroines to ordinary Victorian maidens. Her striking physical beauty cast a spell on everyone who saw her: By all accounts, to see her was indeed to fall in love with her. There was something magical about her stage presence. One contemporary remembered that "when she first appeared the audience gasped—there was a silence, then thunders of applause . . . she seemed a creature of fire and air, she hovered over the stage without appearing to touch it." [8] Inevitably she became Henry Irving's leading lady, and their relationship lasted a quarter of a century.

Her personal life was not so successful. "How could anyone in his kind senses ask such a dear madwoman in marriage," her son later wrote—and yet she was married three times.[9] When she was seventeen, she married G. F. Watts, the middle-aged, testy pre-Raphaelite painter. He painted her portrait, but, we are told, never took her to bed. She left him after ten months of something less than wedded bliss and soon fled London and the stage to become the mistress of Edward Godwin, an architect. Godwin was clearly the passion of her life. She bore him her only two children, both out of wedlock. Their liaison lasted seven years. Then Godwin, it appears, tired of his beautiful companion and their children: He deserted them.

Carroll's 1865 photograph of Ellen Terry (Mrs. Watts) at age eighteen. *(Courtesy Berol Collection, New York University)*

Carroll's 1865 photograph of Ellen Terry. *(Courtesy Gernsheim Collection, University of Texas at Austin)*

Carroll's 1865 portrait of Terry family *(from left to right)*: Tom, Benjamin (father), Florence, Ellen, Kate, Charles, Marion, and Sarah (mother). *(Courtesy Berol Collection, New York University)*

Ellen Terry returned to the stage to support herself and her children, and it was then that she became the reigning queen of the English theater. Having been divorced by Watts while she was living with Godwin, she was now free to marry again; this time she wed an actor, one Charles Wardell, but he soon died. For a time she seemed content with her life on the stage, as Irving's leading lady, perhaps his mistress. But in 1907, when she was fifty-nine, she married one last time, again an actor, this one twenty-five years her junior. But this marriage also did not last: It fell apart after two years. Ellen Terry lived on to 1928, when she died at the age of eighty-one.

It was in the theater that Dodgson first came upon Ellen Terry, and indeed it was in the theater that their friendship took root. Contrary to Victorian custom, Dodgson was devoted to the theater as a civilized and civilizing pastime. His stand on the question shows distinct courage, especially when Samuel Wilberforce, Bishop of Oxford, the cleric who had ordained Dodgson, publicly denounced the theater as dangerous. Dodgson's interest in the stage never flagged; his entire life was punctuated by journeys to London expressly to see a play or two. It was inevitable that he would notice Ellen Terry. In fact, he noticed her in her first appearance on the London stage, as Mamillius in *The Winter's Tale,* at the Princess's Theatre on June 16, 1856, when she was all of nine years old and he twenty-four. Their friendship began eight years later and endured until Dodgson's death.

If we open Ellen Terry's autobiography, we find that almost all her memories of Dodgson are affectionate and respectful, many of them charming. She tells us that he gave her a copy of *Alice's Adventures in Wonderland,* and then, she adds, he "made a progress as the years went on through the whole [Terry] family." [10] She recalls that Dodgson came to see her act and wrote to her "to point out slips in the dramatist's logic which only he would ever have noticed! He did not even spare Shakespeare," she added. She writes of Dodgson's interest in young people who wanted to go onto the stage: "He *really* loved [children] . . . and put himself out for them. The children he knew who wanted to go on the stage were those who came under my observation, and nothing could have been more touching than his ceaseless industry on their behalf." [11] There was, indeed, a veritable parade of young ladies whom Dodgson brought or sent to Miss Terry, either for elocution lessons or as aspiring child-actresses, and if his kindness to these youngsters was "ceaseless," Miss Terry's was even more so, for without complaint or hesitation, she took them in, talked to them, gave them lessons, and on occasion hired them or got them hired to act.

Miss Terry recorded that Dodgson was "one of my earliest friends among literary folk," and she added, "I can't remember a time when I didn't know him. . . . He was as fond of me as he could be of anyone over the age of ten." [12]

If we turn to Dodgson's diaries, we find eighty-three entries about Ellen Terry. The first is, of course, his account of seeing her in her first stage appearance: "a beautiful little creature who played with remarkable ease and spirit" (I:88). From then on he made a point of seeing every play she appeared in. "The beautiful little Ellen Terry appeared [as Puck in *A Midsummer Night's Dream*]," he wrote on January 21, 1858, "making the most perfectly graceful little fairy I ever saw" (I:138). Seven years after he first laid eyes on her, Dodgson noted that "Mr. Tom Taylor knows the Misses Terry, and speaks very highly of them" (I:200). With his photography in mind, he added, "I think I must try to get *them* as sitters." But seventeen months passed before he actually called on the Terrys, presumably with an introduction from Mr. Taylor. The visit was a success, but he recorded that, alas, Ellen Terry, now Mrs. George Watts, was not present (I:224). His hope of meeting Ellen Terry led him to call again on the family on the following day: "Polly and Benjamin met me in the hall, and in the drawing-room I found Miss Kate Terry, Florence, and to my delight, the one I have always most wished to meet of the family, Mrs. Watts. Mr. Tom Taylor called in later to read Miss Terry some of her part in a MS. play . . . and I remained to listen. I was very much pleased with what I saw of Mrs. Watts—lively and pleasant, almost childish in her fun, but perfectly ladylike" (I:225). At the end of the diary entry for that day, Dodgson added, "I mark this day . . . with a white stone."

From then on he felt free to call on the Terrys, and call he did—frequently, on almost every visit he made to London. On April 7, 1865, he stayed to lunch and heard Ellen play and sing (I:228). Three months later, he brought his camera and photographed the Terry family; he also played Castle Croquet with them (I:233). And through all this time, he saw Ellen Terry act and often went backstage to call on her. On June 29, 1866, he recorded that he spent nearly four hours at the Terrys and again played Castle Croquet with them (I:245).

Then, quite suddenly, a change occurs. Mention of Ellen Terry continues, but less frequently and only in connection with the stage. To be sure, he still praises her. "Her acting is simply *wonderful*," he writes after seeing her in Charles Reade's drama about the Tichborne Case, *The Wandering Heir* (II:329), and in the following year, "Mrs. Watts . . . was a perfect treat" in Lord Lytton's play entitled *Money* (II:341). He continues to be a devoted fan of the actress and returns to see her a second and a third time, even when she is acting in dull, uninspired Victorian melodramas. After seeing her in W. G. Wills's *Olivia* (an adaptation of *The Vicar of Wakefield*), he wrote, "Altogether I have not had a greater dramatic treat for a long time . . . she acted with a sweetness and pathos that moved some of the audience (nearly including myself) to tears" (II:370). On another occasion, "Ellen Terry as Ophelia was simply perfect" (II:377). But through all these entries, we have no suggestion of any personal meetings at all.

The estrangement endured until June 1879, until Ellen Terry, divorced by her first husband, had married her second, Charles Wardell. We then read this in Dodgson's diary: "I called on the Wardells, to renew the friendship with Ellen Terry, which has now been broken off for twelve years. . . . She was as charming as ever, and I was much pleased with her husband. . . . I also liked her two children . . ." (II:380). From this point on, the entries are frequent again, and again the friendship bloomed. In 1881, for instance, Dodgson took one of his favorite little girls, Agnes Hull, to see Ellen Terry in a double bill of Dumas's *The Corsican Brothers* and Tennyson's *The Cup.* "I had told Mrs. Wardell I was going to bring Agnes, and had suggested how much it would delight her to have the book of *The Corsican Brothers* . . . sent round to her, inscribed with her name: and at the end of the first act the gift was brought, with a charming inscription, and accompanied by a bouquet of violets, which Agnes declares she will keep the rest of her life!" (II:393).

On another occasion, Miss Terry managed to get Dodgson two seats in the stalls when none was otherwise available, so that he could see her for a second time in *The Cup* (II:395). By January 1883, Dodgson felt on such good terms with her that he took the liberty of suggesting changes in her stage business. "I urged on Mrs. Wardell to get the 'church' scene in *Much Ado* so far altered as to have the love-scene *outside,* and she said she would tell Mr. Irving" (II:414). At another time, Dodgson took a young cousin of his, Minna Quin, to see Miss Terry, in the hope that the famous actress would suggest how Minna could get employment in the theater. Ellen Terry hired the girl on the spot as an extra. "She will 'walk-on' in the Cathedral scene in *Faust,*" Dodgson noted (II:510).

Dodgson continued to see Miss Terry in all her stage appearances, and, from time to time, took his child-friends backstage to chat with her. On August 21, 1897, less than five months before his death, he recorded his last meeting with his actress friend. On that occasion, he took another child-friend, Dolly Rivington, to Winchelsea, where Ellen Terry was then living. Miss Terry sent a carriage to meet them, and they spent the afternoon to-gether in her garden. For part of the time, Dodgson tells us, Ellen Terry and Dolly Rivington were swinging, side by side, in hammocks (II:537–38). The image of his child friend with Miss Terry by her side is the one that Dodgson took to the grave with him the following January. The diary ends on Decem-ber 23, just before Christmas 1897, less than a month before Dodgson suc-cumbed to pneumonia.

We have yet another source of information about the friendship between the actress and the don: the surviving letters. Certainly they corresponded during their thirty-five year friendship. In fact, Dodgson, a compulsive letter writer by nature, did write Ellen Terry long and frequent letters. She must have replied in kind. Dodgson was a hoarder of papers, letters, things, and one would expect him to have kept all the letters he received from so eminent a friend. But he was also a man of strong Victorian sensibility, and he surely destroyed a good many letters, along with the photographs and negatives we know for a fact that he destroyed, lest by keeping them, he would ultimately allow them to fall into strange hands. It is safe to say, knowing Dodgson as we do, that at one point in his life, probably when he was beginning to realize he had passed middle age, he destroyed a good many letters that Ellen

Terry had written to him, letters, one feels sure, he would have liked to have kept. The few letters that he did keep came down through the Dodgson family, and though they were sold at auction in 1932, copies were preserved in the family archives. Sadly, however, they are not very interesting; they are not personal letters, and perhaps they survived only for that reason.

On the other hand, Miss Terry certainly did not destroy the letters she received from Dodgson. When she wrote her autobiography, some ten years after his death, she had his letters before her and quoted from a few. And when the ingenious Langford Reed came along to write a life of Lewis Carroll in the 1930s, he not only got the Dodgson family to let him have a look through the unpublished diaries, but he managed also to charm Ellen Terry's daughter, Edith Craig, into letting him "examine many of the letters which the author of 'Alice in Wonderland' wrote to her distinguished mother." [13] But Reed quoted only bits and pieces of a total of six letters, and one yearns for more. Exactly what happened to those letters is not clear. The actress's daughter lived until 1947, but my guess is that, for one reason or another, she did not retain the letters to the end. Had she done so, they probably would have remained in the Terry-Craig family and ultimately found their way to the Ellen Terry Museum just outside London. I believe that Miss Craig sold those letters soon after Mr. Reed saw them. In any event, by the early 1950s, when Derek Hudson wrote his life of Lewis Carroll, he lamented: "The original letters that [Dodgson] wrote to [Miss Terry] do not appear to have survived." [14]

When I began the search for Lewis Carroll letters, in the early 1960s, I naturally resolved to do what I could to find the letters to Miss Terry. I could not agree with Mr. Hudson that they had not survived; no one would destroy a Lewis Carroll letter at that late date, and certainly not one to the queen of the English theater. And so I searched, in all the obvious places, among the various Dodgson family collections (after all, Miss Craig might have sent the letters back to the family, or the family could secretly have bought them back), and then I approached the descendants of the Terrys and the Craigs, making something of a nuisance of myself.

But no, the letters were not to be found. In the autumn of 1963, I returned to New York from a year's sabbatical leave in England feeling glum and defeated. But not for long, for like Alice, who found the Red Queen by walking in the opposite direction, I found a group of Dodgson's letters to Ellen Terry only after I had given up hope—and I found them not very far away from where I had begun my search. They were, in fact, part of the private collection of Arthur A. Houghton, Jr., and he very kindly permitted me to examine them in his office on Fifth Avenue in New York City and, at my request, supplied me with photographs of them all.

The letters, though not so numerous or so frequent as we would wish them to be, throw a good deal of light upon the relationship that existed between the actress and the don. They certainly go beyond the boundaries of mere acquaintance, and they reveal much of the two persons involved. And as we might expect and even hope, they possess that characteristic Dodgson-esque quality we have come to know so well. Here is one he wrote to Miss Terry from Christ Church on November 13, 1890.

My *dear* old friend,

(*N.B.* "old" doesn't mean "old in *years*" but "old in *friendship*"!) You are really too nice and kind for anything! What *is* one to do with a friend who does about 100 times more than you ask them to do? The very utmost I hoped for was that, after seeing Isa [Bowman] and ascertaining that she had some "teachableness" in her, you would tell me that, if I applied to the manager of such-and-such a theatre, he would give me the address of some good teachers of elocution. It never crossed my thoughts that you would give her lessons *yourself!* Well, you have earned (if such things can in any way repay you) the deep gratitude of *one* old friend, and the rapturous love of *one* enthusiastic child.

And so you have found out that secret—one of the deep secrets of Life—that all, that is really *worth* the doing, is what we do for *others?* Even as the old adage tells us, "What I spent, that I lost; what I gave, that I had." Casuists have tried to twist "doing good" into another form of "doing evil," and have said "you get pleasure yourself by giving this pleasure to another: so it is merely a refined kind of selfishness, as your own pleasure is a motive for what you do." I say "it is *not* selfishness, that my own pleasure should be *a* motive so long as it is not *the* motive that would outweigh the other, if the two came into collision?" The "selfish man" is he who would still do the thing, even if it harmed others, so long as it gave *him* pleasure: the "unselfish man" is he who would still do the thing, even if it gave him no pleasure, so long as it pleased *others.* But, when both motives pull together, the "unselfish man" is *still* the unselfish man, even though his own pleasure *is* one of his motives! I am very sure that God takes real *pleasure* in seeing his children happy! And, when I read such words as "looking unto Jesus, the author and finisher of our faith, who *for the joy that was set before him* endured the cross," I believe them to be *literally true.*

And so in your case, dear friend; I believe that it is real joy to *you* to know that you are filling, full to overflowing, Isa's little cup of happiness; and yet there is no shadow of *selfishness* in what you are doing, but that it is pure, unadulterated, generous *kindness.*

I really believe your great kindness will *not* be wasted on my dear little friend, but that she will take all possible pains to do credit to your teaching.

I wish you could have seen her little sister Nellie play in *Editha's Burglar!* In all my theatrical experience, I have hardly ever seen anything so simple and so sweet.

One thing that made it impossible for me to *bring* Isa to see you, is that I have been ill for the last fortnight, with an aguish attack, and a prisoner to my fireside. But when I *am* able to come to town again, I hope to call, and thank you viva voce for all you are doing for her.

Love to Edy. If she at all desires to have a "stamp-case," she has only to throw out a hint! I'm a capital hand at taking hints!

By the way, I wonder if you ever received a copy of *Sylvie and Bruno,* which I sent to you December 12, 1889? If it failed to reach you, I will send you another copy, as I want you to have the book. Believe me always

Yours affectionately,
C. L. Dodgson
(II:812–14)

And another, also from Christ Church, dated June 7, 1894.

My dear Miss Ellen Terry,

I want to thank you, as heartily as words can do it, for your true kindness in letting me bring Dolly behind the scenes to you. You will know, without my telling you, what an *intense* pleasure you thereby gave to a warm-hearted girl, and what love (which I fancy you value more than mere *admiration:* I know *I* do!) you have won from her. Her wild longing to try the Stage will not, I think, bear the cold light of day, when once she has tried it, and has realised what a lot of hard work, and weary waiting, and "hope deferred" it involves. She doesn't, so far as I know, absolutely *need* (as Norah does) to earn money for her own support. But I fancy she will find life rather a *pinch,* unless she can manage to do *something* in the way of earning money. So I don't like to advise her strongly *against* it, as I would with any one who had no such need.

Also, thank you, thank you, with all my heart, for all your great and constant kindness to Norah. She *does* write so brightly and gratefully about all you do for her and say to her! I was very nearly writing a line to Mr. Irving, to thank him for his most welcome proposal that Norah should stay on: but on second thoughts, never having had the pleasure of meeting him, I will not trouble him with a letter. Perhaps you will *tell* him some time, will you?, how grateful I am.

Once I wrote to you about *Faust,* and was so fortunate, I fear, as to vex you a little, by a remonstrance (probably very unskilfully worded) about the "business" in the chamber scene. I only allude to it again because I noticed the other day, that you have quite altered the "business," and now wholly omit what I had feared might make some of the audience uneasy. Would you mind telling me, some time, whether the alteration is a permanent one, or merely an accidental difference that day; and, if permanent, whether the change is connected at all with my letter?

Our interview the other day was *awfully* short! That isn't *at all* the sort of interview I like best with old friends. Tête-à-tête's are what I like best. Now that I have entered on the stage of being a "lean and slippered pantaloon," and no longer dread the frown of Mrs. Grundy, I have taken to giving tête-à-tête dinner-parties—the guest being, in most cases, a lady, of age varying from 12 to 67 (the maximum I have yet had): and they are *very* pleasant! If *you* were staying in Oxford, I really think (however incredible it may sound) that I should have the "cheek" to ask *you* to come and dine so!

Would you give my love to Norah, when next you see her, and accept the same yourself from

Your affectionate old friend,
Charles L. Dodgson

Oh, and heaps of thanks for treating Norah's sisters to a sight of *Faust.* You have brightened *their* lives also.

(II:1025–26)

They are, you see, delightful letters. But they do not, in fact, answer the critical questions we raised earlier. A great many more letters must have passed between Miss Terry and Mr. Dodgson than those that have come to light. The earliest letter we have is dated January 1, 1889, twenty-four years after Dodgson first saw Ellen Terry act and sixteen years after he first met her. Knowing Dodgson as we do, we know that he wrote her a good many letters during those earlier years. The letters we lack might tell us more about Dodgson's earlier attitude, even perhaps his feelings, toward the actress. And the letters we have do nothing to explain the reason why the relationship was, at one point, to use Dodgson's own phrase, "broken off."

Still another source of information about the friendship presents itself and begs to be tapped. Among the four thousand Dodgson letters that I have collected in the past twenty years, Ellen Terry's name appears frequently— her name, in fact, appears much more frequently than do letters addressed directly to her. Dodgson has reason for discussing Miss Terry with some of his child-friends and with some of their mothers. The letters where he writes about her to others are interesting for the facts they supply; but they are also interesting for psychological reasons. And it is in one of these letters, when Dodgson writes to the mother of one of his recently acquired young girl friends, that he tells us outright the reason for the twelve-year "break" in his friendship with Ellen Terry, and in doing this he reveals, as though impelled by some psychological imperative, the intricate workings of his mind.

In January 1894 Dodgson went to see a young lady friend named Edith Lucy play Bianca in an amateur production of *The Taming of the Shrew*. Two months later, we learn from the diary that "Edith Lucy came to tea [in his rooms at Christ Church], bringing a new friend for me, Miss Dolly Baird [who had played Petruchio in the same amateur production]. She is very pleasant: she wishes to try the Stage" (II:506–508, 510). By now, we can anticipate the course of events that would follow. Indeed, Dodgson would turn to his friend Ellen Terry and plead Dolly's case with her, notwithstanding that Miss Terry was, almost at that very moment, engaging Dodgson's cousin Minna Quin as an extra. Within the month of Dolly Baird's initial visit to Christ Church, Dodgson spends two hours one day on a visit to Dolly's parents, and on the next day, he writes Dolly's mother this letter.

Christ Church, Oxford
April 12, 1894

Dear Mrs. Baird,

There are two questions that I want to put before you for consideration.

The first is as to that friend of mine to whom Dolly wishes to be introduced. I have now introduced to her four of the daughters of my friends of ages between 18 and 25; but in every case, *before* doing so, I told the mother the history of my friend and asked her whether, now she knew all the circumstances, she still wished her daughter to be introduced. In each case the answer was "Yes." So now, before giving any more promises to introduce Dolly, I would like to know what *you* think about it.

If you already know what is popularly said against my friend (which is usually a good deal more than the truth) and, if knowing it, you still wish Dolly to be introduced, I am quite satisfied and no more need be said.

If you do not know of any such tales, current in society, then I think I had better come and tell you the true history (you yourself, I mean; I had rather not talk about the matter to your daughters) and then you can settle what you wish to be done.

The other question is, may Dolly come and dine with me? I ask this, not knowing your views as to "Mrs. Grundy." And you may be sure I shall not feel in the least hurt if you think it best to say "No." It is only in these last two or three years that I have ventured on such unique and unconventional parties. Winifred Stevens was my first guest.

If you say "Yes" and will name a day (I've no engagements) I would come for her about 5½ and would escort her back at any hour you named (but I hope you would fix it as late as you can). Believe me

Sincerely yours,
C. L. Dodgson
(II:1014–15)

For some reason, probably because he was extremely busy these days, Dodgson did not call on Mrs. Baird to tell her the story of Ellen Terry's life, as he had done in the previous four cases. This time, he wrote it down and sent it to Mrs. Baird. The account survives. This is what Dodgson wrote about Ellen Terry:

When she was scarcely more than a child (17, I think), a man nearly three times her age professed to be in love with her. The match was pushed on by well meaning friends who thought it a grand thing for her. From the first, I don't think she had a fair chance of learning her new duties. Instead of giving her a home of her own he went on living as a guest with an elderly couple and the old lady was constantly exasperating the poor child by treating her as if she were still in the schoolroom and she, just like a child, used to go into fits of furious passion.

Quarrels began at once and very soon a separation was agreed on. He cynically told his friends that he found he had never *loved* her; it had only been a passing fancy. He agreed to make her an annual allowance so long as she lived respectably.

This she did for a while, then she rebelled and accepted the offered love (of course without ceremonial of marriage) of another man.

I honestly believe her position was, from her point of view, this:

"I am tied by *human* law to a man who disowns his share of what ought to be a *mutual* contract. He never loved me and I do not believe, in God's sight, we are man and wife. Society expects me to live, till this man's death, as if I were single and to give up all hope of that form of love for which I pine and shall never get from *him*. This other man loves me as truly and faithfully as any lawful husband. If the marriage ceremony were *possible* I would insist on it before living with him. It is *not* possible and I will do without it."

I allow freely that she was headstrong and wild in doing so; and her real *duty* was to accept the wreck of her happiness and live (or if necessary die) *without* the love of a man. But I do not allow that her case resembled *at all* that of those poor women who, without any pretence of *love,* sell themselves to the first comer. It much more resembles the case of those many women who are living as faithfully and devotedly as lawful wives without having gone through any ceremony and who *are,* I believe, married in *God's* sight though not in Man's.

A lady (wife of a clergyman) to whom (before I would introduce her daughter to my friend) I told this story said, "She has broken the law of man; she has *not* broken the law of God."

She lived with this man for some years and he *is* the father of her son and daughter. Then came the result she must have known was possible if not probable and which perhaps her mad conduct deserved; the man deserted her and went abroad.

When her lawful husband found out what she had done, of course he sued for and got a divorce. Then of course she was, in the eye of the law, free to be legally married and if only the other man had been as true as she, I have no doubt, meant to be to him, they would have married and it would have gradually been forgotten that the children were born before the ceremony.

All this time I held no communication with her. I felt that she had [so] entirely sacrificed her social position that I had no desire but to drop the acquaintance. Then an actor offered her marriage and they were married. It was a most generous act, I think, to marry a woman with such a history and a *great* addition to this generosity was his allowing the children to assume *his* surname.

The actor's father, a clergyman, so entirely approved his son's conduct that he came from the North of England to perform the ceremony. This second marriage put her, in the eyes of Society, once more in the position of a respectable woman. And then I asked her mother to ask her if she would like our friendship to begin again and she said "yes." And I went and called on her and her husband.

It really looked as if the misery of her life was *over.* But another misery came on of quite another kind. The man drank. She knew he was addicted to it before she married him but she fancied (very foolishly, I fear) she could cure him. This got worse and worse till they had to live apart and I believe he drank himself to death.

So she is now a widow.

(II:1015–16)

Did Mrs. Baird permit the Reverend C. L. Dodgson to introduce her daughter to the actress Ellen Terry? Certainly. And, just for the record, Dolly Baird went on to become a successful actress herself and later married Henry Irving's actor son, Henry Brodribb Irving.

But what about Dodgson and his relationship with Ellen Terry? What about that letter to Mrs. Baird? For one thing, it answers some of our earlier questions. We know now the reason for the twelve-year break in the friendship. It occurred—not because Miss Terry went into retirement, or because Miss Terry shunned Dodgson's affection or friendship, not because Dodgson thought that Miss Terry would prefer to be left alone. No, the break came because Dodgson himself decided to "drop the acquaintance." The letter also clears up the question of a possible marriage proposal—or to be more accurate an *im*possible marriage proposal. She was, we remember, already married when Dodgson first met her, and the letter to Mrs. Baird makes it clear that her marital difficulties did not bring Dodgson closer to her. They drove him away.

But how does one reconcile the letter to Mrs. Baird, calling Ellen Terry "headstrong" and "wild," telling Mrs. Baird that he had dropped Miss Terry because she had so "entirely sacrificed her social position"—how does one reconcile that letter with the admiring entries in his diaries and with the affectionate letters he wrote to her?

One explanation is the religious one. Dodgson the clergyman, Dodgson the devout servant of God, which he certainly was, was especially sensitive to the sacraments, and even though Miss Terry was a friend, she had, after all, violated the sacrament of matrimony.

But perhaps that is not a satisfactory explanation, for in the letter to Mrs. Baird, Dodgson takes the position that she has sinned against man, not against God.

The indictment on social grounds is more convincing, especially if we take a look at Charles Dodgson, proper Victorian gentleman. During his entire adult life Dodgson was formal to a fault, punctiliously correct in all his dealing with all people, whether they were blood relatives, friends, acquaintances, professional associates, or merchants. On principle he never addressed an adult outside his family by a first name. Social conventions absolutely ruled his life: He lived by them and expected everyone else to do so too. As the years passed, moreover, he became more and more difficult, uncompromising in attitude and in behavior, more prickly, more prudish. He could not abide off-color stories and stormed out of Common Room when they were told. He wrote chidingly to clergymen who, in the course of a sermon, allowed themselves a pun or an amusing anecdote. Time and again he stalked out of the theater in the midst of a performance when he felt a breach of decorum had occurred on the stage. He even made Ellen Terry "furious" once by criticizing her in *Faust,* when, as Margaret, she undressed her child in full view of the audience. A clergyman so entirely bound in as Dodgson was by Victorian strictures might not be able to rise above them in his relationship with an actress. His propriety might indeed eclipse his kindness.

But even the argument that Dodgson became uncharitable under the pressure of social convention is not, to my mind, altogether satisfying. There is a deeper psychological explanation for the harsh judgments he makes of Ellen Terry in the letter to Mrs. Baird. Dodgson was fully aware that his preference for female child-friends created suspicions in some minds. But his friendships with young girls were so important to his happiness—even to his well-being—that he never even entertained the possibility of giving them up. On the contrary, he nurtured them more and more, especially as he grew older and they grew fewer. Clearly nothing in his life was more important: They constituted his ideal reality. For him they were pure, they were sacred, they were indispensable. But he knew full well that because these friendships were unconventional, in order for them to exist and flourish, he had to live an impeccably conventional life, a life beyond criticism. What is more, he had to have more than his neighbor's approval; he had to have his own approval. And given the uncompromising nature of his character, there must never enter into his plans or his actions the slightest deviation from the righteous path. If he permitted a fall from grace in his own life, he would have to permit it in others. He made no room for exceptions anywhere.

Dodgson, consciously or not, had to choose between Ellen Terry, the tainted woman, and his virginal child-friends. His letter to Mrs. Baird tells us his choice in no uncertain terms. His relationship with Miss Terry was real and, I believe, filled with genuine respect and affection on both sides. But hardly love. Charles Dodgson's romantic attachments were reserved exclusively for his young friends, and not even Ellen Terry could be allowed to cast a shadow of impropriety upon that most important area of his life. He valued her friendship, but he required the unspoiled friendships with his young friends.

Is this, then, the whole story of the actress and the don? Isn't there more to know? Yes, certainly there is more. Many more of the letters he wrote to Ellen Terry must still exist somewhere, and I live in hope of someday uncovering them. They will be fascinating to read and to publish. But they will not tell us anything about Dodgson or his feelings for Ellen Terry that we do not already know. They were good friends, the actress and the don, they had much in common and performed many kindnesses for one another. But the relationship never transcended friendship, never entered the shimmering pool of romantic love.

NOTES

1. Derek Hudson, *Lewis Carroll* (London: Constable, 1954), p. 198; 2nd ed. (1976), p. 167.
2. Phyllis Greenacre, *Swift and Carroll: A Psychoanalytic Study of Two Lives* (New York: International Universities Press, 1955), p. 143.
3. Anne Clark, *Lewis Carroll* (London: J. M. Dent & Sons, 1979), p. 146.
4. Stuart Dodgson Collingwood, *The Life and Letters of Lewis Carroll* (London: T. Fisher Unwin, 1898; New York: The Century Co., 1899), p. 355.
5. Quoted in Hudson, *Lewis Carroll,* 1st ed., p. 191.
6. Langford Reed, *The Life of Lewis Carroll* (London: W. & G. Foyle, 1932), p. 90.
7. All the Dodgson letters to Miss Terry that I have found (a few of which appear in this essay) appear in full, with more extensive biographical material and annotations, in *The Letters of Lewis Carroll,* ed. Morton N. Cohen with the assistance of Roger Lancelyn Green, 2 vols. (London: Macmillan; New York: Oxford Univ. Press, 1979). Quotations from Dodgson's diaries that appear in this essay come from *The Diaries of Lewis Carroll,* ed. Roger Lancelyn Green, 2 vols. (London: Cassell, 1953; New York: Oxford Univ. Press, 1954). All citations from these sources will be given in the text, following the quotations.
8. W. Graham Robertson, *Time Was* (London: Hamish Hamilton, 1931), p. 287.
9. Edward Gordon Craig, *Ellen Terry and Her Secret Self* (London: Sampson Low, Marston & Co., n.d.), p. 50.
10. Ellen Terry, *The Story of My Life* (New York: Doubleday, Page & Co., 1909), p. 384.
11. Ibid., p. 386.
12. Ibid., p. 201.
13. Reed, *The Life of Lewis Carroll,* p. 80.
14. Hudson, *Lewis Carroll,* 1st ed., p. 196.

Blessed Rage:
Lewis Carroll and the Modern
Quest for Order

DONALD RACKIN

What should we make of a man who for fifty years kept a meticulous register of the contents of every letter he wrote or received—summaries of well over 100,000 letters? Of a man who maintained a record of the many luncheons and dinners he gave throughout a sociable lifetime, with diagrams showing where each guest sat and lists of just what dishes were served? Of a man who threatened to break off relations with his publisher of thirty years' standing because he found slight imperfections in the eighty-four thousandth copy of one of his popular children's books, then in print for twenty years? These are a few of the curious facts that shape our understanding of Charles Lutwidge Dodgson, that religious Oxford don, obsessive and conservative, who denied publicly throughout his life that he had anything to do with those masterpieces of mad, nonsensical disorder signed by a comic genius called Lewis Carroll.

Wherever we look, the biographical evidence indicates that Dodgson was passionately devoted to order in his everyday affairs and that his rage for order sometimes even bordered on the pathological. But he was by no means unique: We recognize the type all around us. People like Dodgson, people who manifest their extraordinary need for order by obsessively regulating their everyday lives, seem also to manifest through this behavior a deep-seated anxiety about the messiness that surrounds us, an anxiety about the morally random nature of existence. On guard against this apparently mindless chaos that threatens their beliefs and their very sanity, they fill their waking lives with artificial structure—with manufactured systems and rules their wills impose on all the disorderly matter and events they inevitably encounter.

Scientific studies demonstrating the strict mechanical order in nature, like Darwin's explanations of nature's puzzling randomness, variation, and waste (*The Origin of Species,* by the way, was published less than two years before

Dodgson told the first Alice story to his beloved Alice Liddell), cannot even begin to dispel such troubled people's desperate sense of underlying anarchy. Indeed, these troubled souls are likely to find in theories like Darwin's further evidence of ultimate moral chaos; for such strict mechanical order in nature offers little human comfort, little or no power to resolve the anxieties we can suffer in contemplating the morally meaningless process that is nature and our only home. Instead of finding in Darwinian and post-Darwinian science some solution to the metaphysical problems of apparently random natural variety, these obsessively orderly people—and by no means are they always scientifically naive—might very well find there objective, daytime corrobora- tions of their worst nightmares: a chilling panorama of the pointless, mind- less, amoral, and inescapable mechanisms in which science has now placed them firmly and forever. And they might easily find themselves—in their need for a corresponding moral pattern, for individual or collective human significance—alone, terrifyingly alone in a careless, indifferent, absurd uni- verse. When Alice in her Wonderland cries because she is, as she says, "so *very* tired of being all alone here!" [1] she pines not only for the human companion- ship she has lost, but also for some familiar signposts of intelligible order that her fellow humans dream or construct for themselves in their darkness above nature's ultimate emptiness. The religious and metaphysical assumptions that once answered the basic human need for orderly and permanent expla- nations and reasons beyond the reach of reason had thinned out and van- ished for many Victorians during their very lifetimes, destroyed by a natural, childlike curiosity like Darwin's—and like Alice's. The resulting void was terrifying.

Thus, the broadly operative teleological vision that found or mytholo- gized an orderly metaphysical structure within nature's bewildering multi- plicity, fecundity, and waste was swept away in the nineteenth century by modern science hitting its full stride, an inescapable science that now began to demonstrate conclusively the true cold order of nature. Like religion, natu- ral history could no longer serve as a refuge for those who searched for the warm comforts of an intelligible moral pattern in their physical environment. The deep need for such order that Dodgson expressed overtly in his life and covertly in his imaginative works could no longer be satisfied by those genial forays into shapely nature and natural history in which genteel English ama- teurs had indulged before Darwin. It might therefore be symbolically impor- tant that Dodgson's hobbies were usually ordered not naturally, but mechanically—photography, music boxes, mechanical toys, cerebral puzzles and games. In his conscious pastimes at least, Dodgson was wise enough to avoid what his own Cheshire Cat feels is unavoidable—going among mad people—wise enough to avoid journeys to the natural substratum, to that threatening underground beneath his orderly, civilized, conventionally reli- gious existence.

But in Carroll's great and honest literary fantasies, games and toys will not suffice: The ends of his *Alice* games are arbitrary and forced, the search for the Snark is doomed to failure, the Riddle of the Raven and the Writing

Desk—that is, the connection between predatory, amoral nature and polite civilization, between Nature and the Word—has no answer. His human and animal creatures, aside perhaps from Alice, symbolize a *permanent* confusion—not the merely physical, and thus solvable, puzzles of something like Darwin's Galapagos Islands creatures. The explanations that Carroll's fantasies seem to call for from within nature will *never* be found. There can be no *telos,* no final goal or ultimate "meaning" within Alice's biological nature or her natural surroundings: Her natural curiosity and her human need for what she calls "the meaning of it all" (p. 86) make her, like us, a permanent stranger to her natural environment. She will never attain that Eden she calls "the loveliest garden you ever saw" (p. 10). The creatures she meets will always go round and round their mad tea tables and pointless caucus rings, with no possible rationale or goal, no final end to their circles—graphic metaphors for the Darwinian model of nature's instinctual, unthinking, amoral, and endless round of self-preservation and of the permanent schism between the workings of nature and the human mind's need for final meaning. Such comic vignettes epitomize and focus the chaos that pervades the *Alice*s and *The Snark:* Their games are essentially ruleless, circular, and without end—games, undoubtedly, for "mad people."

The fault here lies, of course, in life itself. When Alice complains to the Cheshire Cat that the croquet game seems to have no rules, she couples this with "and you've no idea how confusing it is all the things being alive" (p. 67). A cat literally has no idea of this confusion, but we humans certainly do. For after Darwin, life itself becomes almost by definition a maddening moral confusion. The lovable imp Bruno in Carroll's *Sylvie and Bruno Concluded* (1893), seeing the letters "E-V-I-L" arranged by Sylvie on a board as one of his "lessons" and asked by Sylvie what they spell, exclaims, "Why it's 'LIVE,' backwards!" The narrator sympathetically adds, "(I thought it was, indeed)." [2] Carroll critics often cite this passage as a clue to Dodgson's psychology; but they generally miss its more direct and crucial relationship to Carroll's "backwards" literary fantasies—to the evil confusion in all the living things being alive, to the darkness and the old chaos inherent in living and dying nature after Darwin's simple biological vision has settled on the world, after innocent, childish Darwinian curiosity has enticed us down the rabbit-hole and behind our manufactured, anthropomorphic looking-glasses.

Carroll's comedy, then, contributes to the final destruction of a sustaining vision of nature and human nature in harmony, moving meaningfully according to divine rules toward some divine end. Such a vision hopefully concluded the chief philosophical poem of the age, Tennyson's *In Memoriam* (1837–50). This poem ends with the assertion that the human race (along with all natural creation) moves inexorably along a clear path toward a higher state of being and consciousness, where nature will make complete moral sense "like an open book" and where, ultimately, the seemingly mindless, amoral multiplicity and waste of "Nature red in tooth and claw" will attain the coherent singleness of a cosmos lovingly designed and justly ruled by one God.

> That God, which ever lives and loves,
> One god, one law, one element,
> And one far-off divine event,
> To which the whole creation moves.

The natural moral progress, the sense of unitary, purposeful, God-given order and natural motion within an ultimate rest celebrated here by Tennyson (and by Tennyson's stunning music) were by mid-century already a kind of outdated, forced, wishful thinking for many intellectuals (and probably for Tennyson himself). And, among other things, the *Alice* books and *The Snark* should be understood as representing the completion of this disillusionment— a strangely comical announcement of a new age of dark human consciousness.

Indeed, in Wonderland the sort of progressive evolutionism voiced at the end of *In Memoriam* and echoed in much conventional Victorian literature is treated with particular scorn: For example, a baby can devolve into a pig as easily as a pig can evolve into a baby. In Carroll's comic vision, motion is mere motion without first cause or final goal. And despite Alice's queening and the checkmate in looking-glass chess, no one really wins by progressing logically and by deliberately reaching some known and desired end [3]—or everyone wins, as in the endlessly circular Caucus Race, which in itself nonsensically destroys the very grounds of all teleology. Alice, of course, does progress, but only toward a recognition that she must deny her frighteningly vivid perceptions of nature's endless, careless, amoral, and unprogressive dance. The final chapter of *Wonderland* is called appropriately "Alice's Evidence," and the subtitle of all *Looking-Glass* is *and what Alice found there.* Both titles underscore the fact that Alice gains the evidence necessary to impel her to end her threatening dreams.[4]

In order to survive, Alice—like the orderly Charles Dodgson—must create a meaningful world out of the morally unintelligible void, and often in opposition to clear evidence from the natural world of which we are an inseparable part. Such order is thus made *in spite;* and the spiteful element in Dodgson's rejections of disorder (like his spiteful rejections of babies and little boys because of their natural messiness) remains never far from the surface of his fantasies. Alice's own spitefulness ("Who cares for *you.* . . . You're nothing but a pack of cards!" [p. 97], for example) is one of Carroll's principal means to make her characterization believably human. It also helps explain why modern readers frequently admire what they see as her "heroism." Like many spiteful heroines and heroes of failed causes in stage tragedies, Alice is a not altogether attractive figure. But we still admire her because she unwittingly learns to act heroically when she fails to find the order she seeks in the surrounding natural chaos. She thus becomes for many modern readers what she undoubtedly was for Dodgson: a naive champion of the doomed human quest for ultimate meaning and Edenic order. In the *Alices*, as in modern existential theory, human meaning is made in spite of the void; and, in making her order and meaning out of, essentially, *nothing,* the child Alice spitefully makes—for herself and for us, her elders—sense out of nonsense.

But this is not to say that the *Alice* books are little *King Lears*. For all their tragic implications, they are basically comic. Accordingly, their heroine, besides persevering and fighting back, has the practical good sense of a comic, rather than a tragic, heroine. At the end of each book, she has the good sense to do another necessary human thing, to run away, to deny and suppress her own true nightmares.

In any case, to a certain extent Alice's imposed order becomes all the more admirable and precious because of its seriocomic fragility (the way the *Alice* books have become the cherished, sometimes sacrosanct, possession of troubled adults). The comic tone at the end of *Wonderland,* for example, like the customary tone of Carroll's adult narrator, is so sure of itself because it is ultimately so unsure of itself, because it is forged in shaky anxiety, emerging suddenly and full-blown from the rejection of an orderly person's nightmare of disorder. Like the total rejection of any bad dream we have just broken off, Carroll's concluding pages seem to deny completely the validity of adventures that have all the luminosity of our truest experiences, whose creatures and insanities will continue, we sense, indefinitely after we reject them and wake to our fragile veneer, our dreams of cosmic order. Therefore, the endings of both *Alice* books, contrived and sentimental as they are, are paradoxically appropriate and paradoxically true to our ordinary ambiguous experience. Brazen (and frightened) Alice heroically rejects all her evidence as nonsense and dream; chaos and old night are ironically dispelled by mere teatime and a little kitty cat (both, by the way, fine and delicate symbols of insouciant high civilization); and the final narratives seem to explain away sensibly whatever residual conviction of the adventures' relevance and validity might persist—in dreamers, readers, or writers whose waking moments are shaped by and dedicated to humanly constructed order.

Of course, Lewis Carroll was not alone in this preoccupation with lost visions of cosmic order: The concern is central to Victorian thought. Framed by Carlyle at the beginning and Hardy at the end, Victorian literature offers us a comprehensive gallery of intellectual, emotional, and aesthetic responses to this sense of loss and ultimate anarchy I have been discussing. Carlyle (especially in *Sartor Resartus,* 1830–34, probably the most influential of all serious Victorian books) attempts, with some success, to rant and rave himself and his spiritually bereft audience into a new conviction of immanent supernatural order, of divine design within the seemingly mindless, mechanical, amoral welter of a new society and a new nature without the old God.[5] In a deliberately different key, Hardy writes a postscript to the era in his poem "The Darkling Thrush" (pointedly signed "December 31, 1900")—a picture of the vain human search for coherence, poignantly and ironically underscored by a simple natural image, an aged thrush (like an aged English poet) singing in pointless, isolated joy, flinging "his soul/Upon the growing gloom." For Hardy, as for a great many of his contemporaries, the earlier, rather desperate, Victorian search for a meaningful pattern within nature ("terrestrial things") had failed abysmally. For him, his age culminated in the spirit of his final stanza.

> So little cause for carolings
> Of such ecstatic sound
> Was written on terrestrial things
> Afar or nigh around,
> That I could think there trembled through
> His happy good-night air
> Some blessed Hope, whereof he knew
> And I was unaware.

But in the middle of the period, Lewis Carroll represents something different. His comic fantasies of the 1860s and 70s stand in curious contrast to the attitudes toward ultimate order found in most Victorian literature (Pater is the notable exception). And on this contrast rests, perhaps, Carroll's strongest claim to a place in the rise of modernism. The order that is restored at the ends of both *Alice*s is no "Victorian compromise" between a horror vision of nature's moral disorder and a consoling assertion of some traditional moral order within nature. Missing in Carroll is even that nostalgic sadness, that vain longing, that hopeless but "blessed Hope" Hardy half senses in darkening nature, a spirit that might revive some corresponding, if ephemeral, hope in us. Instead, Carroll's final, above-ground order stands fully isolated, discontinuous with the literal anarchy of Alice's adventures and the metaphysical and moral anarchy they encapsulate. Instead of the typical Victorian compromise, here at the ends of both *Alice* books is a defiant, spiteful, total, and uncompromising rejection of one vision and a complacent, comic reassertion of another—one that, significantly, no longer appears to retain a shred of philosophical validity, even within its own field of play, the adventures themselves.

Like a haughty member of the upper classes staring down an incontrovertible but class-threatening fact, the frame story of each *Alice* book stands in direct, defiant opposition to the body of the book, the adventures themselves. When Humpty Dumpty tells Alice "the question is . . . which is to be master—that's all," (p. 163) he refers to many things. Like Alice's assertion that the "great puzzle" is "Who in the world am I?" (p. 15) Humpty's remark has deep existential, linguistic, political, social, and even economic significance. He is master of his world because he *chooses* to be in spite of the actual circumstances and because in his class-ordered, hierarchical, cash-nexus world, he has the power (words and money) and the elevated position (class and proper diction) to pay for and command obedience—and thus a kind of existence and order. Who "in the world" we are (and who we are "in the world") is a function of how we order (master, boss about, bully, verbalize, and force into a coherent order) our essentially unorderable worlds. Never mind that our mastery over members of lower classes or over the intransigent moral chaos underlying all classes and systems is as fragile as Humpty Dumpty's eggshell and as precarious as Humpty Dumpty's perch. At the end of her Looking-glass adventures, Alice says of their "dreadful confusion" (p. 204), "I can't stand this any longer!" Similarly, at the end of her Wonderland adventures she finally decides she will have no more of their even more dreadful confusion. Like Humpty Dumpty, she decides for herself what to call this dreaded and uncontrollable chaos—and she calls it mere "curious dream," mere "nonsense" (sense though it most certainly seems to be). So too do the ends of both fantasies define as wonderful "nonsense" what we and Alice have just experienced vividly as frightening reality—asserting through their form as well as their content that they too will have none of it. For at this point in the adventures and the narratives there appears no sane choice for humans but to seize power, to impose the fragile, artificial order of above-ground human law and social convention, using their shaky *words* as their primary means of mastery—calling, for example, Alice's ominous "under Ground" a sunny "Wonderland."

Of course, like the White Knight (a most probable candidate for Dodgson's persona behind the looking-glass)—who says of his silly upside-down box "it's my own invention"—we sometimes allow ourselves to recognize that such order and such power are merely our own silly, upside-down inventions of a whole world. But generally we keep up our guard, and such chilling recognitions come to us indirectly and disguised in fantasies, jest, nonsense, and dreams—not straight and not in that daylight we choose to call sober, unadorned everyday life. Besides, we are also well aware, at some level of comprehension, of the final danger: If our eggshell, invented, but coherent waking world falls and is shattered, we too, like that imperious but fragile Humpty Dumpty, may be shattered forever.

Thus, like the aesthetic order of much modern art, the final order of the *Alice* books and *The Snark* is not an order discovered in objective nature, but an order openly imposed upon nature—a human meaning and coherence that frames and shapes a morally shapeless void. Like Wallace Stevens's singer whose song "mastered the night and portioned out the sea," Alice, with her naive declaration that all the assembled disorderly creatures of her disorganized adventures are "nothing but a pack of cards," masters them with language, to satisfy what Stevens calls our "blessed rage . . . to order the words . . . of ourselves and of our origins." [6] Like Stevens's shapely but simple jar, simply placed in the wild nature of Tennessee, Alice's simple final declarations make the forever "slovenly wilderness" of her underground adventures in raw nature take on *her* order, shape, and meaning. Like Stevens's plain jar, her childish declarations of mastery not only take dominion over her particular nightmares of chaos; in a sense, they also take, as Stevens puts it, "dominion everywhere." [7] And for this, many of Carroll's modern readers bless him unaware. For the question is not whether Alice's ordering of night and sea, of herself and her origins, is ultimately valid in terms of physical nature as we post-Darwinians now know it. The question is much more pressing and pragmatic: It has to do with Alice's capability to fulfill her human potential despite her own nature and that nature of which she remains a permanent part.

Conrad's *Heart of Darkness* (1899), a crucial document in the development of modernism, gives us the story of a very pragmatic, simple, rather literal-minded and naive young man who abhors lying, but who finally lies to preserve a precious illusion that gives life some moral order and significance. Rather than tell a dead idealist's naive fiancée that her dying lover's last words as he looked into the very heart of darkness that lay around him deep in the African Congo as well as within his own depraved nature were "The horror! The horror!" Marlow tells this innocent what she needs to hear: "The last word he pronounced," says Marlow, "was—your name." For, as Marlow says, to tell her the truth that he had learned in his surrealistic, underground adventures, to destroy her groundless faith—"that great and saving illusion that shone with an unearthly glow . . . in the triumphant darkness"—would have made their present world "too dark—too dark altogether." Similarly, for Alice (or Carroll) to call her horrible nightmares of dark chaos actual "chaos" would be too horrible, too dark altogether. So she (and her creator) ends these journeys into her own heart of darkness (and ours) by sunnily telling herself (and us) that they were "wonderful," "nice," nonsensical dreams populated by silly playing cards, funny chessmen, and pointless players of pointless games.

Moreover, because she is child, dreamer, liar, and name-giver, Alice is also artist—a special player of very special games.[8] And like many modern artists, she moves toward creating an ominous, rather illusory beauty and order out of dangerous, disorderly, essentially grotesque materials—not by denying the existence of these materials, but rather by shaping them into what she (and we) can call patterned "adventures," through her fully human "blessed rage" for order.

In a sense, then, this naive child-heroine can represent the central spirit behind the twentieth-century dependence on art as a new, if fragile, source for those beautiful visions of coherence that alone make human existence bearable. Wallace Stevens's unnamed singer, "among/The meaningless plungings of water and the wind," could easily be a direct descendant of Carroll's Alice:

> It was her voice that made
> The sky acutest at its vanishing.
> She measured to the hour its solitude.
> She was the single artificer of the world
> In which she sang. And when she sang, the sea,
> Whatever self it had, became the self
> That was her song.
>
> Then we,
> As we beheld her striding there alone,
> Knew that there never was a world for her
> Except the one she sang and, singing, made.

A naive forerunner of the modern artist-hero figure, Alice resists succumbing to the despair elicited by her perceptions of absurdity. Instead of drowning in her own tears (a primal salt sea filled with life and full of all those Darwinian natural creatures—and with an ape significantly in the center of Dodgson's original *Under Ground* illustration), she leads the way to that fantastical shore where games can still be played and tales told. Along with her fastidious creator, Alice persists despite setbacks and finally seems to win the game for us all.

Thus, in his rather singular comic approach to the modern problem of finding new metaphysical order in an intellectual environment hostile to such order, hostile even to the search itself, Lewis Carroll ushers in our age. For his is the voyage on which many of us now find ourselves—a voyage into our own heart of darkness, without the old maps, without even a reasonable hope of replacing them. This is the voyage begun so casually by curious Alice in her *Adventures Under Ground* and extended in its fascinating sequels—*Alice in Wonderland, Through the Looking-Glass,* and *The Hunting of the Snark.* Many modern readers, it seems, will continue to hunt that Snark, to seek—hoping against all hope—a new coherent vision of the human condition.

Florence Becker Lennon writes: "It is because Lewis Carroll sensed the irrationalities, the under side of the carpet, the lions behind the staircase—the beast in man and the indifference of the universe—that he was a great poet. He was able to deal with contradictions and horrors and irrationalities, and to convert them into an art form that gives release to children and adults alike." [9] This release through art—this delicate comic shaping and celebration of the permanent paradoxes of the human condition—is one reason why modern readers, more than ever, cherish their Lewis Carroll, thankful that he accompanies them on their necessary, though pointless, quest for our order and meaning.

NOTES

1. *Alice in Wonderland; Authoritative Texts of Alice's Adventures in Wonderland, Through the Looking-Glass, The Hunting of the Snark,* ed. Donald J. Gray, Norton Critical Edition (New York: W. W. Norton, 1971), p. 17. All subsequent citations refer to this edition. Page numbers are cited parenthetically in the text.
2. Lewis Carroll, *Sylvie and Bruno Concluded* (London: Macmillan, 1893), p. 12. The narrator of both *Sylvie and Bruno* and *Sylvie and Bruno Concluded* is clearly associated with the author.
3. Ivor Davies—in "Looking-Glass Chess," *The Anglo Welsh Review,* 15 (Autumn 1970), 189–91—points out that the apparently ruleless chess of *Through the Looking-Glass* can be made intelligible if the game is played according to the rules of the original ancient Indian chess from which modern chess developed. "At the remote period of its birth in India," writes Davies, chess "belonged to the widespread family of human games based on chance and 'the moves were governed by the casts of dice.' These significant words occur in the very first sentence" of Howard Staunton's *The Chess-Player's Companion; Comprising a New Treatise on Odds, and a Collection of Games* (1849), and Carroll owned a copy of Staunton's treatise. "Not only does the chess become intelligible," writes Davies, "it reveals some-

thing fresh and disturbing about the meaning of the looking-glass world." Davies concludes his article with this paragraph:

> "They don't keep this room so tidy as the other," thought Alice when she arrived behind the looking-glass and discovered a world beyond the care of providence or the decrees of fate. How disturbing if Carroll is suggesting that this "other world" is, after all, the real one and that it is ruled by the principle of uncertainty! A pawn's progress toward the eighth rank is hazardous in the hands of a skilled chess player. In looking-glass chess its survival depends on the casting of unseen dice by an invisible master. No wonder Alice cried as she threw herself down on the last square, "Oh, how glad I am to get here!"

4. A Victorian churchman with Dodgson's Broad Church views would, whether consciously or unconsciously, naturally associate the title "Alice's Evidence" with William Paley's celebrated *Evidences (Natural Theology, or Evidences of the Existence and Attributes of the Deity Collected from the Appearances of Nature,* 1802). Paley's work—usually referred to simply as "Paley's *Evidences*"—served during much of the earlier nineteenth century as one of the principal sources for a logical proof of God's existence based on the argument of orderly design in natural phenomena. Among later Victorian intellectuals, Paley's *Evidences* suffered an almost fatal blow from the "evidences" presented by modern geology and particularly by modern evolutionary theory. Carroll's play on Paley's *Evidences* vs. "Alice's Evidence" constitutes, like much of his comedy, a little joke with cosmic applications. Moreover, the fact that Alice is a little girl operating with the laughable logic of a normal naive child and that Paley was a grown man operating with the formidable but finally laughable logic of a brilliant adult theologian adds several degrees of irony to the jest.

5. See especially Carlyle's crucial chapter "Natural Supernaturalism."

6. Wallace Stevens, "The Idea of Order at Key West" (1935).

7.

Anecdote of the Jar

I placed a jar in Tennessee,
And round it was, upon a hill.
It made the slovenly wilderness
Surround that hill.

The wilderness rose up to it,
And sprawled around, no longer wild.
The jar was round upon the ground
And tall and of a port in air.

It took dominion everywhere.
The jar was gray and bare.
It did not give of bird or bush,
Like nothing else in Tennessee.

[Wallace Stevens, 1923]

8. This notion of the artist as suspect games-player, as artificer and forger of self and cosmos, that I have associated with Carroll and his Alice is probably most familiar in connection with the principal figure in modernist English fiction, James Joyce. And in fact Joyce was tremendously indebted to Carroll: His *Finnegans Wake* (1922–39) depends heavily on Carrollian portmanteau words and abounds in witty allusions to Carroll and Carroll's fantasies. (See, for example,

Anne McGarrity Buki's "Lewis Carroll in *Finnegans Wake*" in this book, and James Atherton's *The Books at the Wake: A Study of Literary Allusions in James Joyce's "Finnegans Wake"* [New York: Viking, 1960]. Atherton demonstrates that "many of the wildest and most startling features of *Finnegans Wake* are merely the logical development, or working out on a larger scale, of ideas that first occurred to Lewis Carroll" [p. 124].)

9. Florence Becker Lennon, *The Life of Lewis Carroll* (New York: Collier, 1962), p. 10.

Punch and *Alice:*
Through Tenniel's Looking-Glass

MICHAEL HANCHER

By now Tenniel's illustrations have become perfect mirror images of the world that Alice discovered down the rabbit-hole and through the looking-glass. They make up the other half of the text, and readers are wise to accept no substitutes, not even those drawn by Arthur Rackham, certainly not those by Salvador Dali. This parity of word and image, unmatched in any other work of literature, fulfills the rules of symmetry set out in the second of Carroll's two *Alice* books, which is itself a reflection of the first. It also satisfies our modern and romantic need to see in literature a hall of mirrors that gives no outlook on the world.

Nonetheless, like Alice herself, I can't help wondering if there isn't something of interest to be found on the other side of the mirror, behind (or before) the impassive surface of Tenniel's realistic fantasies. And so, like her, I will venture back and through.

To "begin at the beginning": Why did Carroll choose Tenniel to illustrate *Alice* in the first place? For one thing, Tenniel had succeeded in such jobs before: for example, in drawing the popular illustrations for *Lalla Rookh* by Thomas Moore (1861). Furthermore, he had achieved solid success as a chief cartoonist for *Punch*, a position that guaranteed his work the attention of thousands of middle-class readers every week. (It was through a colleague on the *Punch* staff, Tom Taylor, that Carroll had first approached Tenniel to draw the *Alice* illustrations.) Many people then, even as now, could be counted on to buy *Alice's Adventures in Wonderland* for the Tenniel illustrations.

Like us, Victorian readers would find much of Alice's strange world to be reassuringly familiar. A difference is that for them the familiarity would come, not from having read the books and studied the pictures at age six, nor from having been overexposed to the reproduction of Tenniel's images in novel contexts (such as IBM advertisements), but from having been granted frequent previews of Wonderland in images drawn for *Punch* by Tenniel and his colleagues on the staff.

Some years ago Frances Sarzano noted in passing that the *Alice* books "harvest the work of early days on *Punch.*" Before that, Marguerite Mespoulet had shown at length that the humanized animals of Carroll's text and of Tenniel's illustrations must have evolved from the grotesqueries drawn by Grandville for the French prototype of *Punch,* the journal *Charivari.*[1] Humanoid and fashionably dressed animals multiply in the pages of *Punch* both immediately before and throughout the period of Tenniel's apprenticeship and ascendancy. What I want to draw attention to here are certain *Punch* illustrations by Tenniel and others that are not so obviously in Grandville's tradition, but that cast their reflex none the less on the pages of Carroll's books.

Since image reflection is our inevitable topic, Tweedledum and Tweedledee are obvious subjects (Fig. 1, which was drawn, like all the *Looking-Glass* illustrations, some time between the end of 1869 and the middle of 1871). Here, on the far side of the looking-glass, each identical twin represents only the other. But on the near side, where Alice begins and ends her journey, both resemble John Bull, that embodiment of everyday England, at an age when he might be styled Master John Bull (Fig. 2; April 27, 1861). Under the anxious eyes of his mother, Britannia (judging from the unusual crest on the ordinary bonnet), Master John is accepting an anodyne small reduction in the income tax from his considerate dentist, William E. Gladstone, then chancellor of the exchequer. He looks almost as distressed as Tweedledee was to be later (Fig. 3).

Like many of the *Punch* drawings by Tenniel to be cited in this article, the Gladstone tax cartoon is unsigned; it does not bear the familiar monogram. (See bottom right corner of Fig. 1 for an example of Tenniel's distinctive monogram.) Tenniel signed his work occasionally from early 1851 (shortly after he joined the Punch staff) until early 1853, and more regularly from August 1862 on; but during the intervening decade his abundant work for *Punch* bore no signature, and much of the early work is unsigned also. Still, there is rarely any question whether a particular drawing is his; the styles in which he worked are distinctive enough.

A few years before this Gladstone cartoon, Tenniel had shown Master John as a boy in Mr. Punch's schoolroom of western nations, being defied by a rambunctious Jonathan (the United States) for having tried to take some toy soldiers (Fig. 4; from the preface to volume 30, dated June 28, 1856). During the previous months the Pierce administration had sharply cooled its relations with Great Britain, partly because British agents had actively recruited soldiers for the Crimean War in the United States. Master John's Tweedle-twin in the background, wearing the paper hat labeled "BOMBA," is

Figure 1 (*Through the Looking-Glass*, Chap. 4)

MASTER BULL AND HIS DENTIST.

Dentist. "DON'T CRY, MY LITTLE MAN! I'M NOT GOING TO DRAW ANY MORE THIS TIME, AND THERE'S A PENNY FOR YOU!"

Figure 2

(*Punch* illustrations courtesy *Punch*)

Figure 3 (*Through the Looking-Glass*, Chap. 4)

Figure 4

Figure 5 THE LATEST ARRIVAL.

Ferdinand II, king of the Two Sicilies, popularly known as "King Bomba," who had been censured by England and France for committing atrocities against his subjects. (Among other things he had ordered the bombardment of major cities in Sicily—hence the nickname.)

As late as 1882, ten years after *Looking-Glass* was published, Tenniel's young John Bull still looks like a prototype for Tweedledee and Tweedledum (see Fig. 5, the New Year's cartoon published January 7, 1882). Tenniel's political cartoons were conservative artistically as well as politically; he did not change his stock of imagery much during his long career. The first historian of *Punch,* M. H. Spielmann, noticed that the way Tenniel drew a locomotive hardly changed, even as actual locomotives evolved into more and more modern forms.[2] The present essay is a broader view of Tenniel's inclination to conserve and renew the imagery of the recent and not-so-recent past.

When relations between Carroll's Tweedledum and Tweedledee deteriorate to the point where the two have to be armed for battle, Tenniel pictures the scene (Fig. 6) in a way that not only responds to Carroll's description but also recalls the supposed mock-heroics of the Chartist movement as they were interpreted for *Punch* by John Leech (Fig. 7; July-December 1848, p. 101).[3] The Chartist includes in one suit of armor the dish-cover breastplate of Tweedledum and the coal-scuttle helmet of Tweedledee. Tweedledum's own saucepan helmet closely resembles the new hat for London bobbies that *Punch* proposed in 1865 (Fig. 8; February 25, 1865, by an unidentified artist). A few years before that, Tenniel had illustrated the transformation of utensils into helmets, as part of a parody of nineteenth-century researches into the history of costume (Fig. 10; June 9, 1860—a specific parody of Fig. 9).[4]

Figure 6 (*Through the Looking-Glass*, Chap. 4)

A PHYSICAL FORCE CHARTIST ARMING FOR THE FIGHT.

Figure 7

Figure 8

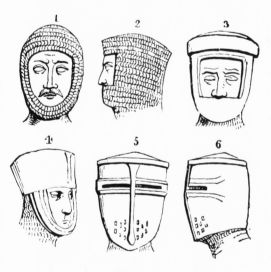

Figure 9

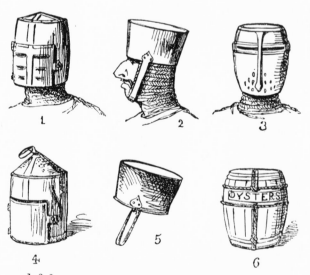

1, 2, 3. HELMETS. TEMP. RICHARD THE FIRST AND JOHN.
4, 5, 6. THE SAME IN THEIR PRIMITIVE SHAPE.
FROM MR. PUNCH'S ARCHÆOLOGICAL MUSEUM.

Figure 10

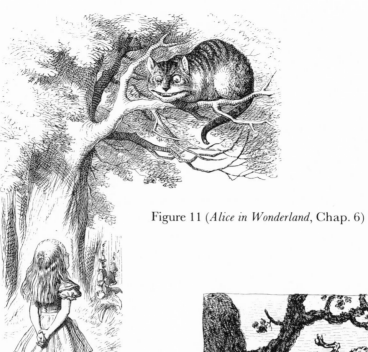

Figure 11 (*Alice in Wonderland*, Chap. 6)

The Republican Rattle-Snake fascinating the Bedford-Squirrel.

Figure 12

"UP A TREE."
Colonel Bull and the Yankee 'Coon.

'Coon. "AIR YOU IN ARNEST, COLONEL?"
COLONEL BULL. "I AM."
'Coon. "DON'T FIRE—I'LL **COME DOWN**."

Figure 13

Figure 14 (*Alice in Wonderland*, Chap. 6)

Figure 16 (*Through the Looking-Glass*, Chap. 6)

THE GIGANTIC GOOSEBERRY.

G. G. "HERE'S A PRECIOUS GO, FROGGY! I THOUGHT BIG GOOSEBERRIES AND SHOWERS O' FROGS UD HAVE A HOLIDAY THIS 'SILLY SEASON,' ANYHOW. BUT THE PRECIOUS TICHBORNE CASE HAVE BEEN ADJOURNED, AND WE'LL HAVE TO BE ON DUTY AGAIN."

Figure 15

The mild hostility between England and the United States that marked the mid-fifties had worsened a good deal by the early years of the Civil War. When the U.S.S. *San Jacinto* stopped the British steamer *Trent* and seized two Confederate envoys, the British responded with threats of war that in the end forced the Lincoln administration to release the two (the so-called *Trent* affair). Tenniel depicted the outcome for *Punch* by showing Abraham Lincoln as a raccoon treed by John Bull—who is now his adult self, and an honorary "Colonel" as well (Fig. 13; January 11, 1862).[5] The vertical relation of the two figures in this cartoon is the same as in the famous illustration, drawn some three years later, of Alice and the Cheshire Cat (Fig. 11); and the perspective is precisely reversed, as is the orientation of the tree branch on which each animal is perched.

Tenniel may have based the design of the Lincoln cartoon on Gillray's rendering of Francis Russell, the duke of Bedford, as a hapless squirrel falling from an aristocratic height into entanglement with the predatory snake Charles James Fox (Fig. 12). This caricature, published in 1795, would have been readily available to Tenniel in a collection of Gillray's work published in 1851.[6]

One of the simpler reflections in the *Alice* books of Tenniel's work for *Punch* is the drawing of Humpty Dumpty addressing the messenger (Fig. 16). Especially as regards the character on the left, it mirrors the contemporary illustration of a giant Grandvillian gooseberry addressing an even more Grandvillian frog (Fig. 15; July 15, 1871), who in turn recalls the demeanor of the frog footman in *Alice's Adventures* (Fig. 14). (The gigantic gooseberry and the background shower of frogs are allusions to stock "filler" items, reporting supposed wonders of nature, which filled the popular press during the slow summer months—when there was usually a dearth of official news— and which *Punch* never tired of ridiculing.) [7]

Perhaps more subtle reflections would have caught the Victorian reader's eye more immediately. Some early readers may have noticed how Tenniel's White Queen and Red Queen (Fig. 17) renew the association in *Punch* of Mrs. Gamp and her imaginary friend Mrs. Harris—the besotted pair from *Martin Chuzzlewit*—who served as emblems of the look-alike *Standard* and *Herald* newspapers (Fig. 18, by Tenniel's mentor John Leech; April 9, 1864). Note the crinoline apparatus displaying itself beneath the White Queen's dress, and beneath Mrs. Gamp's. *Punch* waged a relentless war against the vanity and vulgarity of crinolines, then the current fashion.[8] *Punch* also disdained the

Figure 17 (*Through the Looking-Glass*, Chap. 9)

THE IDLE GOSSIPS.

Figure 18   Mrs. Gamp (to Mrs. Harris, sneering at the Age of Dear Old Pam). "WHAT I SAY IS—HE'S TOO OLD TO BE A CONDUCTOR—WE WANTS SMART YOUNG CHAPS LIKE YOUNG DARBY AND YOUNG DIZZY!" [*See page* 146.

RELIEVING GUARD.

Figure 19

Figure 20 (*Through the Looking-Glass*, Chap. 5)

pope, and loved to show him effeminate and helpless in crinolines (Fig. 19, by Tenniel; September 20, 1862).[9] In general posture this pope is every inch a White Queen (Fig. 20, drawn nine years later).

That *Punch* thought the Papacy to be a caterpillar on the English landscape can be judged from the conjunction of two more or less irreverent images, Fig. 21, by Tenniel (January-June 1855, p. 67), and Fig. 22, by Leech (January-June 1851, p. 35): [10] Taken together, they yielded the now well-known image of the Wonderland caterpillar, preemptory if not quite predatory, enjoying his hookah on a toadstool (Fig. 23). The hookah was a common motif in the fantasies of the *Punch* staff, which often boasted Arabian or Oriental decor; in one instance it was accompanied by a psychedelic mushroom (Fig. 24, by H. R. Howard; October 20, 1860).

Even as in the *Alice* books, orality in *Punch* could take more aggressive forms than placid hookah-smoking. A trope shared by both publications, very common in *Punch,* shows animated foodstuffs in danger. The well-known scene of the Walrus and the Carpenter addressing the oysters (Fig. 25), for example, is a recasting of Tenniel's cartoon of the English beef admonishing the German sausages under the gaze of the French wine (Fig. 26; January 9, 1864).[11] Oysters had been personified before in a *Punch* drawing, perhaps by Tenniel (Fig. 27; July-December 1853, p. 244). The personified beef and wine look forward, also, to the disturbing dinner party that concludes *Looking-Glass,* especially to the personified mutton (Fig. 28), the bottles that turn into birds, and the recalcitrant pudding. When Alice tries to treat the pudding as just an ordinary pudding, and takes a slice out of it, Carroll has it talk back to her much like the pudding in a cartoon by Frank Bellew, Figure 29 (January 19, 1861). Tenniel pictures Alice's pudding only once, as part of the general confusion that ends the banquet (Fig. 30); it is easy to miss in the

Figure 21

THE POPE IN HIS CHAIR.

With Mr. Punch's Compliments to Lady Morgan.

Figure 22

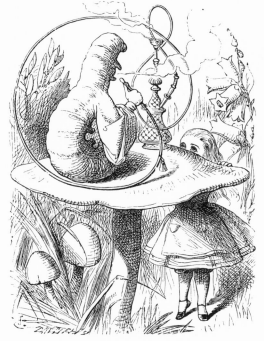

Figure 23

(*Alice in Wonderland*, Chap. 5)

Figure 24

Figure 25 (*Through the Looking-Glass*, Chap. 4)

THE ENGLISH BEEF, THE FRENCH WINE, AND THE GERMAN SAUSAGES.

The Beef. "NOW, LOOK HERE, YOU 'SMALL GERMANS,' DON'T JUMP OUT OF THE FRYING-PAN INTO THE FIRE—THAT'S ALL!"

Figure 26

an Oyster shell   *A lady's Bonnet*

ORIGINAL SKETCH BY MR. PUNCH'S LITTLE BOY.

Figure 27

Figure 28 (*Through the Looking-Glass*, Chap. 9)

lower left-hand corner, opposite the mutton (appropriately), upside-down, a dim look of perplexity appearing on its face/body.

A prototype for all the *Punch* cartoons cited here (and others that are similar) is a drawing by Leech for the 1844 *Punch* almanac (Fig. 31, on the page for February).[12] Leech's mentor George Cruikshank had published a drawing with similar details in his *Comic Almanack* for 1841 (Fig. 32, December).[13] No doubt this tradition of illustration was as influential on Carroll as it was on Tenniel.

When the Carpenter finally sets to work devouring the oysters (Fig. 33), he strikes a pose identical to that of an oyster-eating lawyer in Tenniel's cartoon "Law and Lunacy," drawn almost a decade earlier (Fig. 34; January 25, 1862). A satire on the way that court costs were consuming the large inheritance of an heir said by his guardian to be insane,[14] the drawing al-

A CHRISTMAS VISITOR.

Figure 29

Figure 30 (*Through the Looking-Glass*, Chap. 9)

Figure 31

THE DUKE OF CAMBRIDGE RECEIVING AN INVITATION TO A CHARITY DINNER ON HIS BIRTHDAY.

Figure 32

DECEMBER   A Swallow at Christmas   (Rara avis in terris)

ludes to a proverb on the injustice of the law in the matter of court costs: "A shell for him, and a shell for thee,/The oyster is the lawyer's fee."

This proverb, which associates oysters with the sharp practices of lawyers, occasions a complaint by some high-minded oysters to the reform-minded lord chancellor, Lord Bethell, in a doggerel fable in the manner of John Gay's *Fables* (1727), called "Reversing the Proverb" (June 4, 1864). This fable, which was illustrated by Tenniel (Fig. 36) even while he was working on the illustrations for *Wonderland,* quite likely was noticed by Carroll at the time, and had its echo years later in the pathetic colloquy of the oysters, the Walrus, and the Carpenter. As Lord Bethell was about to enjoy a luncheon of oysters, ale, bread, and butter:

> An Oyster thus addressed my Lord,
> Not in a whistling timid key,
> But in a voice well-trained at sea.
>
> "Ho! Equity's great guard and friend!
> Attention and assistance lend."

Figure 33 (*Through the Looking-Glass*, Chap. 4)

Figure 34

LAW AND LUNACY;
Or, A Glorious Oyster Season for the Lawyers.

THE STRIKE.—HITTING HIM HARD.
Non-Unionist. "Ah, Bill! I was afraid what *your* Union would end in"

Figure 35

REVERSING THE PROVERB.
"The Oyster where it ought to be, | And Shell and Shell the Lawyer's Fee."

Figure 36

> "My Lord," the Oyster said again,
> (Edging away from the Cayenne)
> "We ask relief, nor singly come,
> But in the name of Oysterdom.
> Too long, my Lord, a proverb old
> Links us with justice missed, or sold,
> Too long we've been the ribald type
> Of all who'd give the law a wipe,
> And now we hold it fitting time
> That you should quite reverse the rhyme."

After some discussion, Bethell tells the oyster that he has already accomplished the desired reforms.

> "Henceforth the rhyme that carries smart
> To my poor Oyster's oozy heart,
> Shall in another fashion run,
> And thus be passed from sire to son:
> 'The Oyster where it ought to be,
> And shell and shell the lawyer's fee.' "

> Again he smiled, so says the fable,
> And drew his chair up near the table,
> When all the Oysters, seen and hid,
> Cried, "Eat, and welcome." And he did.

So ends "Reversing the Proverb," on much the same note as Carroll's own fable of oysters, pepper, bread, and butter:

> "O Oysters," said the Carpenter,
>   "You've had a pleasant run!
> Shall we be trotting home again?"
>   But answer came there none—
> And this was scarcely odd, because
>   They'd eaten every one.

The Carpenter's hat (Figs. 25, 33) is, of course, the standard paper cap of the mid-Victorian workingman, which Tenniel had occasion to draw many times; for example, Figure 35 (June 22, 1861; see also July-December 1853, p. 169; April 6, 1861; September 5, 1863; and August 4, 1866). Tenniel's habit of drawing carpenters may have determined his choice of that character type when Carroll put the choice to him. (Having at first objected to the Carpenter, Tenniel finally preferred him to either of the two dactyllic replacements that Carroll had obligingly offered, "Baronet" or "Butterfly.")

Not only the foreground figures in *Alice,* but also the backgrounds, sometimes derive from *Punch.* Two of Tenniel's four drawings illustrating "Father William" are landscapes, and both have their prototypes in the magazine. The field in which Father William does his headstand (Fig. 37) had already served as a resort for Mr. Punch and his family (Fig. 38, by Tenniel; July-December 1856, p. 1); even the hayrake and pitchfork are much the same. When Father William balances an eel on the end of his nose (Fig. 39), he does

Figure 37 (*Alice in Wonderland*, Chap. 5)

Figure 38

so before a background that may perplex the modern reader, but that would have been familiar to anyone who had frequented a riverbank in the middle of the nineteenth century or, failing that, who had read *Punch* or looked at certain lesser nineteenth-century landscape paintings. The structure in the right background is an eel weir or set of eel bucks, wicker baskets used to trap eels—a detail appropriate to a scene in which a man balances an eel on his nose. Leech made eel bucks the dominant elements in the design of his cartoon of Mr. Briggs, the sports enthusiast, setting out on a doomed fishing expedition (Fig. 40; July-December 1850, p. 94). Eel weirs are pictured in *Punch* in July-December 1853, p. 142, and April 23, 1859, as well; Tenniel himself used one again as a background motif as late as April 22, 1876. William Müller did several paintings and drawings that exploit the pictur-

Figure 39 (*Alice in Wonderland*, Chap. 5)

Figure 40

Figure 41

Figure 42

Figure 43 (*Through the Looking-Glass*, Chap. 9)

esque qualities of this rustic architecture, and a painting by Frederick Richard Lee, *Morning in the Meadows* (Fig. 41), shows this minor genre at its most pleasant.

One final background, displayed in Figure 42 (July-December 1853, title page), may suggest how nearly equivalent Punch and Alice were for Tenniel. The romanesque doorway from which Punch distributes his largesse (bound volumes of *Punch*) is virtually the same door at which Alice demands admission to her royal prerogatives (Fig. 43). These are not the only romanesque doorways that Tenniel drew; he was long loyal to the style. But the resemblance is striking nonetheless.

And what of Alice herself? What place does she have in *Punch*'s England? She plays essentially the same role there as her usual role in the *Alice* books, that of a pacifist and noninterventionist, patient and polite, slow to return the aggressions of others. At the end of June 1864, when he had read Carroll's manuscript but probably had not yet begun drawing the illustrations for *Alice's Adventures,* Tenniel put Alice in the center of a patriotic *Punch* title page (Fig. 44, January-June 1864). Only a few days had passed since Palmerston's cabinet had decided, in a narrow but momentous vote, not to intervene against Bismarck in the deteriorating Schleswig-Holstein affair, which had become a war between Germany and Denmark. The decision, which Parliament quickly confirmed, proved Palmerston's earlier vague threats to be empty, but the English public in general greeted it with "relief at having escaped the horrors of war." In Figure 44 Tenniel fittingly images that relief in domestic terms. The English cannon stands at the ready, but only to protect the domestic scene; and the British lion is changed from a ferocious agent of war to a noble household pet, suitable to amuse children of either sex.[15]

In decorating that militant animal with the garlands of peace, Alice is much more at her ease than she is later in *Alice's Adventures* when she confronts the officious Do-Do-Dodgson (Fig. 45). But though her demeanor is thus subtly different in the two images, the figure and the posture are essentially the same. Of course no reader in the middle of 1864, when this *Punch* frontispiece appeared, could have recognized Alice in this, her first appearance. And by the time, a year and a half later, that she finally appeared as herself in *Wonderland*, the old image from *Punch* would have slipped from memory. Yet, like the absentminded White Rabbit, the Victorian reader might well suppose that he already knew who Alice was.

Alice is not the only veteran from *Punch* to appear in Figure 45: The ape peering out from behind the Dodo has the same features and aspect as the villainous King Bomba, shown in Figure 46 (October 11, 1856) seeking the support of Russia after having been censured by England and France.[16]

Conversely, Figure 44 is not Alice's only appearance in *Punch*. *Punch's Almanack* for 1865, published more or less simultaneously with *Alice's Adventures*, contains a page for July and August on which Alice figures as the astrological sign Virgo, in the form of a statue of the modest and long-suffering Joan of Arc (Fig. 48). The facial aspect and Pre-Raphaelite hair are virtually the same as in Figure 47, which shows Alice undergoing one of her early ordeals. A late-summer harvest scene is depicted in the tapestry hang-

Figure 44

Figure 45 (*Alice in Wonderland*, Chap. 3)

BOMBA'S BIG BROTHER.

Emperor of Russia. "THEY SHAN'T TAKE AWAY HIS PLAYTHINGS, THAT THEY SHAN'T"

Figure 46

Figure 47 (*Alice in Wonderland*, Chap. 4)

PUNCH'S ALMANACK FOR 1865.

Figure 48

(*Courtesy Royal Academy of Arts, London*)

ing behind this statue, and Tenniel plays wittily with the frames of these disparate art objects by having the virtual reality of the statue impinge on the virtual reality of the tapestry. The mower closest in the foreground appears amazed to discover, behind a sheaf of wheat, this heroic image of maidenhood. The amazement may be in part the shock of recognition, for this mower and his colleagues look much like the gardeners who painted the Queen's roses red (Fig. 49), and on whose behalf Alice courageously intervened.

Opposite this Virgo stands Leo, the British lion, whom we have already seen paired with Alice in Figure 44. But unlike the mowers in the tapestry,

Figure 49 (*Alice in Wonderland*, Chap. 8)

Figure 50 (*Through the Looking-Glass*, Chap. 7)

Figure 51

Figure 52

CONSTANTINE PRY'S VISIT TO ENGLAND.

"JUST DROPPED IN—HOPE I DON'T INTRUDE—OFF AGAIN TO-MORROW."

this figure does not put in an appearance in *Wonderland*. When he does appear in *Looking-Glass*, opposite the Unicorn (Fig. 50), he wears a bemused look, which is called for in the text, and a pair of spectacles, which are not. ("The Lion had joined them . . . he looked very tired and sleepy, and his eyes were half shut. 'What's this!' he said, blinking lazily at Alice. . . ." [Chap. 7].) The spectacles are an old attribute, dating from 1853 at least (January-June,

p. 57), some twenty years before. In Figure 51 the lion and the unicorn are at odds also, the English lion remonstrating to a Scottish unicorn that he ought not to be displaced from the Royal Arms of the United Kingdom by "an obsolete quadruped calling itself the Lion of Scotland," as five Scotsmen had recently proposed. The squib accompanying this drawing is cast in the form of a letter from "The British Lion" to the lord responsible for the royal arms. The tone is one of formal indignation, like that of a typical letter to the *Times;* evidently this lion is at home in his study, so the pair of spectacles is quite in order. A few years later they help in reading a newspaper, no doubt the *Times* (Fig. 52; June 13, 1857).[17]

It is unlikely that Alice, before and after her visits to Wonderland and through the looking-glass, ever paid much attention to the *Times;* her standard for a worthwhile book, at least, called for an ample stock of "pictures and conversations." The *Times* during this period was long on Parliamentary debates and law reports—which involve conversations of a peculiar sort—but it was very short on pictures. This lack was in large part supplied by *Punch,* which after its early salad days of radicalism settled down to provide a comic and largely visual supplement to the somber and verbal newspaper of record—so that Tenniel gradually became the quasi-official political cartoonist of England. If indeed Alice would not have looked at the *Times,* she might well have looked at *Punch* now and again, not so much for the conversations as for the pictures, in some of which she would have recognized herself and her world, as in a looking-glass.

NOTES

1. Frances Sarzano, *Sir John Tenniel,* English Masters of Black-and-White (London: Art and Technics, 1948), p. 18; Marguerite Mespoulet, *Creators of Wonderland* (New York: Arrow Editions, 1934).

2. M. H. Spielmann, *The History of "Punch"* (London: Cassell, 1895), p. 471.

3. Though Leech, like Tenniel, did not sign all his work, this cartoon is recognizably his.

    Carroll's text specifies much of the detail in Tenniel's illustration: "things . . . such as bolsters, blankets, hearth-rugs, table-cloths, dish-covers, and coal-scuttles"; also the saucepan-helmet (Chap. 4). Though the twins strangely enough find these things in a "wood," they are the domestic items that a Victorian child would most readily convert into armor for war games.

4. Figure 9 is from Chapter 18 in the series "Punch's Book of British Costumes," which ran from February 4 to December 29, 1860. The many illustrations for the series are unsigned, but most, if not all, of them are by Tenniel. It is possible that he wrote some of the letterpress as well; cf. Spielmann, *History,* pp. 355, 372. (Tenniel had made a special study of costume when an art student.)

    From time to time the series cites the authority of (among others) F. W. Fairholt, author of *Costume in England* (London: Chapman and Hall, 1846; 2nd ed., 1860). Several of the illustrations for the series are silently copied (with ironic commentary) or adapted from illustrations in Fairholt's history. Figure 9 obviously derives from Figure 10, which appears on p. 159 of the first edition.

5. From about 1839 a member of the Whig party in the United States might be called a coon because of the raccoon emblem of the party; Lincoln had been a Whig until the party disintegrated after the 1856 election. There may also be a racist slur implied in the cartoon.

   Tenniel, incidentally, was not the sole author of his political cartoons. The basic "idea" for each cartoon was usually invented by the *Punch* editorial staff at their weekly meeting. Tenniel illustrated the ideas of others—for *Punch* as for *Alice*.

6. *The Works of James Gillray* (London: Henry G. Bohn, 1851; rpt. New York: Benjamin Blom, 1968), p. 136. See also Mary Dorothy George, *Catalogue of Political and Personal Satires Preserved in the Department of Prints and Drawings in the British Museum*, vol. 7 (London: British Museum, 1942), pp. 198–99 (No. 8684).

7. In *Creators of Wonderland*, pp. 44–45, Mespoulet compares Tenniel's drawing of the frog footman to two drawings by Grandville.

8. The joke on the *Standard* and *Herald*, morning and evening papers that were much the same because under the same management, dates back to a squib accompanied by a cartoon by Leech, published in December 1845, p. 262; see Spielmann, *History*, pp. 211–13. The crinoline was a later addition, calculated to keep Mrs. Gamp in the rear-guard of fashion. and Tenniel perpetuated this detail in cartoons of Mrs. Gamp published July 16, 1864, August 11, 1866, and August 22, 1868.

   In Figure 18, "The Idle Gossips," Mrs. Gamp and Mrs. Harris are complaining of Palmerston's failing health, and looking forward to his replacement as prime minister by either Benjamin Disraeli or the earl of Derby.

9. Pius IX was made uneasy by the prospect of the French emperor, Napoleon III (right), withdrawing his forces from Italy and leaving Rome to the mercy of Victor Emmanuel II (left, trying to remove traces of Garibaldi's recent unsuccessful campaign). In this and many similar cartoons Tenniel reduces the pope's triple crown to a mobcap, to go with the crinoline.

10. This representation of the pope as a Mohammedan alludes to an extended controversy that involved Nicholas Wiseman and Sydney Morgan. In Morgan's travel book *Italy* (1821), she reported that some French antiquarians had impugned the supposed Chair of St. Peter by uncasing it and discovering on it the inscription, in Arabic, "There is but one God, and MAHOMET is his prophet." Wiseman, then rector of the English College in Rome, rejected her account in a pamphlet (1833). In the general controversy that attended his elevation in 1850 to cardinal archbishop of Westminster, the topic was revived, occasioning a pamphlet by Lady Morgan that went through four editions in 1851.

11. Caption: "THE ENGLISH BEEF, THE FRENCH WINE, AND THE GERMAN SAUSAGES./THE BEEF. 'Now, look here, you "small Germans," don't jump out of the frying-pan into the fire—that's all.' " The frying pan is labeled "SCHLESWIG and HOLSTEIN."

   The beef is John Bull; the bottle is Napoleon III. Bavaria and the other lesser German states (here the "small Germans"—small German sausages) were at that time resisting a scheme by Prussia and Austria that would have given nominal protection to long-standing Danish claims in the duchy of Schleswig. England here warns them of the dangers of intransigency.

12. Caption: "THE DUKE OF CAMBRIDGE RECEIVING AN INVITATION TO A CHARITY DINNER

ON HIS BIRTHDAY." On the table, a stack of papers marked "INVITATIONS"; beside it, a box marked "DINNER PILLS." Framed paintings of a pig and a hare are on the wall. February 24, 1844, was the seventieth birthday of Adolphus Frederick, duke of Cambridge, a son of George III and uncle of Queen Victoria. The duke was "most generous with his time . . . to an almost incredible number of charitable causes" (Roger Fulford, *Royal Dukes: The Father and Uncles of Queen Victoria* [London: Collins, 1973], p. 300). Apparently much of that time was spent banqueting, at the expense of the various foods shown here presenting an invitation inscribed "I.O.U."

13. *The Comic Almanack . . . First Series, 1835–1843* (London: Chatto, 1912), facing p. 289. For a dozen years *Punch's Almanack* imitated and competed with Cruikshank's *Comic Almanack,* and in the end it was the survivor.

    Caption: "DECEMBER—'A Swallow at Christmas' (Rara avis in terris)." Swallows being normally associated with summer, "a swallow at Christmas" must be a proverb or pseudo-proverb for rarity—here given a punning interpretation. Note the walking roast and pudding.

14. The cartoon is reprinted and the case identified in John Tenniel, *Cartoons from Punch* (London: Bradbury and Evans, n.d.), n.p.

15. The quotation is from Keith A.P. Sandiford, *Great Britain and the Schleswig-Holstein Question, 1848–64: A Study in Diplomacy, Politics, and Public Opinion* (Toronto: Univ. of Toronto Press, 1975), p. 118.

    My account of the title page supposes that it was produced after the cabinet had announced its nonintervention policy in Parliament on June 27. There is some evidence, perhaps unreliable, that it was designed before then.

16. The Russian bear has the spindly legs and military boots that Tenniel regularly ascribed to Czar Alexander II. The bandaged paw alludes to setbacks suffered in the Crimean War.

17. The Grand Duke Constantine, brother of Czar Alexander II, had paid a perfunctory courtesy visit on Queen Victoria, one "divested of any show or state," on June 1 (the *Times,* May 29, 1857, p. 10; June 1, 1857, p. 9). The surname is taken from the hero of John Poole's farce *Paul Pry* (1825), who was constantly making a nuisance of himself, and forever saying "I hope I don't intrude."

After Innocence:
Alice in the Garden

TERRY OTTEN

I

What fascinates us about the *Alice* stories, what attracts us as children and yet also intrigues us as adults, may well be the extraordinary ambivalence of the viewpoint. For Alice seemingly exists between two worlds, one of childlike fantasy and one of prescriptive absolutes. Seen psychoanalytically, she moves somewhere between the two most profound early stages of consciousness, the Oedipal period and puberty. Given the precociousness she exhibits for a child her age (seven in *Alice in Wonderland* and seven and a half in *Through the Looking-Glass*), she betrays the myopic vision of seven to ten year olds, who psychologists tell us undergo an intense literal-mindedness. As Donald Rackin notes, Alice "has reached the stage of development where the world appears explainable and unambiguous, that most narrow-minded, prejudicial period of life where, paradoxically, daring curiosity is wedded to uncompromising literalness and priggish, ignorant faith in the fundamental sanity of things." [1] Viewed theologically, or existentially, the issue lies deeper: Alice's naive point of view raises fundamental questions about the relationship between childhood and Original Sin. Here, at least, critics part company.

The Victorian attitude toward children was itself divided. In a post-Romantic age when children—via the legacy of Blake, Wordsworth, and others—were accorded idyllic grace, the relationship between the child figure and the Fall was understandably muted, despite a strongly evangelical bent toward fundamentalistic, Augustinian doctrine. Carroll, Robert Pattison suggests, could not "tolerate the idea of children as part of the world of sin, and in *Alice in Wonderland,* the heroine stands resolutely apart from the machinery of Original Sin." To Pattison, Alice remains innocent even though Wonderland itself "is the world after The Fall . . . a world of death where living creatures are perverted from their natural functions." [2] But it is difficult to accept Alice's innocence in light of her raw assertions of power and her dominant will. We sense that she has already moved beyond the quiet, unassailable, but unearned innocence of Blakean childhood. Far from being "the romantic pastoral child, the symbol of Blake's innocent life," as Peter Coveney contends,[3] Alice reflects a postlapsarian state by her very protestations of innocence. She is neither a conscious villainess nor an unsuspecting victim, neither a child of Rousseau nor a child of Calvin; and it is this remarkable duality, this paradoxical nature that allows her both to judge and to be judged. Naively an image of the fallen adult society that she embodies at an age when she wholeheartedly embraces its values and assumptions, Alice barely retains the most precious gift of childlike innocence—a potentially redemptive imagination that gives her passage to Wonderland.

We therefore can identify Alice's point of view as symptomatic of both innocence and experience: innocence because she is not so bound by the fallen world that she cannot yet enter Wonderland; experience because, although she "falls" into Wonderland, she unknowingly brings with her the destructive power of adulthood. This may explain the division among critics who find her either a mistreated heroine or a rather malicious snob. Rackin represents those who find Alice morally superior to the bizarre characters who lie in the Kafkaesque realm of Wonderland. Like Pattison and others, he sees the "underworld" as the fallen garden that Alice must finally transcend. Against this argument stands the less frequently stated idea that Alice is the truly fallen creature who threatens the regenerative world of the unconscious. James Kincaid articulates this thesis in his essay suggestively entitled "Alice's Invasion of Wonderland." To him, Alice's "rude and tragic haste" to achieve queenship in the "underside of consciousness" marks "the loss of Eden." [4] For some critics, then, Wonderland seems the reflection of innocence—a garden of sorts—for others the terrifying world of experience. Glimpsed one way, Wonderland and the looking-glass world portray the fallen garden; viewed another way, the fallen garden is the repressive culture that Alice leaves.

Perhaps Carroll's own ambivalence, his outward conventionality and inward, quiet rebellion, corresponds to his dual vision of Wonderland and attests to the competing opposites that inevitably emerge from the Fall. But, whatever the cause, Alice's delicate balance depicts a tense dialectical pattern: on the edge of sexual consciousness yet not conscious, tottering between innocence and experience—already having embraced the fallen world above the rabbit-hole with all its constraining powers but not yet having *consciously* chosen it. At the beginning she is still naive, still unaware of her potential will to power. She is on the cutting edge of a new state of being, a fact made manifest by her being too big to remain in the "womb" and too small to leave it. In effect, Alice's fall is the Fall in reverse—that is, a return to the Garden. She carries the knowledge of an adult consciousness with her, and such knowledge creates a fixed world of time and space. Although she cannot avoid the mockery of time in Wonderland, Alice, nonetheless, moves linearly in a place where clocks and maps seem inoperative but are constantly present—present both because they reflect the adventures Alice has already had in time and because they remind us that Wonderland and the looking-glass world exist in just that precarious moment before the alarm of consciousness shatters them forever.

We have, then, a heroine innocent only insofar as she has remained unconscious of her potential for evil, who visits a garden peopled by creatures parodying the fallen characters of her own world. In Wonderland, threats, violence, and cruelty are always neutralized. If characters battle, no one loses. Allusions to death are true causes neither for alarm nor for despair. Death appears comically at the end of the rat's tail (tale), for example; and the Gnat speaks of death in the most unapprehensive terms.

> A new difficulty came into Alice's head. "Supposing it couldn't find any?" she suggested.
> "Then it would die, of course."
> "But that must happen very often," Alice remarked thoughtfully.
> "It always happens," said the Gnat.[5]

Except where Alice is concerned, the limits of mortality seem nonexistent or irrelevant. Her growing consciousness alone terrorizes Wonderland—and it gives testimony of the Fall.

To illustrate the tension between Alice's unwitting "fallen" vision acquired by means of age and experience in the adult world and the still innocent vision of her dream consciousness, we can examine a few representative episodes in the two Alice stories. Again, this dialectic between competing realities can best be understood as depicting a Fall in reverse, for the measure of Alice's innocence is her ability to journey into Wonderland and the measure of her fallen nature is her inability to remain there.

II

In a memorable phrase, Claire Rosenfield says of the boys in *Lord of the Flies,* "they degenerate into adults." [6] Alice's "degeneration" manifests itself the moment she falls down the rabbit-hole. She asserts her flawed knowledge of school subjects, manners, and moral platitudes. Though utterly naive, she betrays a proclivity for violence, moral tyranny, and unswerving absolutism. Her vocabulary reflects her linear assumptions about truth. Allusions to longitude, latitude, "antipathies," maps, and books of rules, expose her effort to circumscribe reality. Both a prelapsarian Eve "curiouser and curiouser" to enter the "lovely garden" and a fallen Eve instinctively aware of death (seen in her fear of killing someone with the marmalade jar, her reference to Dinah, her apprehension about "poison," and, especially, in her fear of extinction), Alice arrives at the existential question: " 'Who am I?' Ah, that's the great puzzle!" (pp. 15-16). Already divided against herself, Alice "was very fond of pretending to be two people." An authoritarian *and* a rebel, like Blake's Urizen and Orc, "she remembered trying to box her own ears for having cheated herself in a game of croquet she was playing against herself"

(p. 12). Paradoxically aware but ignorant, she acts out her fallen nature while retaining an unearned innocence.

Certain themes continually illustrate Alice's degeneration into adulthood. Her attitude toward other people illustrates the moral folly of her normal world. She fears being Mabel because Mabel lives "in that pokey little House" and has "ever so many lessons to learn!" (p. 17). Later, she feels no remorse in knocking the Rabbit into the cucumber-frame or in kicking Bill out of the chimney. Challenged by the Caterpillar's rude questions about her identity, she appears more piteous than threatening, especially when she unintentionally insults him by complaining that "three inches is such a wretched height to be" (p. 41). But, in fact, her humility comes from her diminished height. She conceals her judgment ("I wish the creatures wouldn't be so easily offended!' ") only because she is not in a position of power. When in control of authority, she seldom hesitates to use it.

A superb illustration of her duality occurs at the end of Chapter 5, when she eats the mushroom and finds herself towering far above the trees with a neck able to "bend about in any direction, like a serpent" (p. 42). In the ensuing encounter with the Pigeon, Alice once again faces the existential question. Accused of being a serpent, Alice claims to be a little girl. She is of course both. "In this scene," Nina Auerbach writes, "the golden child herself becomes the serpent in childhood's Eden." [7] When the Pigeon asks if she has tasted an egg, Alice replies, "I *have* tasted eggs, certainly . . . but little girls eat eggs quite as much as serpents do, you know" (p. 43). With stunning simplicity the Pigeon replies, "if they do, why, then they're a kind of serpent: that's all I can say" (p. 43). As James Kincaid observes, "it doesn't matter if Eden is destroyed by purposeful malignity or by callous egotism and ruthless insensitivity that often pass for innocence." [8] The truth is, Alice is no more innocent than her flawed humanity will allow her to be. The Pigeon knows cannibalism when she sees it, even if Alice does not. If Alice provokes our sympathy, it is not because she is victimized by others, but rather because she is victimized by herself. Eve and the serpent, like Adam and the serpent, are one.

Perhaps the most telling episode in *Alice's Adventures in Wonderland* occurs at the Duchess's house. Here too Alice garners our sympathy *and* our judgment. In her attempt to save the baby from abuse, Alice assumes moral responsibility: "Wouldn't it be murder to leave it behind?" (p. 49). But her compassion coexists with her "civilized" nature: " 'Don't grunt,' said Alice, 'that's not at all a proper way of expressing yourself.' " When she discovers the child to be a pig, Alice gratefully puts the creature down and surmises: " 'If it had grown up,' she said to herself, 'it would have made a dreadfully ugly child: but it makes a rather handsome pig, I think.' And she began thinking over other children she knew, who might do very well as pigs . . . saying to herself 'if one only knew the right way to change them—' " (p. 50). As Kincaid and others have noted, Alice's potential for tyranny is nowhere more apparent than here. "Alice is transformed into a kind of Circe," says Roger Sale, "turning all those she controls into swine." [9] Devoid of all but self-deception, Alice, like the boys in *Lord of the Flies,* becomes a child of darkness as well as of light.

The dialectical pattern repeats itself throughout the tale—in her attempts at poetry, which transform nursery rhymes into poems abut death; in her frequent allusions to Dinah, which change a child's pet into a beast of prey; in her constant concern for rules, which attempt to reduce the openness of Wonderland to constrictions of time and place. As the unwitting defender of civilization, Alice usually suffers glorious rout. To her literal mind, time is the servant of order; to those at the Mad Tea-Party, as Donald Rackin remarks, it is "a person, a kind of ill-behaved child created by men." [10] Alice's reductiveness gives way to expansiveness. Her efforts to apply constraints to reality—to establish rules for the croquet match, meaning for the Duchess's moral aphorisms, and sense for the Mock Turtle's outrageous puns—seldom succeed. Existing in the dream state, like Marlow in *Heart of Darkness,* Alice experiences "that commingling of absurdity, surprise, and bewilderment . . . that notion of being captured by the incredible which is the very essence of dreams."

Withal, however, there remains Carroll's marvelous comic detachment and his reassurance that man's cruelty to man can never be enacted here. Even if the King had not whispered to the host of those sentenced to execution "You are all pardoned" (p. 73), we would know they are—"they never executes nobody, you know" (p. 74), the Gryphon informs us. The world of the imagination, in short, for all the references to time, to law, to rule, to schooling and manners, to child abuse and death, maintains the virtues of openness and incompletion. Unending in its possibilities and protected by its fantasy, the Garden can redeem with truth the temporal society it mimics. Though time is a constant theme in Wonderland, it is, in fact, for Alice alone that time exists. Her tendency toward closure betrays her fallen condition. Unlike the creatures whom she treats with careless malice, Alice reveals her divided nature: her potential for kindness and disdain, compassion and judgment. Though she can temporarily visit Wonderland, she cannot long remain there. She has nearly outgrown her innocence altogether.

The end of *Alice in Wonderland* reveals Alice's tenuous state of becoming. Lionel Morton says of the trial of the Knave of Hearts, Alice's " 'You're nothing but a pack of cards!' is more devastating than 'Off with his head' " because "it destroys a whole world. . . . Alice's awakening is the end of the story and the breaking of the spell of the half-unreal love that has united Alice and her Scheherazade. . . . With the end of the story time resumes its power." [11] Peter Coveney finds in Wonderland "the claustrophobic atmosphere of a children's Kafka" and labels the story "the frustrated 'quest' for the 'Garden' which in the event is peopled with such unpleasant creatures." Hence, he concludes, we feel "a sense of shock" to find Alice's "innocent life blighted with 'dead leaves' " at the end of the story.[12] But the destructive power resides in Alice herself, not in the dreamworld of the imagination. The "fallen leaves" appear in the *external* world, not in Wonderland—and they existed there before Alice entered the "underside of consciousness."

III

Perhaps few would agree with W. H. Auden that *Through the Looking-Glass* is "even better" than *Alice in Wonderland*,[13] but no one can ignore the difference in its tone and substance. Yet Carroll resumes his narrative with a clear sense of continuity, for Alice—as in Wonderland, far more mature than her age suggests—continues the cycle of becoming from childhood to adulthood. In effect, Alice in the Looking-Glass world is Alice in Wonderland once removed. The differences in the stories reveal, not contradiction, but logical progression.

The obvious contrasts between Wonderland and the looking-glass world—outside/inside, light/dark, summer/winter—signal Alice's evolving character. In some respects she has already assumed the obligations of an adult. Lionel Morton points out that Alice is a sort of mock-maternal figure mothering Dinah's newly born kittens rather than being mothered by her sister.[14] Nor is Alice's identification with the Red Queen without meaning. In Wonderland Alice had understandably rejected the terrifying power of the Queen; now she all but seeks it. Consequently, the action varies. The journey in Wonderland remains marvelously quixotic. In the looking-glass world, the squares of the chessboard and Alice's will to be crowned Queen determine the action. Morton concludes that Alice *is* the Red Queen: "the Queen is the desire to dominate and to punish, which began the whole dream and caused all the mischief. This desire is also the desire to grow up and be an adult, as Carroll sees it."[15] In Blakean language, the journey through the looking-glass marks the final passage from a rapidly fading innocence to an assertive selfhood (for Blake the essence of sin)—*Through the Looking-Glass* portrays the consequences of a fall. Yet, paradoxically, such a fall is the unavoidable condition of mortality.

Even from the beginning, Alice plays Urizen, Blake's mythological figure representing the rational faculty attributed to the "nobodaddy" god of the Old Testament. Her first words are judgmental: "Oh, you wicked little thing! . . . Really, Dinah ought to have taught you better manners!" (pp. 107–8). She threatens to put the kitten out in the snow and to save "all your punishments for Wednesday week" (pp. 108–9). Her proclivity for violence also surfaces when she recalls frightening her old nurse "by shouting suddenly in her ear, 'Nurse! Do let's pretend that I'm a hungry hyaena and you're a bone!'" (p. 110)—an ironic echo of the many cannibalistic expressions in *Alice in Wonderland*. More aggressive and confident, Alice does not now fall accidentally down the rabbit-hole, but wilfully enters the mirror. Symbolically, she has moved from what John Vernon labels a garden consciousness to a map consciousness. Vernon describes the dialectic between "the unity of opposites and the wholeness of experience" envisioned in the Garden and the "separation of opposites and the fragmentation of experience" in the adult psyche embodied in the Map.[16] The tension between these opposite appeals provides clear evidence that Alice has ventured beyond innocence.

In Wonderland Alice experienced a pattern of stretch and shrink: stretch because she was challenged by new knowledge; shrink because she was humiliated by her ignorance. Within the looking-glass the conflict dissolves, for Alice is too "wise," too confident, and too superior in her attitude. In The Garden of Live Flowers she identifies with the Tiger-lily, who terrorizes the other flowers. The Tiger-lily trembles "with excitement" when the daisies shout together because "They know I can't get at them!" But in defense of the tyrant, Alice whispers ominously to the daisies, "If you don't hold your tongues, I'll pick you!" (p. 122). Finally impatient with the flowers, she decides to go meet the Red Queen, "for, though the flowers are interesting enough, she felt it would be far grander to have a talk with a real Queen" (p. 123). Impressed by power, she sets out on the chessboard, admitting, "I wouldn't mind being a Pawn . . . though of course I should *like* to be a Queen, best" (p. 126).

The series of events that follows traces Alice's steps to the Eighth Square. Though offered redemptive self-knowledge in various encounters on the way, Alice journeys unabated toward a single goal—queenship. Her intent to meet, and finally to be, a queen ironically identifies her with the other symbols of power, and especially with the Queen of Hearts and the Red Queen. The queens express comically an authority that Alice reenacts in earnest. If Dinah embodies her unacknowledged will to power in the first book, the quest for queenship portrays it overtly in the second book. Though challenged by the "Garden" consciousness of various characters, Alice never veers from her course.

One example of Alice's inability to respond to the "Garden" is the episode with the Gnat. With the possible exception of Sissy Jupe's futile attempt to define a horse for Mr. Gradgrind in *Hard Times,* no moment in literature so cogently reveals the conflict between childlike imagination and reductive reason. The Gnat struggles vainly to deny Alice's devotion to certainty, logic, and definition. Baffled by his wisdom, Alice holds to her Urizenic assurances. When the Gnat asks what insects she rejoices in, Alice can only reply, "I don't *rejoice* in insects at all. . . . But I can tell you the names of some of them" (p. 132). The conversation goes on,

> "Of course they answer to their names?" the Gnat remarked carelessly.
> "I never knew them to do it."
> "What's the use of their having names," the Gnat said, "if they won't answer to them?"
> "No use to them," said Alice; "but it's useful to the people that name them, I suppose. If not, why do they have names at all?"

As we see reflected later in the Humpty Dumpty episode, names are an imposition of order for Alice, a means of exercising control over other creatures. That is, for Alice—as for Gradgrind and the utilitarian society he represents—names constitute what Martin Buber would call an I-It relationship, in which other beings become objects capable of being manipulated.

When Alice offers to list some insects she knows, the Gnat converts dictionary definitions into poetic truths: "a Rocking-horse-fly. It's made entirely of wood, and gets about by swinging itself from branch to branch"; "a Snap-dragon-fly. Its body is made of plum-pudding, its wings of holly-leaves, and its head is a raisin burning in brandy"; and "a bread-and-butter fly. Its wings are thin slices of bread-and-butter, its body is a crust, and its head is a lump of sugar" (pp. 133–34). Against the Gnat's transcendent definitions stands Alice's morbid sense of mortality. She theorizes about why "insects are so fond of flying into candles" and expresses her fear that the Bread-and-butter-fly might die for want of "Weak tea with cream in it."

Finally the Gnat asks Alice if she would be willing to lose her name. Her selfhood firmly established, Alice "anxiously" answers, "No, indeed." The Gnat then puns by remarking that Alice's governess could not call her to lessons if she had no name:

> "Well, if she said 'Miss,' and didn't say anything more," the Gnat replied, "of course you'd miss your lessons. That's a joke. I wish *you* had made it."
>
> "Why do you wish *I* had made it?" Alice asked. "It's a very bad one."
>
> But the Gnat only sighed deeply while two large tears came rolling down its cheeks. (p. 135)

Surely the Gnat weeps for her lost innocence. Bound by her acquired distrust of insects, by her reductive dictionary definitions, by her elemental fear of death, by her own self-definition, Alice mirrors her fallen condition—her commitment to Urizenic principles of order and to an unredemptive selfhood.

Suggestively, Alice's ensuing brief journey through the woods "where things have no names" marks a further rite of passage from innocence to experience. Empson associates the dark woods with death and sexual awakening. Perhaps so. In one sense, however, Alice has already been acquainted with death and has frequently received and issued threats of death. In another sense her self-consciousness *is* raised dramatically in the scene: "I know my name now," she claims with resolve—"I won't forget it again" (p. 137). Furthermore, the appearance of the Fawn gives significance to the moment. When she enters the woods, Alice speaks with and "lovingly" holds the Fawn. When they come out of the woods, though, the Fawn cries out, "You're a human child!" and runs away in fear. The association of the child with gentle animals is of course a conventional symbol of innocence. Alice's disassociation exposes her emerging state of being.

While continuing to parody adult follies (as in the mock battles between Tweedledum and Tweedledee, the Lion and the Unicorn, and the Red Knight and the White Knight), the characters seem less threatening to Alice as the book goes on. But while Alice moves with increasing surety, she continues to show her susceptibility and fear when her comic antagonists penetrate her easy assumptions. Her apprehension that she may be part of the Red King's dream, as Tweedledee tells her, provokes both insistence—"I am real!" (p. 145)—and tears. She rapidly changes the subject. She does so again later when Humpty Dumpty tells her that seven-and-half is "An uncomfortable sort of age" (p. 162). Humpty tells her she should have left off at seven and Alice replies, "one ca'n't help growing older." His response—"One ca'n't perhaps . . . but *two* can. With proper assistance, you might have left off at seven!" (p. 162)—has led Richard Kelly to remark, "Humpty's chilling phrase, 'with proper assistance,' is a grim reminder that Alice is in a post-lapserian [sic] world and that innocence is indeed a fragile commodity." [17]

Alice's innocence has indeed been lost. Whereas Humpty can rejoice in unbirthdays, Alice is compelled forward in time, driven across the board to the Eighth Square (suggestively the number *after* the mystical number seven), where identity and death coexist. Declaring the independence of time and language, Humpty counters Alice's necessity for fixity and certainty. Against his imaginative interpretation of "Jabberwocky" (Humpty assures her he "can explain all the poems that were invented—and a good many that haven't been invented yet"—p. 164), Alice can offer only the reductive fact of death: *"somebody* killed *something:* that's clear, at any rate—" (p. 118). Unconscious, but nonetheless aware, of the fallen world, Alice sees through postlapsarian lenses.

Her sight is at once wise in the way of the world and deficient in grace. Her end—selfhood and queenship—justifies her means. The scene with the White Knight illustrates the point. To Martin Gardner, "of all the characters Alice meets on her two dreamy adventures, only the White Knight seems to be genuinely fond of her and to offer her special assistance. He is almost alone in speaking to her with respect and courtesy." He concludes that "we hear loudest in this episode that 'shadow of a sigh' that Carroll tells us in his prefatory poem will 'tremble through the story.' " [18] The sorrow that Gardner finds stems from Alice's compulsion (and perhaps her need) to achieve queenship. Carroll, as biographers have noted, found the line between childhood and adulthood, innocence and puberty, difficult to acknowledge. Perhaps in injecting himself into the story in the person of the White Knight, he utters his modest protest against the deterministic forces that drive his heroine. For, however unknowingly, Alice *does* abandon the impotent White Knight and, figuratively at least, the precarious and gentle world he represents. Says James Kincaid, this "deeply kind" figure may provoke laughter, but "we must take him seriously." His song parody of Wordsworth's "Resolution and Independence" exactly parallels Alice's insensitivity to him: "The point of the poem is the cruelty of self-absorption, precisely the same self-absorption that allows Alice to joke about the disappearing friend—'It wo'n't take long to see him *off,* I expect'—and then skip away thoughtlessly: 'and now for the last brook, and to be a Queen! How grand it sounds!' " [19] Alice cannot remain a child forever, of course, so we cannot make her into some kind of villainess because of her treatment of the White Knight. Nonetheless, her will to power sadly justifies an unconscious cruelty. As Blake well knew, Experience is purchased at the cost of Innocence.

When Alice finally arrives at the Eighth Square, she undergoes a last ironic "test," a climax to all the mock rituals, the parodies of learning, and the satires on authority that form the sum and substance of the tales. She thinks the whole affair "grand" when she finds herself, newly crowned, sitting between the Red Queen and the White Queen. Her every expectation of sovereignty is marvelously ridiculed. Unable to answer the queens' questions, to play the game of nonsense that totally lambastes the privileges of rank and position, Alice laments, "I wish Queens never asked questions" (p. 195). When the examination ends, the Red Queen shows a side of queenship that Alice seems to know little about—kindness. She tells the new queen to sing the White Queen a lullaby ("She's tired, poor thing!"), but Alice can no more sing the song than she could join in the humor—"I don't know any soothing lullabies." As the two queens sleep on Alice's shoulders, she characteristically defines queenship by the book: "I don't think it *ever* happened before, that anyone had to take care of two Queens asleep at once! No, not in all the History of England—it couldn't, you know, because there never was more than one Queen at a time. Do wake up you heavy things!" (p. 197). As always, Alice measures the fantasy world against her knowledge and finds the world wanting. All the more insistent on her reign, she goes on to "Queen Alice's," announces her royalty to the old Frog, complains about the missing servant, and stamps her foot in irritation. She has become the "real" queen she has sought to be, an authoritarian with the overriding power to enact her will.

To some, perhaps most, Alice's enactment of the will to power at the dinner is a positive gesture. It strikes out against chaos, they contend; or, in Robert Pattison's language, it "overturns the false order of Wonderland with the faith and assurance of the symbolic logician destroying a fallacious syllogism." [20] Truly one cannot remain in Wonderland, and we are given little choice in deciding between growing and retreating into childhood. Yet even if Carroll did not suffer the prolonged commitment to Neverland that Barrie did, he seemingly was keenly aware of the price to be paid for the loss of innocence—and he depicts Alice's "victory" with no little irony. When the Red Queen parodies the rules of etiquette by scolding Alice for wanting to slice the Mutton before she has been introduced and orders it off along with the pudding, Alice decides the Red Queen should not "be the only one to give orders." When all goes awry, she pulls out the tablecloth, not so much resolving the chaos as participating in it. That is not all, of course. Alice turns "fiercely" upon the Red Queen, "catching hold of the little creature in the very act of jumping over a bottle. . . . She took it off the table as she spoke and shook it backwards and forwards with all her might" (pp. 204–5). The violence expressed in the dream suddenly explodes in the external world, where it is truly frightening—however much Alice coyly pretends to fuss over her kitten, whom the Red Queen becomes, for waking her from "such a nice dream." Lionel Morton incisively states that Alice "cannot really shake off the Red Queen, because the Queen is in her, not the kitten: the Queen is the desire to dominate and to punish. . . . This desire is also the desire to grow up and be an adult, as Carroll saw it." [21]

When Alice observes Dinah, the image of her predatory self, cleaning the white kitten, she remarks, "Do you know you're scrubbing a White Queen? Really, it's most disrespectful of you!" She plays the governess-judge-queen, ordering the kitten to confess, sit up straight, and curtsy. Then, she recalls the "quantity of poetry" she heard about fishes and concludes ominously, "To-morrow morning you shall have a real treat. All the time you're eating your breakfast, I'll repeat 'The Walrus and the Carpenter' to you; and you can make believe it's oysters, dear!" (p. 208). As Kincaid points out, "The Walrus is a very apt caricature of Alice." [22] The poem's comic portrayal of the Walrus's mock sympathy for the oysters and, by implication, the whole of the savagery and cruelty everywhere apparent in Wonderland and the looking-glass are transposed in a world no longer protected by regenerative humor.

Throughout the *Alice* books, Alice exists in opposing realities, a fallen— and so, divided—character. The tension moves her from humiliation to the assertion of power in an abbreviated moment of becoming. Elizabeth Sewell finds Carroll's "deep sense . . . to be very close to that of Blake, who sees in the logical, rational Urizen a power beautiful when balanced by other powers of the mind, lethal when developed in independence and isolation." [23] It is precisely Alice's comfortable faith in the pure light of reason and guaranteed existence that renders her deficient in Wonderland and dooms her to destroy it—and concomitantly to pay undue allegiance to a fallen adulthood. Alice's fall-in-reverse, her return to the innocence of the garden, can prove redemptive only to the degree she can recover from the "Autumn frosts" of time. "We are but older children, dear," Carroll writes in the prefatory poem to *Through the Looking-Glass*, "who fret to find our bedtime near" (p. 103). If the innocence of childhood remains, it abides in the memory of a lost childhood, whose vision alone can do battle with the Urizenic realities of a fallen world— "except ye become as little children." So long as it exists within the self, it can resist the "shadowy hermaphrodite" who Blake warns us threatens to circumscribe our being. Though the *Alice* stories do not guarantee the triumph of the imagination in Alice's growing up, they give credence and meaning to the most ancient of myths—and remind us once more that "a little child shall lead them."

NOTES

1. Donald Rackin, "Alice's Long Journey to the End of Night," *PMLA*, 81 (1966), 314.

2. Robert Pattison, *The Child Figure in English Literature* (Athens: Univ. of Georgia Press, 1978), pp. 156, 159.

3. Peter Coveney, *Poor Monkey: The Child in Literature* (London: Rockliff, 1957), p. 195. Nina Auerbach argues that Alice "explodes out of Wonderland hungry and unregenerate" ("Alice and Wonderland: A Curious Child," *Victorian Studies*, 17 [1973], 46).

4. James Kincaid, "Alice's Invasion of Wonderland," *PMLA*, 88 (1975), 92–99.

5. *Alice in Wonderland: Authoritative Texts of Alice's Adventures in Wonderland, Through the Looking-Glass, The Hunting of the Snark,* ed. Donald J. Gray, Norton Critical Edi-

tion (New York: W. W. Norton, 1971), pp. 15–16. All subsequent citations refer to this edition. Page numbers are cited parenthetically in text.

6. Claire Rosenfield, " 'Men of Smaller Growth': A Psychological Analysis of William Golding's *Lord of the Flies*," *Literature and Psychology*, 11 (1961), 100.

7. Auerbach, p. 43.

8. Kincaid, p. 92.

9. Roger Sale, *Fairy Tales and After from Snow White to E. B. White* (Cambridge: Harvard Univ. Press, 1978), p. 115.

10. Rackin, p. 320.

11. Lionel Morton, "Memory in the Alice Books," *Nineteenth-Century Fiction*, 33 (1978), 304–5.

12. Coveney, pp. 197–98.

13. W. H. Auden, "The Man Who Wrote Alice," *New York Times Book Review*, February 28, 1954, p. 4.

14. Morton, p. 305.

15. Ibid., p. 306. William Empson writes simply, "Wonderland is a dream, the Looking-Glass is self-consciousness" ("The Child as Swain," in *Some Versions of Pastoral* [1935; rpt. New York: New Directions, 1960], p. 257).

16. John Vernon, *The Garden and the Map: Schizophrenia in Twentieth-Century Literature and Culture* (Urbana: Univ. of Illinois Press, 1973), p. xiii.

17. Richard Kelly, *Lewis Carroll* (Boston: Twayne, 1977), p. 105.

18. *The Annotated Alice: Alice's Adventures in Wonderland and Through the Looking-Glass,* ed. Martin Gardner (New York: Clarkson N. Potter, 1960), p. 87.

19. Kincaid, p. 99.

20. Pattison, p. 158.

21. Morton, p. 306.

22. Kincaid, p. 95.

23. Elizabeth Sewell, "The Nonsense System in Lewis Carroll's Work and in Today's World," in *Lewis Carroll Observed: A Collection of Unpublished Photographs, Drawings, Poetry, and New Essays,* ed. Edward Guiliano (New York: Clarkson N. Potter, 1976), p. 66.

"If you don't know what a Gryphon is":
Text and Illustration in
Alice's Adventures in Wonderland

RICHARD KELLY

Some literary characters are more easily visualized than others, so much so that we would hardly fail to recognize them in the flesh—or, in the illustration. We can easily conjure up the image of Mr. Pickwick, even if we never saw the delightful illustrations of Hablot Knight Browne. Similarly, Sherlock Holmes is recognizable without the fine drawings of Sidney Edward Paget. These characters, like so many other nineteenth-century figures, are so richly described by their creators that the illustrations serve the reader more as pleasant visual reminders than as definitive portraits. The illustrations to Lewis Carroll's *Alice's Adventures in Wonderland,* on the other hand, are inextricably wedded to the total performance of the work. Even in the first version of the Alice story, *Alice's Adventures Under Ground,* Carroll's own drawings were an integral part of the book. Instead of describing his character in detail, he depended upon his sketches to do that work for him. Later, when Tenniel agreed to illustrate the book, Carroll again relied upon the drawings to establish the physical details of his characters. Browne's and Paget's illustrations for Dickens and Doyle are largely ornamental,[1] but Tenniel's drawings for *Alice's Adventures* are fundamental to the reader's total perception of the characters; it is Tenniel's illustrations and not Carroll's descriptions that provide the definitive portraits of the characters with whom we are now all familiar.

In working out his drawings for the book, Tenniel had to deal with three factors of immediate importance: the thirty-seven drawings that Carroll had already done for *Alice's Adventures Under Ground,* Carroll's personal supervision of the new drawings, and of course, the text of the revised and enlarged Alice story itself. When Carroll first thought of getting Tenniel to illustrate the

Alice story, he wrote to the dramatist Tom Taylor requesting a letter of introduction to the *Punch* artist and said that if Tenniel "should be willing to undertake them [the illustrations], I would send him the book [*Alice's Adventures Under Ground*] to look over, not that he should at all follow my pictures, but simply to give him an idea of the sort of thing I want." [2] Even a cursory glance at the two sets of illustrations makes clear that Tenniel was not restricted in his work by Carroll's illustrations. He adds other characters, new arrangements of old ones, new faces, bodies, clothes, animals, and expressions. Carroll's rather crude sketches of the White Rabbit and the Caterpillar (Figs. 1 and 11), for example, bear only a rough resemblance to Tenniel's richly detailed drawings of the same creatures (Figs. 2 and 10). When Carroll added Chapters 6 and 7 ("Pig and Pepper" and "A Mad Tea-Party") for his expanded version of the story, he did not provide Tenniel with sketches of the Duchess, Cheshire Cat, Mad Hatter, March Hare, or Dormouse. Working under Carroll's careful supervision, Tenniel made preliminary pencil sketches of these and other characters to accompany the new text.[3] Figures 3, 4, and 5, for example, show the development from Carroll's original drawing to Tenniel's finished and remarkably faithful illustration. The extent to which Carroll controlled the specific details of Tenniel's drawings is unknown, but it is known that he had his hand in every stage of every drawing—making suggestions until they got on Tenniel's nerves. Years later Tenniel wrote to Harry Furniss, who was about to illustrate *Sylvie and Bruno*: "I'll give you a week, old chap; *you* will never put up with that fellow a day longer." [4] It is problematic whether Carroll or Tenniel was the inspiration behind the original renderings, but the fact remains that Tenniel's illustrations provide almost all of the visualization of Carroll's characters. It is in this regard that Tenniel's work, unlike that of Browne, Paget, and many other noted illustrators of the period, has its special artistic impact. In this essay I look at how each major character is described in the text and, in turn, at what the Tenniel drawings add to the essence of the book; finally, I offer several explanations for why Carroll abandoned language for pictures in *Alice's Adventures in Wonderland.*

Within a total of forty-two illustrations, here are how many times each of the major characters appear: Alice—23; the White Rabbit—6; the Mad Hatter—5, the Cheshire Cat—4; the King of Hearts—4; the Queen of Hearts—3; the Dormouse—3; the Duchess—2; the March Hare—2; and the Caterpillar—1. While it comes as no surprise that Alice appears in over half of all the illustrations, it is surprising indeed that Carroll almost totally ignores her physical description. Without the benefit of the illustrations, we would know precious little about her appearance. In Chapter 1 she refers to her head, shoulders, feet, eyes, and bodily size, but always in general terms so as not to distinguish her from any young girl. In Chapter 2 she provides a detail about her hair: " 'I'm sure I'm not Ada,' she said, 'for her hair goes in such long ringlets, and mine doesn't go in ringlets at all' " (p. 37).[5] Thus we discover that Alice has straight hair, but we have to wait until Chapter 7 to learn of its length: " 'Your hair wants cutting,' said the Hatter" (p. 94). In Chapter

Figure 1 (*Alice's Adventures Under Ground* [Carroll], Chap. 1)

Figure 2 (*Alice in Wonderland* [Tenniel], Chap. 1)

Figure 3 (*Alice's Adventures Under Ground*, Chap. 10)

Figure 4. Tenniel's preliminary pencil drawing heightened with ink and Chinese white. (*Courtesy Harcourt Amory Collection, Harvard University*)

Figure 5 (*Alice in Wonderland,* Chap. 8)

10 we are informed, thanks to the Gryphon, that Alice is wearing shiny shoes, which she keeps bright by blacking. Finally, in Chapter 12, Carroll notes that Alice "tipped over the jury box with the edge of her skirt" (p. 153), and in Alice's sister's dream we learn that Alice has "tiny hands" and "bright eager eyes" (p. 162). In summary, all we know of Alice's appearance is that she had long, straight hair, shiny shoes, a skirt, small hands, and bright eyes. Given such paltry details, she becomes a nondescript Everygirl.

The White Rabbit, on the other hand, is described with a little more detail than is Alice. In Chapter 1 we are told of "a white rabbit with pink eyes" (p. 25) who "actually *took a watch out of its waistcoat-pocket*" (p. 26). In the next chapter Carroll says that the rabbit was "splendidly dressed, with a pair of white kid gloves in one hand and a large fan in the other" (pp. 36–37). The next description does not come until Chapter 11, when the White Rabbit has "a trumpet in one hand, and a scroll of parchment in the other" (p. 143). But the image we all have of this colorful creature is largely Tenniel's. In the first illustration of the rabbit (Fig. 2) he is wearing the waistcoat with the watch that Carroll mentions, but he is also sporting a checkered jacket, a Gladstone collar, and a cravat and is carrying under his arm a folded umbrella. It is not clear if he is wearing gloves, though he does have human hands. The next illustration gives a rear view of him running down a dark hallway, the fan and gloves on the floor behind him. In the third illustration (Fig. 6), the one in Chapter 11, he holds the scroll in his left hand and the trumpet up to his mouth, but his costume has been completely changed. He now wears a tunic covered with hearts and topped with a large round ruff, the sort worn by Sir Walter Raleigh and Queen Elizabeth, and there are large bows on his sleeves. The frontispiece shows his right profile in the same dress. In Chapter 12 he appears for the last time in the illustration depicting the cards flying up at Alice (Fig. 7). Partially hidden behind Alice's skirt, he appears for the first time in the nude—or more accurately, in the fur. Carroll does not mention this detail in his story, but Tenniel's drawing captures the essential transformation of dream into reality not only by showing the playing-card people reverting to "nothing but a pack of cards" (p. 161) but by undressing and dehumanizing the animals, especially the highly civilized White Rabbit. Tenniel here goes beyond the rendering of characters and pictorially reinforces a major theme of the book, the play between dream and waking. It was the White Rabbit that led Alice from her sister's sleepy book ("it had no pictures or conversations in it" [p. 25]) and from an ordinary afternoon to the mad dreamworld of Wonderland. The reader first sees the White Rabbit standing fully dressed at the head of Chapter 1 and last sees him as an ordinary rabbit in the book's final illustration. These two drawings thus frame the story and support its narrative structure as the reader, like Alice, emerges from a dream-vision that reveals the fundamental instability of one's perceptions. The sudden appearance of the animals out of their clothes in the final drawing captures Alice's rejection of the mad sanity of Wonderland for the dull world of reality. The reader's imagination, however, has been shaped by Tenniel's many earlier drawings of the civilized White Rabbit and now

Figure 6 (*Alice in Wonderland*, Chap. 11) Figure 7 (*Alice in Wonderland*, Chap. 12)

Figure 8 (*Alice in Wonderland*, Chap. 7)

refuses to relinquish those memorable pictures for a mere biological bunny. The last drawing divests the White Rabbit not only of his clothes but of his unique character; he becomes just one of many undistinguished animals—and what's more, Tenniel makes it rather difficult to see him mixed in with the other creatures and peering from behind the dominant figure of Alice.

In expanding the earlier version of his story, Carroll added the memorable trinity of the Hatter, Hare, and Dormouse. The image of the Mad Hatter has entered the popular culture and is almost universally recognized. He has been carved out of English soap, featured in a Disney film, molded in ceramics, and stands as the logo for the elegant Mad Hatter Restaurant on Nantucket Island. Tenniel's powerful and influential creation of this character owes little to Carroll's description of him. In Chapter 7, where he is introduced, the only detail we are given about his appearance is that "he had taken his watch out of his pocket" (p. 96). The three illustrations that accompany the chapter provide the specifics of his now famous image: the top hat ("in this style 10/6″), the Bertrand Russell face, the polka-dotted bowtie, Gladstone collar, and checkered vest and trousers (Fig. 8). The only other description Carroll provides comes in Chapter 11, where the Hatter, as the first witness in the trial of the Knave of Hearts, appears "with a teacup in one hand and a piece of bread-and-butter in the other" (p. 146). It is only after the King exclaims, "Take off your hat" (p. 147) that we learn from the text that the Hatter is wearing one. The Hatter's two companions, the March Hare and the Dormouse, are not described at all. Again, we depend upon Tenniel to visualize them for us. The Dormouse appears in three illustrations and the Hare in two. While the Dormouse looks very much like an overfed, sleepy squirrel, the Hare is given human characteristics. Except for his rabbit head, his body is that of a human. He is dressed in a jacket, striped trousers, and bowtie and wears a random arrangement of weed stalks on his head. As the embodiment of the phrase "Mad as a March Hare," the rabbit's physical appearance clashes with his civilized surroundings of china teacups, white tablecloth, and Alice's stuffed chair. Half human and half rabbit, he sits at the table in the first illustration (Fig. 8) as if he were civilized, but in the background of the drawing are the trees and the woods to which his and the Dormouse's animal natures belong. The illustrations are also useful in reinforcing the theme of timelessness developed in the text. It is always teatime here, and the drawings support this idea by reproducing the images of teacups and by emphasizing the circle in the saucers, plates, and the Hatter's hat in each picture. Even later in the trial scene, the Hatter is seen holding his teacup—though there is now a piece bitten from it, and it no longer has a perfectly round rim: perhaps a subtle visual sign that the end of Alice's "timeless" dream is approaching.

In describing the Cheshire Cat, however, Carroll captures its essential mystery in just two sentences. He introduces it in Chapter 6 as "a large cat, which was lying on the hearth and grinning from ear to ear" (p. 83) (Fig. 9). Later, we see Alice's response to the creature: "It looked good-natured, she thought: still it had *very* long claws and a great many teeth." Its subsequent partial appearances add to its elusive nature, and Tenniel's illustrations here reinforce Carroll's terse descriptions. It is interesting that while Tenniel draws a wonderfully sinister grin and curious eyes for the cat, he does not show its claws, even though Alice called especial attention to them. He does, on the other hand, add a detail to Carroll's portrait by making the cat a

Figure 9 (*Alice in Wonderland*, Chap. 6)

Figure 10 (*Alice in Wonderland*, Chap. 5)

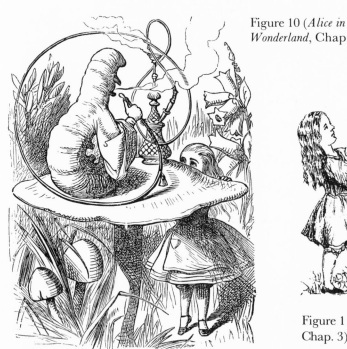

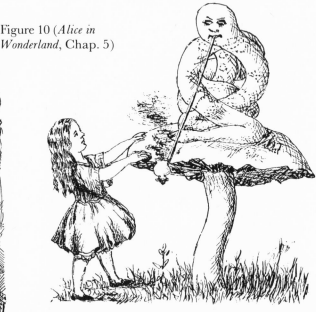

Figure 11 (*Alice's Adventures Under Ground*, Chap. 3)

common striped one, in contrast to Alice's own Dinah (in *Through the Looking-Glass*), who is all black.

Like the Cheshire Cat, the Caterpillar is briefly but memorably described. As Alice stretched herself on tiptoe and peeped over the edge of the mushroom, her eyes "immediately met those of a large blue caterpiller, that was sitting on the top, with its arms folded, quietly smoking a long hookah, and taking not the smallest notice of her or of anything else" (Chap. 4, p. 66). Tenniel's illustration of the Caterpillar in profile (Fig. 10) does not show its arms to be folded, though in Carroll's own drawing (Fig. 11), which gives a frontal view, the "arms" are folded but the drawing is anatomically confusing. Tenniel's illustration captures the mystery and aloofness of the creature by shading its face in profile. Furthermore, he cleverly suggests both a nose and a chin in his drawing of the Caterpillar's forward feet.

The position of the illustration of the Caterpillar at the head of Chapter 5 has a significant effect upon the reader's response. The themes of metamorphosis, growth, and sexuality are all prefigured in the drawing. The tube from the hookah, for example, forms a near circle around the Caterpillar, suggesting the chrysalis mentioned by Alice. Furthermore, the Caterpillar towers over Alice, whose eyes merely reach the edge of the mushroom. This arrangement supports the Caterpillar's superiority and authority and emphasizes Alice's childlike size, out of which she will soon grow to threaten the Pigeon. It is noteworthy that this time only her neck grows to "an immense length" (p. 74). The suggestion of the phallus here is pictorially foreshadowed in the drawings of the three mushrooms. The subjects of sexuality and growth are thus appropriately related to the mysterious and shadowy Caterpillar even before the reader comes to the first sentence of the chapter.

The most grotesque figure in Wonderland, the Duchess, is another character nearly invisible in the text who puts in a dominating and unforgettable appearance in the illustrations. When we first meet the Duchess, in Chapter 6, she is "sitting on a three-legged stool in the middle [of the kitchen] nursing a baby" (p. 82). While the stool is not visible in the accompanying illustration (Fig. 9), it presumably supports the Duchess. She is holding the baby but is not nursing it in the primary sense of the word—namely, giving it suck. It is true, of course, that in the nineteenth century the word *nurse* also meant "to fondle" and "to care for," and that is clearly the sense of the word that Tenniel has in mind in his drawing. How much more grotesque the scene would have been had he followed the more basic and natural definition of the word. In any event, the image of this monstrous female is derived in large part from Tenniel's illustration. She is wearing a dress with a floral print and an enormous hat, under which we see her black wavy hair and huge face with an equally huge pocketlike mouth. Her head is about four times as large as Alice's and she has very masculine features. These grotesque proportions are nowhere mentioned by Carroll, and of course, since the "Pig and Pepper" chapter is an addition to the original manuscript, Carroll had not drawn any pictures of the Duchess. The only feature that Carroll does focus on in the text is her sharp little chin. He tells us that "the Duchess was *very* ugly"

(p. 120) and mentions the uncomfortably "sharp little chin" three times (pp. 120, 121, 122). Curiously, neither of the two illustrations with the Duchess show her to have a chin that is either sharp or little. Rather, her jaw is very broad and fleshy. It seems, in this instance, that Carroll left the realization of the character to Tenniel and approved of what he created.

Even though she appears only twice in the illustrations, the Duchess is one of the most dominant visual figures in the book. The antithesis of conventional Victorian motherhood, she commands the central position of the drawing. Rather than looking to her crying baby, she stares coldly and threateningly out at the reader. Her strong masculine features and exaggerated head size undermine her maternal pose and make her a ponderous, grotesque, and seemingly immovable figure. Her ambiguous sexual nature is further developed in Chapter 9, where she appears with her hand around Alice's arm. Wearing a sinister grin and with her eyelids half open, she appears to be seducing the young girl. Alice makes it clear in the text that the Duchess's increasing physical contact makes her very uncomfortable. William Empson sees this scene as one in which "the middle-aged woman [is] trying to flirt with the chaste young man." [6] Given the Duchess's massive and masculine features, however, her sexual ambiguity at this point makes her an even more troubling creature than Empson allows.

Two other characters in the "Pig and Pepper" chapter go undescribed in the text—the lantern-jawed, grimacing cook whose face is hidden under the shadow of a large bonnet and the rather unpleasant and unhappy looking baby who is howling and sneezing. The Duchess flings the baby at Alice and says "Here! You may nurse it a bit, if you like!" Again Tenniel interprets the word *nurse* in a general way and depicts Alice simply holding the pig-child. Nevertheless, she is holding it in the typical nursing position, which very subtly reinforces a grotesque maternal relationship. This drawing (Fig. 12) provides an interesting parallel with the one in which the Duchess is holding the baby. The Duchess holds up the baby's head with her right hand, and the other picture reverses this by having Alice support the pig-baby's head with her left hand. Neither the Duchess nor Alice look at their infants, but rather stare out at the reader. Alice's expression reminds one of Oliver Hardy's occasional eye-contact with the audience that puts him on their side as a witness to the farcical, madcap proceedings.

In drawing the King and Queen of Hearts Tenniel reproduced the essential features of those characters from the traditional playing cards. The Queen of Hearts is basically an auditory creature, characterized by her recurrent shouting "Off with her head!" Carroll tells us only that her face turned crimson, that she glared at Alice, and that she frowned "like a thunderstorm" (p. 123). Tenniel fixes her face in a perpetual scowl, her brow casting dark shadows over her menacing eyes. The King of Hearts, on the other hand, maintains a more neutral expression characteristic of the face on the playing card. Carroll adds a few appropriate details by having the King put on his spectacles during the trial and wear his crown over his judicial wig: "the judge, by the way, was the King; and, as he wore his crown over the wig (look at the frontispiece if you want to see how he did it), he did not look at all comfortable and it was certainly not becoming" (p. 144). Carroll's direct reference to the frontispiece clearly acknowledges the important interdependence of illustrations and text.

The Mock Turtle is only partially described by Carroll, who informs us that this creature has "large eyes full of tears" (p. 126) and "drew back one of his flappers across his eyes" (p. 131). The bizarre nature of the Turtle, however, is envisioned by Tenniel, who shows it to have the head, hind hooves, and tail of a calf. Martin Gardner explains that Tenniel drew his Turtle this way because mock turtle soup is an imitation of green turtle soup, which is customarily made of veal.[7] The Mock Turtle's associate, the Gryphon (Fig. 13), has a ready-made image from Greek mythology, and Carroll makes little attempt to describe it. He simply states: "If you don't know what a Gryphon is, look at the picture" (p. 124). When one looks at Carroll's own drawing, however (Fig. 14), the Gryphon resembles a rat with a bird's beak and talons more than it does the traditional figure from mythology, and the Mock Turtle appears simply as a rather scrawny turtle. Nevertheless, Carroll's advice applies even more forceably to all of the characters discussed above: Look at the pictures. The illustrations appear to be in exactly the right places in the text so that the reader could see his way along the story. Several of the chapters, for example, have illustrations placed ahead of the text, thereby fixing in the reader's mind what certain characters look like before they

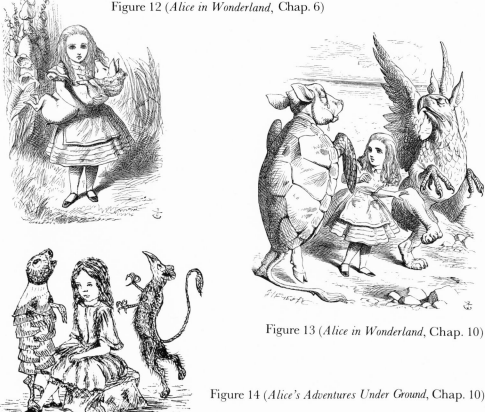

Figure 12 (*Alice in Wonderland*, Chap. 6)

Figure 13 (*Alice in Wonderland*, Chap. 10)

Figure 14 (*Alice's Adventures Under Ground*, Chap. 10)

appear in the text. More frequently, the illustrations appear at points in the text where a character or a scene is briefly described or where language seems inadequate to render a character. The first illustration of the Gryphon, for example, is placed right after Carroll's advice to the reader to look at the picture, "if you don't know what a Gryphon is."

Why did Carroll abandon language for pictures to define the physical appearance of his major characters? Several reasons may be inferred. For one thing, since the book was originally written for a child, there is the obvious reason that children simply enjoy looking at pictures. Illustrations help to win a child's interest in a book, and publishers demanded drawings to enhance the sales appeal of their volumes. Furthermore, there was a brilliant tradition of illustrated books in the nineteenth century, especially those designed for children, including such notable works as Grimms' *Fairy Tales* (1823), illustrated by George Cruikshank; Lear's *Book of Nonsense* (1846); Ruskin's *The King of the Golden River,* illustrated by Richard Doyle; Thackeray's *The Rose and the Ring; or the History of Prince Giglio* (1855), illustrated by the author; and *The House that Jack Built* and *The History of Cock Robin* (1865–66), illustrated by Walter Crane. Many stories first appeared in popular illustrated magazines for children, such as *The Boy's Own Magazine, Aunt Judy's Magazine, The Boys of England,* and *Chatterbox.* In light of this tradition, a book like *Alice's Adventures in Wonderland* was simply expected to contain illustrations.

Second, as Phyllis Greenacre has pointed out, Carroll exhibited a scoptophilic interest that was expressed both in his writing and his photography: "The spirit of both *Alice* books is that of an unplanned sight-seeing trip through a marvelously strange country." [8] The titles of both works, she continues, "re-emphasizes the voyeuristic theme." At the outset of the story, Alice expresses her dissatisfaction with her sister's book "without pictures or conversations." And once down the rabbit-hole she discovers a small passage about the size of a rathole and "knelt down and looked along the passage into the loveliest garden you ever saw." The rest of her journey resembles a museum tour of Ripley's Believe It or Not, with one bizarre spectacle following another—the illustrations standing like photographs of Carroll's mental picture of the characters and scenes.

A third reason for Carroll's exchange of illustrations for verbal descriptions can be adduced from Elizabeth Sewell's observation that "the aim of Nonsense is to inhibit one half of the mind, and nothing more hinders the dream or imagination than to have its pictures provided." [9] Ambiguity and imaginative embellishment are rendered impossible once the stark line drawings of Tenniel are fixed in our minds. By their precision and detail, the illustrations lead to our detachment from the characters. We "know" them in one glance and, with the exception of the Cheshire Cat, they hold little depth and mystery. Most of the creatures represent a class: the Caterpillar, the Red Queen, the White Rabbit. Their abstract, impersonal nature is perfectly suited to their roles in the text—where, with mathematical precision, they articulate the logic of Wonderland.

A fourth reason, and perhaps the most important one, is that *Alice's Adventures in Wonderland*, unlike the works of Dickens or Doyle, is not a piece of traditional fiction that derives its power from creating the illusion of reality and believable characters who interact with one another. Carroll's work is far more abstract and focuses upon language itself. Insofar as the text is concerned, the Mad Hatter, the Caterpillar, the Cheshire Cat, and many of the other characters define themselves through their dialogues as witty masters of the language who seem eager to engage in verbal jousts with their curious visitor. They are intellectual creatures who play with language in a very sophisticated manner. By separating their language (the text) from their bodies (the illustrations), Carroll reinforces the essence of nonsense, namely, that it is a game and the playthings are words. Instead of human characters with complex emotions, the illustrations render the characters as fixed objects. As Sewell puts it, "if people are things in the Nonsense game, they must, when they meet, treat one another as such, and this involves detachment from any form of affection or kindliness. Relationships between them will be matter-of-fact but not matter for feeling." [10]

Susanne Langer draws an interesting distinction between discursive and presentational forms that sheds light on the relationship between text and pictures: "Language in the strict sense is essentially discursive; it has permanent units of meaning which are combinable with larger units; it has fixed equivalences that make definition and translation possible; its connotations are general so that it requires non-verbal acts, like pointing, looking, or emphatic voice-inflections, to assign specific denotations to its terms." In directing the reader to "look at the picture," then, Carroll avoids the ambiguity of language that would damage the nonsense game. As Langer points out, pictures are nondiscursive and untranslatable, do not allow for definitions within their own system, and cannot directly convey generalities. A picture, she says, "in itself represents just one object—real or imaginary, but still a unique object." [11] The illustrations, then, help to establish the characters as "things," unchanging and unchangeable figures in a swirl of abstract linguistic play, marvelous puppets who speak the language of the master wit, Lewis Carroll.

There have been numerous artists after Tenniel who set forth their versions of Alice and her associates: Mabel Lucie Atwell, Peter Newell, Arthur Rackham, Charles Robinson, Thomas Maybank, Harry Furniss, Fritz Kredel, Salvador Dali, and Ralph Steadman—to name a few.[12] Since Carroll did not provide visual guidelines for artists in his text, most of the illustrators fell under the pervasive influence of Tenniel and have not succeeded in displacing from the imaginations of the public the images that were constructed over a century ago. The greatest single rival of Tenniel today must certainly be Walt Disney, whose film version of the *Alice* story has shaped millions of young people's conceptions of the characters. While the Disney artists draw heavily upon Tenniel's illustrations, they have softened and sentimentalized the original drawings and rendered them rather bland. One hesitates to guess what future generations will see when they think about Alice and her mad acquaintances, but one would like to hope that Tenniel's masterful rendition of Carroll's rather abstract wonders will continue to anchor the imagination in the ground of nonsense.

NOTES

1. This is not to say that the illustrations of Browne and Paget, or of other illustrators of nineteenth-century fiction did not influence readers' visual conception of characters, but that they were strictly limited by the authors' elaborate verbal descriptions. In the first chapter of *Pickwick Papers* Dickens quickly establishes the basic portrait of his hero and continues throughout the novel to add details of dress and expression that fix a clear image in the reader's mind of exactly what Mr. Pickwick looks like. Even in the 1940s motion-picture version of the novel all of the characters are remarkably true to Dickens's (and Browne's) original portraits. Like Browne, Paget remained faithful to the text in his many illustrations of the Holmes stories and our present image of Holmes—with his deerstalker cap, a long caped overcoat, magnifying glass, and pipe—is based essentially upon Doyle's own words. The only major departure from the original portrait came in 1899, when William Gillette, in his melodrama *Sherlock Holmes,* introduced the full-bent pipe. The actor found that he could not speak his lines with a straight pipe (the shape depicted by Paget) and thus contributed a memorable detail to the imagined portrait of the great detective.
2. *The Letters of Lewis Carroll,* ed. Morton N. Cohen with the assistance of Roger Lancelyn Green, 2 vols. (London: Macmillan; New York: Oxford Univ. Press, 1979), I: 62.
3. See *Tenniel's Alice: Drawings by Sir John Tenniel for Alice's Adventures in Wonderland and Through the Looking-Glass* (Cambridge, Massachusetts: Harvard College Library and the Metropolitan Museum of Art, 1978).
4. Quoted in *Early Children's Books and Their Illustration,* ed. Gerald Gottlieb (Boston: David Godine, 1975), p. 233.
5. All quotations from *Alice's Adventures in Wonderland* are taken from Martin Gardner's *The Annotated Alice: Alice's Adventures in Wonderland and Through the Looking-Glass* (New York: Clarkson N. Potter, 1960). Page numbers are cited parenthetically in text.
6. William Empson, "The Child as Swain," in *Some Versions of Pastoral* (1935; rpt. New York: New Directions, 1960), p. 264.
7. *The Annotated Alice,* ed. Gardner, p. 124.
8. Phyllis Greenacre, *Swift and Carroll: A Psychoanalytic Study of Two Lives* (New York: International Universities Press, 1955), p. 213.
9. Elizabeth Sewell, *The Field of Nonsense* (London: Chatto and Windus, 1952), pp. 111–12.
10. Ibid., p. 141.
11. Susanne Langer, *Philosophy in a New Key* (New York: The New American Library, 1951), p. 89.
12. See Graham Ovenden and John Davis, *The Illustrators of Alice in Wonderland* (London: Academy Press; New York: St. Martin's Press, 1972; rev. ed. 1979).

Toward a Definition of *Alice*'s Genre: The Folktale and Fairy-Tale Connections

NINA DEMUROVA

The two slender volumes of *Alice* by Lewis Carroll hold a special place in world literature. The number of critical appreciations of them alone bears witness to this. Among various aspects and problems analyzed by students of Carroll, that of genre occupies the least prominent place. We all agree, of course, that the two *Alice* books are literary fairy tales; and it has been suggested, although not pursued significantly, that they belong to late Romanticism. However, such general comments do not seem adequate; the very originality of Carroll's method suggests specific types of genre-forming characteristics. Let us try to single out some of them at least.

The problem of the genre of the *Alice*s is, in fact, the major problem of Carroll's poetics. What follows are a number of preliminary, tentative remarks in connection with this wide and complex theme. In this essay I look at the *Alice*s in the context of the tradition of fairy tales in the nineteenth century, noting the changes and reinterpretations evidenced in Carroll's work; I look at Carroll's use of folklore and nursery rhymes, including indirect influences on Carroll's work—among them possibly that of Edward Lear; and finally I look at the literary dialogue that is so much a part of the fabric of the *Alice*s. I proceed from the assumption that Carroll's work developed within the framework of late Romanticism, varying in a few major points from the classical pattern of early nineteenth-century Romantic writing. One may say, in fact, that his work presents a somewhat reduced variation on the usual Romantic pattern of a lonely hero's (or heroine's) wanderings in strange lands full of wonders.[1] The reductions were brought about by a number of different causes, not least among them the particular stability of the Victorian age as compared with the Romantic period.

I

In England—unlike Germany or other continental countries, where such popularity had come earlier—the genre of literary tales gained wide popularity
only by the middle of the nineteenth century. John Ruskin's *King of the Golden
River* (written in 1841, published ten years later), Thackeray's *The Ring and the
Rose* (1855), Charles Kingsley's *Water Babies* (1863), Charles Dickens's "The
Magic Fish-Bone" (*Holiday Romance,* 1868), to name but a few, all drew on the
rich tradition of English folklore. Rehabilitation of the theory of the fairy tale
as a genre—pitting the fantasy of folklore against the didacticism of utilitarian and religious writing—had been attempted by the early Romantics in
England as far back as the beginning of the nineteenth century, although it is
true that in their own work the English Romantics made little use of the
prose fairy tale, their interests lying in other genres. However, the acknowledgment of the fairy tale in Romantic theory of the early nineteenth century
and the introduction of various other folklore forms in poetic practice prepared the soil for the later blossoming of the literary folktale in England. An
important dimension of the development of the new genre in England
emerged when writers became acquainted with Romantic, especially German, prose. Equally stimulating were the first translations of Grimms' (1824)
and Anderson's (1846) fairy tales.

The writers who took up the genre of literary fairy tale developed it in
accordance with their individual ideas and concepts. Ruskin, Kingsley, and
MacDonald used the folktale "morphology," with its various functions of
character-types,[2] to create their own fairy-tale narratives in the spirit of
Christian ethics and morals—remaining, on the whole, within the folktale
structure, with the kind of reductions, changes, and assimilations that are
permissible there. "Confessional" and "superstitious" changes or substitu-
tions (to use Propp's terminology again) are of special importance in the
context of these writers' tales.[3] Dickens's and Thackeray's fairy tales have a
different character, since both these writers introduce an element of parody,
and not infrequently, self-parody. They blend, phantastically, typical themes
of their own realistic narratives with mock-romantic and fairy-tale motifs,
adding a rich dosage of irony and satire; yet, they retain the most important
characteristics of folktale structure.

Alice in Wonderland and *Through the Looking-Glass* are, undoubtedly, close to
this English ironic development of the fairy-tale tradition. However, they, in
their turn, differ substantially from other English literary fairy tales of the
period. There is, primarily, a certain difference in the functional character of
Carroll's irony itself. In Dickens's and Thackeray's fairy tales, irony is directed against popular second-rate books of melodrama or adventure, as well
as against certain aspects of their own works. In both cases one finds in their
fairy tales ironic models based on themes, characters, and motifs they or
other writers have used elsewhere, and their irony serves primarily the aim of
parody (or self-parody). Carroll's irony has, in principal, a different quality.
In its very character it stands closer to that more general category that, in

relation to German Romantic writers, is known as "Romantic irony." To quote from N. Berkovsky, who made a special study of German Romanticism: "Irony, on the purely cognitional level, meant that the particular method of perceiving reality, practiced in the given work, was considered as nonfinite by the author himself, although attempts to go beyond it were also seen as purely subjective and hypothetic." (Translations throughout are mine.) This is why Tieck in his conversation with Keppke drew his attention to the double nature of irony: "It is neither mockery nor sneering, as the terms are usually understood; but, rather, profound earnestness that is connected with joking and true joy." Irony is both the sorrow of impotence and the merry breaking of positive "frontiers." [4] This sort of irony includes the elements of parody and self-parody, but it goes further than that.

With a varying degree of probability, one may assume that Carroll knew the fairy tales written by his contemporaries. Leaving aside, for lack of factual data, the question of whether Carroll knew Thackeray's *The King and the Rose* at the time he was writing *Alice in Wonderland* from 1862 through 1865 (Dickens published his "Magic Fish Bone" three years later), suffice it to mention that by the time *Through the Looking-Glass* was published in 1871, Carroll must have been acquainted with it. He must also have known Ruskin's fairy tales as well as Kingsley's. He was acquainted with Ruskin, who taught at Oxford, and was on friendly terms with the Kingsleys and the MacDonalds. In the texts of the two *Alice*s we may find not a few passages echoing certain episodes of these writers' tales.[5] Still, the similarities do not extend beyond a number of details. Religious or didactic allegory within the fairy-tale structure was never attempted by Carroll.

Under Carroll's pen the folktale structure undergoes certain changes. One such change occurs as early as the very first chapter of *Wonderland*, which presents what Propp calls an "initial situation." Alice's departure down the rabbit-hole is sudden and in no way premeditated; it is quite spontaneous— ". . . burning with curiosity, she ran across the field after it [the Rabbit]," etc. Neither is it brought about by "misfortune," "villainy" or "insufficiency" (which Propp calls also "lack" or "shortage"), situations that traditionally inaugurate the plot of the folktale.[6]

In fact, Alice feels the insufficiency only when, looking through the keyhole, she sees the beautiful garden beyond the locked door. It is then that Carroll introduces a series of minor insufficiencies, connected with the changing proportions between Alice's height, the height of the table on which the key lies, the size of the keyhole, the width of the little passage leading to the garden, etc. Eliminating the main insufficiency (toward the end of Chapter 7 when Alice, at last, unlocks the door with the little golden key and gets through to the beautiful garden) does not lead to denouement, since the beautiful garden proves to be a kingdom of chaos and fear.

The Queen's croquet party; Alice's meeting the Duchess, the Gryphon, and the Mock Turtle; the trial and the waking up are yet to follow. None of these episodes is prepared for by what proceeds it; none forms a pair with any of previous ones. Neither the knotting nor the unknotting of the tale is caused by any of the traditional devices. It is true that sometimes the folktale can also do without the traditional insufficiency—which may become apparent only later, after the hero's necessary departure; so that in this respect, at least, *Wonderland* exhibits a certain closeness to the traditional pattern. But the arbitrariness (from the traditional point of view) of the unknotting, or denouement, represents a drastic change from the folklore norm. The rigid structure of cause and effect, characteristic of the folk fairy tale, is openly broken in *Wonderland.* The book does not end when Alice succeeds in eliminating the main insufficiency, nor because she does so—the dream simply ends, and with it the fairy tale.

Other functions of different dramatis personae—these molecules that make up the fairy tale—also undergo similar transformations. They are not completely discarded or broken, they are still felt, but their quality and interrelations are radically changed. In both *Wonderland* and *Through the Looking-Glass* we come across "donors" who test, interrogate, or attack the heroine "in preparation for receiving either a magical agent or helper." [7]

In *Alice in Wonderland,* these are the blue Caterpillar, who provides Alice with the magic mushroom; the White Rabbit, in whose house Alice finds the bottle with the magic drink, etc. In *Through the Looking-Glass* there is the White Queen, who makes Alice run and who later explains to her the rules of the chess game; there are also the two queens, who ask Alice questions and riddles and then invite her to her own feast. Of all these, it is only the Caterpillar who actually plays the part of a donor as it should be played. Even then, characteristically, the results of the interrogation, or test, have no bearing whatsoever upon what follows. Alice, in fact, has not answered any of the Caterpillar's questions, so that the receipt of the magic agent, i.e., the mushroom, is quite unexpected, not only for the reader but for Alice herself.

The donor role differs from the traditional fairy-tale pattern to an even greater extent with the other characters Alice encounters. The White Rabbit, who at first takes Alice for somebody else, sends her upstairs, inadvertently helping her to find the little bottle with the magic potion. Later, when—suddenly and catastrophically grown—she takes up the whole house, he leads an attack, giving her, again inadvertently, another magical agent, i.e., the pebbles that, turning into little cakes, enable her to grow small again. Perhaps what is important here is not so much the inadvertency of donation, for this sometimes happens in the folktale too, but rather the fact that the donor himself never learns about his own particular function. In different interrogations and tests suggested by either or both of the two queens, Alice also fails—at least from the queens' point of view. Nevertheless *after* these interrogations, tests, and trials—but not *because* she has succeeded in them—Alice invariably learns what further steps she should take. The cause-and-effect pattern in all of these episodes is extremely weak.

The impression is created in the reader that Carroll is playing with these traditional elements of folktale and that finally, in the process of this game, he destroys them, though they are never totally excluded. "Contrariwise," they are invariably present, as if to afford the author the possibility of playing with them and to make them undergo these significant changes. Here again, the dream device is instrumental in destroying these traditional elements.

To a certain extent, a number of other personages in the two tales may also be considered variables of donors. They also interrogate the heroine and make her undergo different tests; however, they don't present her with the magical agent, but simply send her on to the next donor. The Queen in *Wonderland* plays the role of the hostile donor; her function is also weakened, however, since she only threatens attack and execution, but never carries out her threats.

Other functions of the traditional fairy tale undergo similar changes in Carroll's two tales. This affects "spacial translocation between two kingdoms," or "guidance." A tunnel, i.e., a "stationary means of communication," is made use of at the beginning of *Wonderland,* whereas in *Through the Looking-Glass* another type of "transference" is used. Similarly weakened is the important function of "struggle," in which, according to Propp, "the hero and the villain join in direct combat." Here it takes the form of verbal competition, and sometimes comes quite close to a squabble.

The weakening of these and certain other folktale functions is carried through not only with the help of disorganization of cause-and-effect patterns and of disorganization of the type and interrelation of primary folktale elements, but also with the help of ironic interpretation of all the events that take place, a particular romantic characteristic that Carroll possessed in the highest degree. The dream device, mentioned above, forms one of the tale's most effective methods too.

Carroll's fairy tale, for all its outward similarity to the humorous folktale, is in fact very unlike it. This could be accounted for by a cardinal difference in the very quality of laughter in Carroll's work.

In his interest in folklore, Carroll did not limit himself to fairy tale alone. He turned his attention to nursery rhymes as well—which he also interpreted in his own way. The nature of these interpretations varies however.

A few nursery rhymes are directly incorporated into the text. This occurs mostly in *Through the Looking-Glass* (Humpty Dumpty, The Lion and the Unicorn, Tweedledum and Tweedledee), but the concluding chapters of *Alice in Wonderland,* in which the trial of the Knave of Hearts takes place, are also based on an old nursery rhyme. Its first stanza is cited in the text, whereas the second one, in which the Knave brings back the tarts and vows he'll steal no more, is not taken into account at all. Carroll not only includes these nursery rhymes in his fairy tale, he develops them into episodes and chapters, keeping the peculiar spirit of folklore events and characters intact.

Apart from direct citations and borrowings from nursery rhymes, one may trace some other direct or indirect folklore influences. One of the channels for these could be the limericks of Edward Lear (although this is merely conjectural, since we do not know whether Carroll read Lear). The Carroll/

Lear similarity is sometimes very striking, however. Indeed, it seems not at all impossible that some of Carroll's imagery was suggested by Lear's nonsense, such as his early *Book of Nonsense* (1846)—which is itself indebted to the folklore tradition of madmen and eccentrics.[8]

> There was an Old Man of Coblenz,
> The length of whose legs was immense;
> He went with one prance, from Turkey to France,
> That surprising Old Man of Coblenz.
>
> There was an Old Man with an owl,
> Who continued to bother and howl,
> He sat on a rail, and imbibed bitter ale
> Which refreshed that Old Man and his owl.
>
> There was an Old Man of Leghorn,
> The smallest as ever was born;
> But quickly snapt up he was once by a puppy,
> Who devoured that Old Man of Leghorn.
>
> There was an Old Man who said, "Well!
> Will nobody answer this bell?
> I have pulled day and night, till my hair has grown white,
> But nobody answers this bell!"
>
> There was an Old Man with a beard,
> Who sat on a horse when he reared;
> But they said, "Never mind! you will fall off behind,
> You propitious Old Man with a beard!"

"The Old Man of Coblenz" may have inspired the episode in which Alice bids good-bye to her legs, and the similarity is further enhanced if one compares the drawings of the two authors. Lear's other "old men" may have suggested Carroll's "aged man a-sitting on a gate" from the White Knight's ballad, whereas the White Knight himself, who is constantly falling off his horse, has something in common with those old men of Edward Lear's who suffer similarly through poor horsemanship. It is, perhaps, not completely incidental that both Lear and Carroll identified themselves, in a way, with these unfortunate characters. In Lear's drawings they invariably looked like him, whereas Carroll's White Knight has not a little of self-parody.

The number of these examples could be multiplied, but I shall not cite many; it is sufficient for my purpose just to mention the fact of certain similarities between Lear's and Carroll's nonsense. It could well be that Lear's limericks were instrumental in Carroll's acceptance of one of the aspects of the old folk tradition of madmen and eccentrics. This, of course, is only one possible explanation. Others are to be looked for in a certain affinity in the mental makeup of the two writers and in the aims they set for themselves within the peculiar literary context of the period.

II

Apart from traditional fairy tales and nursery rhymes, Carroll's muse drew upon another treasure-house of national folklore. In Carroll's *Alice* a few characters came to life that owe their natures—and, in fact, their very existence—to old proverbs and sayings: the March Hare, the Mad Hatter, and the Cheshire Cat, as well as a few others. The proverbial stupidity of oysters was "revived," according to R. L. Green, "to a new life" by Tenniel's cartoon in *Punch* (January 19, 1861), and may have suggested the oyster sequence in "The Walrus and the Carpenter." [9] It is, indeed, difficult to overestimate the importance of these characters in Carroll's fairy tale. Deeply rooted in the national consciousness, under Carroll's pen they turn into extended metaphors that define the nature of these personages and their very behavior, providing the structure for the story and its development.

Carroll's madmen and eccentrics have a special place in his fairy tale. They are, directly or indirectly, connected with that "powerful and wild" [10] folklore tradition that constitutes one of the most brilliant features of the English national self-consciousness. It is these madmen and eccentrics (and apart from Alice and a few minor characters, that description embraces practically all the characters in the two books) who inhabit—and indeed, one almost feels entitled to say *create*—that particular "antiworld," that "irreality," [11] that topsy-turvydom that is the very essence of English nonsense. One could discern distant echoes of the roaring carnival laughter of bygone ages, preserved by folklore tradition. It is true that the laughter is heard as a faint and very distant reverberation, "the carnival is undergone in solitude" and "translated into the subjective language of the new epoch." [12]

Scholars who are to some extent familiar with M. M. Bakhtin's theory of carnival and carnival laughter may feel tempted to perceive Carroll's nonsense in the light of this theory. Could it not prompt an answer to the paradox that has been mystifying critics of different trends for so many years? Could it not help us to understand the contradiction between Dodgson's lawabiding personality, his addiction to meticulous order, his piety, on the one hand, and the very essence of his fairy tales on the other—which are "unlawful," "irreligious," topsy-turvy?

Bakhtin's conception proceeds from the underlying premise that in the medieval and Renaissance consciousness, the world was dual. The official, serious world was countered by the world of carnival ritual and pageantry—based on what Bakhtin terms carnival laughter. The carnival presented a completely different, patently unofficial, aspect of the world—of man and human relations extraneous to church and state. It was another world and another life on the other side of all officialdom. It was this life and this world of which all medieval people were more or less a part and in which they lived at certain seasons. It is a duality of a particular kind, and a full comprehension of that duality is essential for an understanding of both medieval and Renaissance culture. To ignore or to underrate the people's laughter in the Middle Ages would be to distort the picture of the whole subsequent historical development of Western culture.[13]

The history of laughter during subsequent periods of the history of culture in general, and of English culture in particular, still awaits investigation. Here we can only point out that Bakhtin's theory may suggest new ways of interpreting Carroll's nonsense. In it, perhaps, resound echoes of the second world of the Middle Age and the Renaissance, conveyed through folklore into the middle of the nineteenth century. Bakhtin's remark on the "element of play" in carnival forms may be important for a better understanding of Carroll's work. "Because of their visual, concrete and sensual character and the presence of a strong play element, they [i.e., the carnival forms] stand close to imaginative arts, to theater and pageantry . . . ," writes Bakhtin. "But the main carnival core of this culture is not purely art, theater, or pageantry; in fact, it does not belong to the sphere of art at all. It exists on the borderline between art and life itself. It is, in fact, life itself, taking a specific play form." [14]

Here again, in the subjective, reduced, formalized devices of Carroll's nonsense, one may distinguish echoes of a strong folk tradition. The first fairy tale that was narrated to the Liddell girls was, in fact, a kind of game in which everybody present participated—the audience not just listening passively, but suggesting themes, moves, and clues. This tale was also *shown* to the audience—not in action, it is true, but in a series of drawings (presenting dramatis personae as well as the mise-en-scène) that Carroll later reproduced in his manuscript of *Alice's Adventures Under Ground.* The first episodes of *Alice in Wonderland* were narrated orally—improvised, as it were, as a kind of commedia dell'arte is improvised: prompted, to a large extent, by what has just happened to the participants, who appear in it as some sort of masks with accompanying names, nicknames, characteristic gestures, etc. Later, in the literary, final version of *Alice,* this improvised freshness was somewhat reduced, but it is still felt even now, constituting one of Alice's major charms and peculiarities. One may also speak of a specific theatrical or dramatic quality of *Alice.* With the exception of initial descriptions—in which the author seems to lay down the conditions of the game, the time and the place of dramatic action (slightly longer in *Wonderland,* where he was just feeling his way, than in *The Looking-Glass*)—the two *Alice*s fall, easily and naturally, into scenes: The participants first conduct a dialogue, which often takes the form of a competition, quarrel, or squabble, and this is followed by actions characteristic of a burlesque or a puppet show. The knights in *The Looking-Glass* hit each other furiously with clubs that they hold with their arms, as if they were Punch and Judy. The Cook throws everything within her reach at the Duchess, the fire irons, saucepans, frying pans, plates, dishes. The Duchess, in her turn, throws the baby at Alice. In fact, in the two *Alice* books somebody is always hitting, banging, beating, kicking, teasing, threatening, scolding, or killing (but not quite) someone. Many of Carroll's jokes and puns, especially those on the death theme, show ties with the fairground tradition. Here again, one may find traces of the popular open-air theater of long ago—partially preserved in Carroll's day in the popular fairground and puppet tradition.

The squabbles of the actors in the *Alice*s are singularly laconic, dynamic, and expressive. In fact, Carroll reveals an extraordinary genius for theatrical dialogue. His descriptions and introductions to scenes are invariably short, his use of detail invariably sparing; he never says anything that is not strictly necessary for action and dialogue. His dialogue is always a kind of duel (not necessarily verbal); it is a competition in which his dramatis personae realize themselves. Alice's thoughts are no less expressive and dramatic; as a rule, they are presented as inner monologues.

The illustrations play a specific role in the text of the two tales as Richard Kelly and others have demonstrated in essays in this volume. They make up for the economy of description, which otherwise might have been felt to be a flaw, and from the very beginning Carroll's story is patently oriented toward them. They not only illustrate the text, but develop it—being a necessary and organic part of the story. A comparison of Carroll's own drawings for *Alice's Adventures Under Ground* with Tenniel's illustrations (as well as their letters to each other) shows how close Tenniel's illustrations were to Carroll's concepts. In fact, many of Tenniel's illustrations realize the ideas of Carroll's sketches.

Finally, in creating his topsy-turvy world, Carroll, more than anybody else, follows what Charles Lamb called the *wild* spirit of folklore. Carroll turns the situations upside down and inside out, making the cause follow the effect; he alienates attributes and parts of the body and creates things and creatures that cannot, and should not, be imagined; he *realizes* worn-out idioms and phrases and breathes new life into old metaphors; he parodies; he laughs at death; etc., etc. I am far from suggesting that Carroll's nonsense is a direct development from folk carnival tradition. Bakhtin develops his brilliant theory upon the material of archaic cultures that constitute a different stage of development from that of the nineteenth century. Nonetheless, I feel it not completely irrelevant to point out the possibility of some genetic connection of Carroll's fairy tales with this old tradition.

III

Another powerful element in the *Alice*s is that of literary dialogue, which is constituted by parodies, allusions, borrowings, quotations, etc. Carroll seems to be carrying on a never-ending dialogue with invisible interlocutors, many of whom are long deceased. A level of this kind is found in every work of literature, since they all take part—directly or indirectly—in a kind of dialogue that is the essence of every culture. What draws our attention in Carroll's fairy tales is, primarily, the multitude of intonations and the types of dialogue inferences.

Critics often speak of parodies in the *Alice*s; among these they cite "Father William," the lullaby sung by the Duchess, "How doth the little crocodile . . . ," and "Beautiful Soup" from *Alice in Wonderland,* and "The Walrus and the Carpenter," "The Aged Aged Man," and the chorus in the Queen Alice chapter from *Through the Looking-Glass.* However, the term *parody* in relation to these poems can hardly be considered completely accurate. True, all of these poems are, in one way or another, connected with some original text, which can be sensed through Carroll's apparently lowering parody. But in each particular case, the degree and the type of connection with the original is different. Sometimes Carroll's poems follow the original very closely, making use of its vocabulary, arrangement of lines, and general structure, while in other cases they preserve only a few details of the original—the rhythmic pattern, or meter for example. In fact, Carroll's attitude toward the original and the aims of his parody varies.

In "Father William," for instance, Carroll seems to lower the text of Southey's didactic poem "The Old Man's Comforts and How He Gained Them." Southey's moralizing and edifying reflections give place to Carroll's happy nonsense—following a rule that is openly and provocatively stated in the second stanza.

> "In my youth," Father William replied to his son,
>   "I feared it might injure the brain;
> But, now that I'm perfectly sure I have none,
>   Why, I do it again and again." [15]

Keeping the same heroes and the question-and-answer pattern of Southey's poem, and retaining a number of descriptive phrases, the meter, and the rhyme scheme, Carroll transforms Southey's original into an irresponsible "standing on one's head." What are the aims of this transformation? The answer seems to be self-evident: satire. Carroll, one is tempted to say, mocks at Southey's dull didacticism and pious moralizing. But here we have to face a difficulty, since Southey's dull and pious moralizing was far from being alien to Carroll. In fact, when Carroll was not busy writing nonsense, he thought, felt, and wrote in exactly the same vein as Southey. In his sermons and letters, in the serious and, in many ways, autobiographical portions of *Sylvie and Bruno,* even in prefaces to his nonsense books, Carroll enlarged upon the same themes. Could it be, then, that the object of Carroll's parody were certain formal aspects of Southey's poetry that were indeed far from being perfect? But, in that case, Carroll would have followed another course, placing satiric emphasis directly upon these formal elements.

We are faced with the same sort of problem when we consider "How doth the little crocodile, . . ." which the reader feels (or, at least, felt in Carroll's day) contains echoes of Watts's "Little busy bee"; or when we examine "Tis the voice of the Lobster, . . ." which again follows Southey's original. Carroll, who wrote at length and with feeling on the necessity of avoiding idleness, for idleness breeds sinful thoughts, could hardly have satirized Watts's poem, which he must have found congenial. The same can be said about "Twinkle, twinkle, little bat, . . ." based on Jane Taylor's "Star"; Carroll's general agreement with the poem's sentiment did not stop him from parodying the poem.

In the Duchess's lullaby, Carroll seems to depart even further from the original than in the poems discussed above; but his position and approach seem unchanged. In "The Walrus and the Carpenter," as well as in the White Knight's song, "Beautiful Soup," and the "Lobster Quadrille," the connection with the original is still more distant and is only imperfectly felt. The satirical elements are practically absent; the underlying text is hardly perceived at all and is felt only in intonation, or in a particular turn of phrase. Perhaps this is so because here Carroll uses the texts of Wordsworth and Tennyson, poets whom he admired greatly, and who, from a poetic point of view, were superior both to Southey and to the children's poets of the former decades.

The question arises as to whether Carroll presents in these poems a kind of poetic synthesis—an attempt to express through parody his attitude toward the chosen poet.[16] I believe that this question should also be answered in the negative. Carroll's "parodies" form an important part in the "intellectual holiday," strictly limited both in time and space, that G. K. Chesterton wrote about.[17] Satire and synthesis are present in Carroll's parodies only in a certain sense: only in that degree to which the reader tends to read them in; and what is more important, only in that degree to which they were allowed in by that particular dual, carnival quality that—with all the modifications of its forms—was characteristic of Carroll's work. It is also possible that there was a measure of deep, unconscious ambivalence in Carroll's attitude not only toward such poets as Southey, Taylor, or Watts but even toward Wordsworth, and Tennyson, and that this ambivalence found its expression in his nonsense parodies. Following Eric Partridge, who has spoken of Lear's echoing words,[18] these parodies could be called echoing poems.

The dialogue, or echoing, character of Carroll's *Alices* is not limited to poetic parodies alone. It has been pointed out that the question concerning cats and bats was probably suggested by Norman MacLeod's "Gold Thread" (1861), whereas a tiny golden key may have been suggested either by George Macdonald's poem "The Golden Key" (published in *Victoria Regis,* 1861) or by his "famous allegorical fairy story of the same name," which Carroll may have read in manuscript by 1862.[19] There are some distant echoes as well of William Roscoe's "Butterfly's Ball" (1806) in the scene with the blue Caterpillar and the mushroom. *Through the Looking-Glass* enlarges on still another theme suggested by George Macdonald (among others) in his romantic story of Cosmo Verstahl, a poor student of Prague University, which was included in his *Phantastes* (1858). Carroll's White Knight reminds us of the Knight in the Rusty Armour in Macdonald's "faerie romance," and, possibly, of Don Quixote.[20] It has been noted that in the opening paragraphs of *Through the Looking-Glass* Carroll was subconsciously recollecting the beginning of a parody of Dickens's *Cricket on the Hearth* that was published in *Blackwood's Magazine* in November 1845,[21] whereas quotations from Dante's *Divine Comedy* and Virgil's *Aeneid* have been found in *Alice in Wonderland.*[22] These quotations and allusions are of particular interest for the Carrollian student, since a few of them introduce a new interpretation of the original images and themes. Quotations, "others' words," incorporated into the new text live a double life; they do not altogether lose the connection with their source, yet they may present a kind of comment upon the new text in which they appear. Carroll's tale reverberates with these distant others' voices—which add, in a new and quite unexpected way, to the misleadingly simple melodies of *Alice*.

Of special interest are reminiscences of Shakespeare, whom Carroll knew well and loved. Roger Lancelyn Green has pointd out not a few hidden quotations from Shakespeare that are used in the dialogue.[23] To these should be added Alice's conversation with the Gnat ("Looking-Glass Insects"), in which one may hear an echo of Hotspur's and Glendower's words in *1 Henry IV:*

> "What sort of insects do you rejoice in, where *you* come from?" the Gnat inquired.
>
> "I don't *rejoice* in insects at all," Alice explained, "because I'm rather afraid of them—at least the large kinds. But I can tell you the names of some of them."
>
> "Of course they answer to their names," the Gnat remarked carelessly.
>
> "I never knew them do it."
>
> "What's the use of their having names," the Gnat said, "if they wo'n't answer to them?"

(p. 132)

Compare *1 Henry IV* (Act III, Scene i, lines 53–55):

> *Glendower.* I can call spirits from the vasty deep.
> *Hotspur.* Why, so can I, or so can any man;
> But will they come when you do call for them?

Perhaps more important than such details is the underlying principle. The method of diffused metaphor that is so characteristic of Shakespeare's work in general—and of *A Midsummer Night's Dream* and *The Tempest* in particular—forms the foundation for the two *Alices*, while Carroll's treatment of time and space also offers a few similarities with Shakespeare's.

Finally, I could go on probing more and more levels diffused throughout the *Alices*. I could follow Martin Gardner's masterful lead in interpreting and unraveling Carroll's scientific intuitions; I could build upon Elizabeth Sewell's brilliant study of nonsense based upon the principles of game; or I could travel the linguistic course previously traversed by M. V. Panov and R. D. Sutherland, among others. The scientific, the nonsensical, the linguistic—one thing is perfectly clear about these two books, with their unexpected twists and depths: Carroll's fairy tales realize in most original and unexpected forms both literary and scientific types of perception. And this is why philosophers, logicians, mathematicians, physicists, psychologists, folklorists, politicians, as well as literary critics and armchair readers, all find material for thought and interpretation in the *Alices*. Perhaps this is the reason why *Alice* is, according to Louis Untermeyer, the most inexhaustible tale in the world.[24]

NOTES

1. See U. R. Vogt's interesting discussion of different folktale functions in *Problemi Romanitisma* (Moscow: Iskusstvo, 1967), especially pp. 77–92.

2. See Vladimir Propp, *Morfologia skaski* [1928], 2nd ed. (Moscow: Nauka, 1969), p. 166; published in English as *Morphology of the Folktale,* trans. Laurence Scott, 2nd ed. (Austin: Univ. of Texas Press, 1968). Propp defines functions as actions of the character-types related to the general importance of action in the folktale. He suggests that character-type functions are an unchanging element of the folktale, invariably found in it regardless of other details, including plot, and they thus provide the most important pattern of the folktale. The number of actions of character-types is strictly limited, their sequence is fixed, and some of them are arranged in pairs (departure and return, lack of something and the elimination of this lack, etc. Propp identifies a series of functions in the folktale, such as "departure" (the hero leaves home), "lack or insufficiency" (one of the members of the family lacks something or wants something), "testing" by a donor (the hero is tested, interrogated, even attacked, before receiving a "magic agent" from the donor), etc.

3. Vladimir Propp, "Transformatsiia volshebnykh skasok," in *Folkor i deistvitel'nost'* (Moscow: Nauka, 1976), pp. 153–73. Propp discusses different types of modifications in the folktale over time and speaks, among other things, of "confessional" or "superstitious" assimilations that occurred when elements or people with religious or superstitious aspects were incorporated into the folktale (e.g., the devil instead of a dragon).

4. See N. Berkovsky, "Nemetzky romantizm" [German Romanticism], *Nemetzkaya romanticheskaya povest* (Moscow: Academia, 1935), I, xxx.

5. Nina Demurova, "O literaturnoy skazke victorianskoy Anglii (Ruskin, Kingsley, MacDonald)" [On the literary fairy tale in Victorian England], *Voprosy literatury i stilistiky germanskikh yazykov* (Moscow: 1975), pp. 99–167.

6. See Propp's *Morfologia skaski* [*Morphology of the Folktale*].

7. See note 2, above, and Propp's *Morfologia skaski,* p. 40.

8. It might be enlightening to recall the publication dates of Lear's and Carroll's major works, as the two nonsense writers may have influenced each other in their later years:
    1846 *A Book of Nonsense* (Lear)
    1865 *Alice in Wonderland*
    1871 *Nonsense Songs, Stories, Botany and Alphabets* (Lear)
    1871 (December) *Through the Looking-Glass*
    1872 *More Nonsense Pictures, Rhymes, Botany, etc.* (Lear)
    1876 *The Hunting of the Snark*
    1877 *Laughable Lyrics* (Lear)

9. Roger Lancelyn Green, *Lewis Carroll* (London: Bodley Head, 1960); rpt. as "Alice" in *Aspects of Alice,* ed. Robert Phillips (New York: Vintage, 1977), p. 27.

10. K. I. Chukovsky, *Ot dvukh do pyati* [*From Two to Five*], 11th ed. (Moscow: Detskaya kniga, 1956), p. 258. The "powerful and wild" distinction is Chukovsky's; see his book for a discussion of this concept.

11. These terms are quoted from D. S. Likhackev and A. M. Panchenko *"Smekhovoi mir" drevnei Rusi* [*The "World of Laughter" in Ancient Russia*] (Leningrad: Nauka, 1976), p. 17.

12. Mikhail Bakhtin, *Tvorchestvo Fransua Rable i narodnaya kul'tura Srednevekov'a i Renessansa* (Moscow: Goslitisdat, 1965), pp. 43–44; published in English as *Rabelais and His World,* trans. Helene Iswolsky (Cambridge, Massachusetts: MIT Press, 1968).

13. Ibid., p. 8.

14. Ibid., pp. 9–10.

15. *Alice in Wonderland: Authoritative Texts of Alice's Adventures in Wonderland, Through the Looking-Glass, The Hunting of the Snark,* ed. Donald J. Gray, Norton Critical Edition (New York: W. W. Norton, 1971), p. 37. All subsequent citations to the *Alice* books are to this edition. Page numbers are cited parenthetically.

16. See V. Novikov. "Zachem i komu nuzhna parodia," *Vosprosi literaturi,* No. 5 (1976), p. 194; A. Morosov, "Parodia kak literaturny zhanr," *Russkaya literatura,* No. 1 (1960); and N. Tynianov "O parodii," *Poetika. Istoria. literaturi Kino* (Moscow: Nauka, 1977), pp. 284–310.

17. G. K. Chesterton, "Lewis Carroll," in his *A Handful of Authors,* ed. Dorothy Collins (London and New York: Sheed and Ward, 1953).

18. Eric Partridge, "The Nonsense Words in Edward Lear and Lewis Carroll," in *Here, There, and Everywhere* (London, 1950).

19. See Roger Lancelyn Green's commentary in his edition, *Alice's Adventures in Wonderland / Through the Looking-Glass and what Alice found there* (London and New York: Oxford Univ. Press, 1971), p. 254.

20. See John Hinz, "Alice Meets the Don," *South Atlantic Quarterly,* 52 (1953), 253–66; rpt. in *Aspects of Alice,* ed. Phillips, pp. 143–55.

21. See Kathleen Tillotson, "Lewis Carroll and the Kitten on the Hearth," *English,* 8 (1950), 136–38.

22. Green, ed., *Alice's Adventures,* pp. 256, 261.

23. See Green's notes to his edition of *Alice's Adventures.*

24. Louis Untermeyer, Introduction to *Alice in Wonderland/Through the Looking-Glass* (New York: Collier, 1962), p. 5.

Carroll's Narratives Underground: "Modernism" and Form

ROGER B. HENKLE

Critics in nineteenth-century England had a special term for fiction like Lewis Carroll's *Alice* books that did not fit into the customary formal definitions of the novel. They were "sports"—that is, oddities, or hybrids of accepted generic formulas. Laurence Sterne's *Tristram Shandy* was a sport, and so was Emily Brontë's *Wuthering Heights*. Now our categories for the novel have so expanded, or have become so sophisticated, that *Tristram Shandy* can be seen to be a significant link in the tradition of the self-reflexive novel—the novel that plays with assumptions about its own form. *Wuthering Heights* has been designated a "romance"—something akin to the novel—and in recent years it has been treated as a "mainstream" novel, largely because psychological and feminist interpreters have allowed us to see that it is an intensified and stylized rendition of cultural stresses of the early Victorian period. Carroll's *Alice* books, however, would still be sports if we were to continue to use the term. They have been impossible to integrate into the development of the novel, and thus we have had to place them in separate categories: fantasy, or children's literature. Yet they do not sit easily in those genres either, for they contain a great deal of overt social criticism of social manners, of Victorian morality, of Darwinism, and of ideas about time, language, and logic that one normally does not find in such literature. Nonetheless, they do not provide enough social density, or enough analysis of human motivation and psychology within complex Jamesian textures, to fit the normal criteria of the nineteenth-century English novel. The *Alice* books seem to be neither social fictions nor psychological fictions—at least not seriously so. They are presumably whimsical expressions; if they respond to the culture, they do so in fitful, playful ways.

The *Alice*s do, of course, contain such powerful psychological undercurrents that they have had telling effects on both adult and child readers throughout the more than 100 years since their publication. Although life in *Alice in Wonderland* and *Through the Looking-Glass* may only whimsically resemble life in England during the 1860s, and although all the characters may be parodies of human traits rather than fully realized human beings, we know that crucial anxieties of childhood and adolescence—associated with growth in size, with stability of identity, with loss of control, etc.—inform both books. *Wonderland*'s episodes are knit together by the motif of uncontrolled fury: The Mouse's tale warns us of its consequences; the Queen of Hearts, by Carroll's own description, embodies it. Violence erupts with alarming frequency, cannibalism is never far from one's mind, and both books end in chaos and brutishness. The adult creatures, Humpty Dumpty, the Mad Hatter, the queens, the Duchess, are all remarkably curt and rude in their dealings with Alice, and yet are capable of dissolving into the most unnerving childishness and petulance. And Alice finds that all her tried-and-true means of controlling her circumstances are to no avail in this puzzling, rapidly metamorphosing world. Because of these characteristics, and because the *Alice* books organize and change themselves through psychic tensions rather than through the more customary means of social behavior, they more closely resemble what we have come to call modernist fiction than nineteenth-century social-realist fiction.

A case can be made, in fact, for *Alice in Wonderland* and *Through the Looking-Glass* as forerunners of the modernist novel. What we call modernism was a reaction against the representational and social orientation of nineteenth-century art. While the major novelists of the Victorian period generally either followed George Eliot's lead in stressing the importance of making clear, intelligent readings of one's social milieu—exploring in detail the ways in which egoism, spots of commonness, and weakness collaborate toward decisions that have fateful social, and ultimately individual, consequences—or else followed Henry James's procedure of examining the subtle workings of motive and feeling in a scrupulously analyzed and depicted set of fully realized human interrelationships; the avant-garde movements of Ezra Pound, Wyndham Lewis, and T. S. Eliot fought themselves free of the need for art to deal with such contexts. In radical formal experimentations, and in "classicism," the modernists sought to liberate expression from the formulas of representation, and from the sentimentalism that clouded the vision of bourgeois humanism. The novelists D. H. Lawrence, Ford Madox Ford, and James Joyce—and later William Faulkner and Graham Greene—developed fictions that were organized by the undercurrents of psychic and thematic tensions, because the realist and naturalist modes had finally glutted themselves on the banality of the phenomenal: in debased language, in tedious social settings, in absorption with the everyday concerns of an unimaginative nonvital sociality. *Women in Love, The Good Soldier,* or *Absalom, Absalom!* can only be understood if we suspend our normal inclination to interpret the social surface—the narrative of events and story—and attempt instead to gauge what lies beneath that surface: the tensions of polar relationships, the schizophrenically repressed anxieties, the contained furies. The passionate expressions of such novels are removed or displaced from situational presentation; they no longer manifest themselves through the familiar means of social experience. Beneath the routine and the insignificant debris of ordinary life lies the genuine human expression and human contact. The novels are organized by means of what Nathalie Sarraute calls "sub-conversations." The surface interaction of characters, that which takes place on a social level and which normally made up the texture of the realistic novel, is no longer the real interaction. For that social scene has long ago become a vacant lot littered with discarded ideas, received notions, clichés, banalities, publicity jargon, role-playing. The essential expression—be it interaction among characters or the unfolding of a psychic warp—occurs underground, sometimes in nonverbal or preverbal "events," or in the strains: the silences and the outbursts.

None of this means, of course, that what transpires on the surface of the modern novel is inconsequential. Rather, it means that we can no longer interpret the text according to our customary assumptions: i.e., that it replicates social reality in a familiar way; that behavior is motivated by familiar motives; that change in human nature occurs through the process of social experience. Instead, the surface narrative functions either as a diaphragm against which the tensions pulse or as an overburden upon which are registered the seismic shocks of the underlying fractures. Or the surface materials, the objects, the characters, the actions are representations or correlations of underlying psychic or conceptual forces and movements. In the latter case, characters often become counters or tokens in fields of force, bearers of personally charged meaning rather than full, complex "independent" beings. Fictional characters are now fragments of projections of the psychological state or states that truly motivate the novel's expression.

Without subjecting oneself to the insidious evolutionist fallacy of looking upon nineteenth-century works as precursors or developmental stages on the way to the modern novel, one can legitimately characterize the *Alice* books as works in which the narrative surface is formed largely by the tensions between it and the underlying psychic matter. There is a crucial difference, however, between a modernist's attitude toward the imperatives of everyday life—social decorum, morality, the manner of individual expression—and Carroll's more Victorian outlook, which necessarily further complicates any analysis of the generic characteristics of the *Alice* books. For one thing, modernism emerged from a series of avant-garde movements that were openly defiant of the bourgeois cultures they were rejecting, and that were self-consciously "aesthetic"—asserting the primacy of art and of form over social content or ethical considerations. Carroll could scarcely be called avant-garde; he had little interest or background in aesthetics, and throughout his life he was conformist, sometimes even ultraconservative, in his attitudes toward social change. Carroll dug in his heels at nearly every reform of curriculum or requirements at Oxford, for example, and used his celebrity later in life to condemn irreverence. He peppered the letter columns of newspapers with prudish lamentations over licentiousness in the theater. His criticisms of contemporary mores were oblique; nonsense and children's tales were used to cover up his sense of being out of tune with his times. If there were fault to be found, he usually found it first within himself.

In fact, what creates the unique tensions in the *Alice* books is Carroll's very Victorian insistence on the central importance of the issues of moral choice and social behavior. A modernist writer would most likely deny this centrality—or would at least put ethical issues on different terms, into new, more relativistic perspectives. For Carroll those issues cannot be dismissed or even reformulated; they simply must be agonized over. The agonizing in *Through the Looking-Glass* most obviously takes the familiar Victorian form of sentimentalization. From the saccharine opening and closing poems of the book—which speak of the "happy summer days' gone by, and vanished summer glory," of aging and loss—to the dispirited humor of the Gnat, and the frequent reprises of the pathos of growing old in "The Aged Aged Man" poem and in the White Knight's fuddled behavior, we are subjected to a heavy overlay of sentimentality, which is often an emotional distension of the moralizing temperament.

The concern over morality and social action also takes another form: that of analysis of the element of rationality in the making and carrying out of ethical or personal decisions. Those questions of responsibility, of intentionality, of attention to the consequences of one's acts, that are so critical to the examinations of ethical issues in the writings of Dickens, George Eliot, and Hardy also figure constantly in *Through the Looking-Glass*. Behind the adventures of Alice lies the issue of predestination, for the possibility remains that she exists only as an object of the sleeping Red King's dream. Alice's control over the course of her own fate is frequently in question; certainly she wishes to advance along the chessboard, linear pattern of growth toward adulthood that is signified by becoming a queen, but she is ambivalent about it also, especially since so much seems to be out of her power. And as if reminding us of the problematic quality of intentionality's role in our behavior, Alice takes hold of the end of the pencil with which the White King is writing, and writes for him—until at last he pants out: "I really *must* get a thinner pencil. I can't manage this one a bit: it writes all manner of things that I don't intend—" [1] Yet in these and other instances, subterranean, almost unconscious, impulses figure more largely than they do in Victorian realistic novels. It is the Red King's *dream* that may control Alice's behavior. It is, similarly, a source of power of which we have no cognitive awareness that moves the White King's pencil, or that affects many of the creatures in looking-glass world. Thus we have different levels of compulsion operating within the novel; in the episode with Tweedledum and Tweedledee, for instance, Alice finds herself unaccountably dancing: "But it certainly *was* funny" (Alice said afterwards, when she was telling her sister the history of all this), "to find myself singing *'Here we go round the mulberry bush.'* I don't know when I began it, but somehow I felt as if I'd been singing it a long long time!" (p. 139). Here Alice wonders at behavior that seemed to have no conscious decision attached to it at all. At the same time, Tweedledum and Tweedledee *must* have a brief fight, and the crow must come to darken the sky and frighten them, because it is prefigured in the nursery rhyme about them, which Alice recalls and wishes upon them. Again the power to govern their behavior is taken away from the twins, but it manifests itself in a conscious, articulated form—the rhyme—and it is in the forefront of Alice's mind. Similarly, we are uneasily aware, as Alice *and* Humpty Dumpty are, that the nursery rhyme about him will cause him to topple from the wall, and that all the king's horses and all the king's men will not be able to put Humpty together again.

The nature of these explorations of causation and intentionality, of control over one's behavior and one's fate, draws attention to the particularly complex interaction between what seem to be more modern qualities of fiction, in which we are aware that the narrative is shaped by underlying or unconscious patterns, and qualities that are more typical of Victorian writing, in which aspects of choice, value, consequence, etc., are foregrounded and subjected to rational examination. The generic tensions are thus acute in *Through the Looking-Glass,* because the preoccupation with rational exploration of ethical choice and social consequences cannot be denied, yet the dynamics that govern the configurations of narrative action do not seem to be fully accounted for. To a certain extent, Carroll seems to be using the *Alice* books to explore, albeit tentatively, the conclusions about human psychology that Henri Bergson was to reach a few decades later in his *Time and Free Will,* a work that was undeniably influential in changing literary characterization in the twentieth century, and that made Victorian formulations of morality and social responsibility highly problematic. Bergson discards the notion of choice; he insists that the human mind never comes to certain crossroads at which one course of action is decided and another rejected, and that thinking is instead a continual flow of states of mind that contain complexities of inclination that phase into each other. We become disposed toward courses of action or behavior patterns—and often give ourselves the illusion of making a decision, or of engaging in the highly reasoned, self-conscious process that we associate with motivation—partly because of social pressure and partly because of our desire to believe in control of our actions.[2]

The episode in *Through the Looking-Glass* called "Wool and Water" provides a particularly striking breakdown of the accustomed relationships between motive or feeling and social/moral consequence. Alice complains during the episode that "things flow about so" (p. 154) for it presents the most unsettling series of metamorphoses in the book. The chapter opens as Alice, in the woods, watches the White Queen's shawl being blown across a brook; the Queen spreads out her arms and goes flying after it. When the Queen retrieves the shawl and puts it on, she seems to have been transformed into a sheep, and is in a small, cramped shop. The shop has many shelves, but as Alice looks hard at any shelf to see precisely what is on it, the objects disappear. The sheep-queen begins to knit with as many as fourteen pairs of needles, and they turn into oars in her hands, for now they are in a little boat, gliding between tall river banks among beds of elusive reeds. As they drift, Alice is pulled from the boat into a bed of rushes, but nonetheless finds herself next still *in* the boat. At the mention of the word *choice,* the oars, the boat, and the river vanish, and Alice is back in the shop again, reaching, as the episode ends, for the egg that will materialize as Humpty Dumpty, the protagonist of the next chapter. Nowhere in the *Alice* books do we have quite such a dizzying breakdown of the sequential connections between activities. And it is in this episode that the Queen propounds her vexing looking-glass logic:

> "The rule is," the Queen said, "jam to-morrow and jam yesterday—but never jam *to-day.*"
>
> "It *must* come sometimes to 'jam to-day,' " Alice objected.
>
> "No, it can't," said the Queen. "It's jam every *other* day: to-day isn't any other day, you know."
>
> "I don't understand you," said Alice. "It's dreadfully confusing!"
>
> "That's the effect of living backwards," the Queen said kindly: "it always makes one a little giddy at first—"
>
> "Living backwards!" Alice repeated in great astonishment. "I never heard of such a thing!"
>
> "—but there's one great advantage in it, that one's memory works both ways."
>
> "I'm sure *mine* only works one way," Alice remarked. "I ca'n't remember things before they happen."
>
> "It's a poor sort of memory that only works backwards," the Queen remarked.
>
> (p. 150)

The presentation of these disorienting paradoxes is characteristic Carroll, for an unconventional view of psychology, one that turns motivation and consequence upside down, is played with as an idea. Carroll—who brooded so often over the transient, disconcerting caprices of the mind; who invented "pillow-problems" to keep the mind from wandering in the dark hours of the night; who equated sleep and insanity; who wrote so often of "losing one's head"; who did himself love to play with little girls and to invent games in order to evade the tedious obligations of adulthood—brings to the forefront the possibilities that the mind does not work as rationally and sequentially as most of his fellow Victorians assumed. And typically, Carroll casts the issue into a problem of logic; he objectifies a psychological issue into a subject for rational discourse. He takes a concern that has very troubling implications for his time and projects it into an intellectual game, a curiosity of reverse logic.

Bergson would diagnose this as a natural consequence of his theory that we do not engage in conscious decision making, even though we base our ethics and our social behavior on the illusion that we do. Bergson argues that we divide into unconscious and projected selves.

Hence there are finally two different selves, one of which is, as it were, the external projection of the other, its spatial and, so to speak, social representation. We reach the former by deep introspection, which leads us to grasp our inner states as living things, constantly *becoming*, as states not amenable to measure, which permeate one another and of which the succession in duration has nothing in common with juxtaposition in homogeneous space. But the moments at which we thus grasp ourselves are rare, and that is just why we are rarely free. The greater part of the time we live outside ourselves, hardly perceiving anything of ourselves but our own ghost. Hence our life unfolds in space rather than in time; we live for the external world rather than for ourselves . . . we "are acted" rather than act ourselves. . . . We generally live and act outside our own person in space rather than in duration, and . . . by this means we give a handle to the law of causality, which binds the same effects to the same causes.[3]

Bergson's formulation might explain Carroll's choice of the format of the *Alice* books, in which internal impulses do seem to be spatialized into the actions of the book's creatures and cast into socialized frames. It further accounts for the generic inconsistencies of the *Alice*s that we have been describing, for we could say that although the primary forces shaping the narrative are those of unconscious or dimly apprehended impulses—anxieties and desires—the surface of the text consists of projections that spatialize and socialize this content (or at least what is perceived of the content) by casting them as ideas for intellectual play, or as abstracted social issues.

But such an explanation would only make sense if we could say with confidence that the *Alice* books deal with the split in a single, individual consciousness, either Alice's or Carroll's. Superficially, it appears that both books dramatize the anxieties and the aspirations of Alice. The "Wool and Water" episode, for instance, deals with a child's fear of disapproval by adults: a normal concern of growing up. The curtness and impatience—indeed, the inexplicable eccentricity—of the adult creatures such as the White Queen accords with a child's difficulty in understanding adult behavior, and her normal apprehensions about how to behave. Metamorphosis is a rather common element in fairy tales, representing the mystery of change and development, and the elemental, pantheistic quality of a child's imagination. The frustrations in the shop as Alice reaches for objects only to have them retreat from her grasp may reflect the ambivalence she now feels about her desire for possession of things; her fear of disapproval of her childish urges to take and consume. And when Alice is toppled from the boat while reaching for ever more beautiful rushes, it reminds her that she can no longer uninhibitedly gratify all her old urges, and perhaps emphasizes that the old innocent ways of behaving are now fast vanishing.

Similarly, the larger pattern of *Through the Looking-Glass* conforms to those of narratives about growth and integration into society. The motif of the book is advancement to an adult status, through a series of psychologically revelatory experiences, many of them involving adolescent anxieties and rites of passage, some (such as the episode in the wood of forgetfulness) addressing issues of identity and name. The book is framed, as we have noted, by poems about the passing of the summers of youth, of becoming "but older children," and it is deeply imbued with tones of regret and loss. The great appeal of the Alice books to children can be attributed to their ability to sense the psychological pressures of adolescence. The dynamics of *Alice in Wonderland* and *Through the Looking-Glass* are those of the fairy tale, and *Wonderland*—and, we can assume, *Looking-Glass*—evolved as the narratives of a storyteller who was uniquely attuned to the sensibilities of children.

Neither book is, of course, a fairy tale proper, for fairy tales, as Bruno Bettelheim states, are "the result of common conscious and unconscious content having been shaped by the conscious mind, not of one particular person, but the consensus of many in regard to what they view as universal human problems." [4] *Through the Looking-Glass* differs from the fairy tale in another, more crucial respect, however, and that is in the depiction of adulthood in the critical episodes of self-definition and discovery that the child's consciousness must undergo. Vladimir Propp, in his effort to map out a morphology, or characteristic structural pattern, of the folk tale, or fairy tale, contends that in almost all cases, the secondary figures (such as the adult creatures in *Looking-Glass*), exist to perform specific functions in the psychological and narrative progression of the tale. Such figures inhabit clearly designated spheres of action, as helpers in the case of many adult figures, or as villains, or as assigners of significant tasks or rites of passage. [5] None of the adults in *Looking-Glass* can be truly said to have such an assigned sphere of action. In most cases, they are troublingly amorphous in their roles, often impotent figures such as the White Queen or the White Knight; often unreliable, even treacherous, figures but without clearly evil qualities. Ambivalence riddles their portraiture. These characterizations relate to the issue of choice and ethical/social decision making that we have found to be so complex in the book, for presumably in a story about the development toward adulthood and social integration, Alice or any child looks upon adult figures for guidance. Grown-ups supply the rational explanations or the life examples that assist in the child's development. But this is not the case in *Looking-Glass*, where Humpty Dumpty contorts all rationality into solipsistic game-playing, and the Gnat, the queens, the kings, and the White Knight are, all of them, incompetent. Thus the normal dynamics of fairy tales associated with maturation are not fulfilled; rather than a tension between Alice's childish impulses and the expectations of intelligent choice and action, there is a tension between Alice's urges and the equally capricious impulses of adults.

In Bettelheim's study of the psychology of fairy tales, he rarely cites instances of total breakdown and incompetence on the part of the projected adults of the tale. There are instances in which the father figure is not strong, in order that the child will learn of the human limitations of adults, and of course, tales dealing with the experiences of prepuberty may often establish the mother as a wicked stepmother, but rarely is the weakness and the melancholy, the incapacity for adulthood, persistently emphasized as it is in *Through the Looking-Glass*. In addition, there is a disconcerting role reversal in this book and in *Wonderland*, for in both cases Alice often acts more adult, more rational, better integrated, than any of the adult figures. Delightful as it is for the child reader to perceive that he behaves more rationally and with greater inner strength than do most grown-ups, such a reversal confounds the customary psychological pattern of the fairy tale.

In fact, the resistance to adult integration constitutes a second, and very strong, psychological motif in the book. The melancholy tone bespeaks resistance against the expectations of adulthood, and the argument is made that grown-ups are "but older children," whose whimsicality is but a sad reflection of the earlier exuberance of childhood play. It is the adults in *Looking-Glass* who insist on being silly, on having fights, on turning the feast at the close of the book into the chaos of a spoiled birthday party. The White Knight stumbles morosely through his roles, begging Alice to watch after him until he has gotten out of sight: "I think it'll encourage me, you see" (p. 190). The appeal of the *Alice* books to an adult audience can be attributed to this extra dimension; it evokes our own self-doubts and regressions. It is both an escape from and an articulation of the anxieties of adulthood. As I have discussed elsewhere, Carroll was beset by concerns at the time of writing the *Alice* books over his failures to work as diligently as he should and his incapacity to fulfill a religious vocation. These anxieties manifest themselves both thematically, in the tentative explorations of escapism and alternative ways of behaving in both books, and in the depictions of adult characters.

Consequently, instead of the Bergsonian division of one psyche, we have in *Looking-Glass* an instance of two psychological patterns—one associated with the concerns of a growing child, the other with the anxieties of an adult—being posed against each other. The two patterns exist in the book as undercurrents—subterranean psychic flows influencing and intruding upon the narrative—and as surface projections. And the issue of adult integration assumes broader implications than an individual psychology, for Carroll has abstracted his own self-doubts into those that he believes (apparently rightly) are shared by many adults. The power of the Alice books both in their own time and later attests to the success with which he has converted internalized anxieties into larger cultural projections. Writing many years later about the *Alice*s, Carroll acknowledges the double themes working in the books, the nature of their "contrast," and the broader implications of his portraits: "And the White Rabbit, what of *him?* Was *he* framed on the 'Alice' lines, or meant as a contrast? As a contrast, distinctly. For *her* 'youth,' 'audacity,' 'vigour,' and 'swift directness of purpose,' read 'elderly,' 'timid,' 'feeble,' and 'nervously shilly-shallying,' and you will get *something* of what I meant him to be." The Red Queen of *Looking-Glass* was intended to embody the "concentrated essence of all governesses," and the White Queen "seemed, to my fancy, gentle, stupid, fat and pale; helpless as an infant; and her just *suggesting* imbecility, but never quite passing into it." [6]

The dynamics of the *Alice* books are thus more complex than they would be if they were depicting the pressures of one unconscious set of emotions against the narrative surface. And these crosscurrents increase the complexity of the form of Carroll's works. Certainly the novelistic form that the *Alice*s might seem—because of part of their subject matter—to mimic most closely, that of the nineteenth century novel of individual growth and development, cannot adequately serve as a generic model for books that not only reject the central assumption of such development (the possibility of adult integration) but dramatize firm resistance to it. The conceptual basis for the dominant fictional form of the century—the social/developmental novel—has been denied.

The Russian critic Mikhail Bakhtin, in his study of Dostoyevsky's poetics, sees the same rejection, for much the same reason, of the social/developmental novelistic paradigm in Dostoyevsky and notes as well an intriguingly similar adaptation of form. He contends that Dostoyevsky also rejected the dominant mode of nineteenth-century fiction because that mode implied social integration. Dostoyevsky's major works do not organize themselves in terms of an evolution toward adjustment to defined social roles and positions, but rather presents theaters of psychic and ideological interaction and conflict, leading to no organic integration. Bakhtin believes that Dostoyevsky conceives his worlds spatially, depicting the inner contradictions and psychological compulsions of individuals in a series of encounters with alter egos, caricatures of themselves, foils, etc. Dostoyevsky's "little men," his nonheroes and underground men, resist the categorization in social terms that traditional novels assume, for their primary assertion is the *indeterminacy* of the individual—his playfulness, oddity, perverseness. Bakhtin calls the form of Dostoyevsky's novels "dialogic," that is, works in which the characters assert a kind of independence and represent or engage in dialogues. Bakhtin assumes that normally characterization serves to dramatize the issues that organize the novel: The protagonists enact the central theme of their development of growing awareness; secondary characters represent facets of the crises facing the protagonists. They both serve the author's theme. In the dialogic novel, the characters are allowed to represent warring, sometimes inconsistent, positions or psychologies, and these are not necessarily harmonized to a central theme; the characters are allowed to speak and behave as if they were not subject to the author's single, governing vision. Obviously Carroll's two-dimensional creatures do not achieve that degree of complexity, but one can feel within the novel the anarchic pulls of differing sensibilities, and even as unrealistic tokens they do engage in a kind of dialogic interplay.

Bakhtin's theories about the forms that Dostoyevsky adapts proves to be even more intriguing when they are compared with the *Alice* books, for Bakhtin suggests that the "dialogic novel" borrows from the older narrative modes of the Socratic dialogue and the Menippean satire. The Socratic dialogue was a vehicle for discussion of various points of view on a subject, leading to an understanding of its nature. In later adaptations, particularly in symposia, it was used to present ideas and notions, such as those the Carroll characters articulate, about cause and effect, language, naming, logic, etc. Clearly the Socratic dialogue form allows for that objectification of ideas and that play with them that characterize the method of the *Alice* books. The Menippean satire provides a form to accommodate even more experimentation with ideas, using legendary or fantastic figures and improbable situations in order to elaborate the potentialities of various positions. Inventiveness and ideational play are the characteristics of the mode. Menippean satire adapts various generic elements of adventure, dream, fantasy, comedy, all for the purpose of exploring ideas and human truths from unusual perspectives, and it often incorporates highly topical material. The interplay of these elements undermines a tragic view of man and his situations, Bakhtin contends; the individual loses "singleness of meaning." [7]

Such elements abound in the *Alice* books. As I have suggested, the books are heavily burdened with abstracted conceptual material; issues such as those of cause and effect are thrust into the surface narrative as topics for dialogue. Yet other material emerges through the literary play, in fantasy and dream, where it is subject to the crosscurrents of the inconsistent anxieties of child and of dissatisfied adult. And gripping the entire affair is Carroll's resistance to social integration and his covert doubt about the assumptions of motive and causality that fortify conventional English morality.

There is, on the other hand, no evidence that Carroll was consciously adapting such sophisticated literary forms for his *Alice* books, which did emerge as oral creations, and which he always referred to as entertainments for children. Carroll's literary sensibility was often rather lamentable. He was not a literary man; nothing in his letters or diaries suggests that he addressed generic considerations in composing fiction. Yet he was, after all, an Oxford don, a man educated in the classics. The dialogic forms that Bakhtin refers to were undoubtedly a part of Carroll's literary learning, and could readily be assimilated to his purpose in discovering a vehicle to present such conflicting and emotionally charged material as we find in the *Alice* books.

We have, then, an Oxford don's version of the fairy tale. Its unique combination of formal elements, its mixing of genres, results less from attempts to graft modes of literature together or to work toward some variation on the novel of his time than from the need to accommodate highly volatile emotional and conceptual material. This is probably characteristic of many evolutions of literary form. In Carroll's case it suggests that we cannot really fit the *Alice* books into some sort of subgenre called the "children's book," because they are clearly more complex in their structural handling of their material than what we have assumed of children's books. (Of course, this alerts us to the possibility that there are tensions generated by adult anxieties operating in other major children's books of the mid-nineteenth century, such as those of George MacDonald and Charles Kingsley, in which case we may want to revise what we have been accustomed to say about such literature.) Our investigation also suggests that the movement toward what we have designated as modernism in fictional presentation took place in the nineteenth century from vastly more complex motives than the conscious desire to clear away the old social surface, to shed manners, ethical concerns, bourgeois materialism, etc. We have uncovered another source of novelistic variation besides the self-conscious avant-gardism of the late nineteenth century—and in what seemed like an unlikely place.

NOTES

1. Lewis Carroll, *Through the Looking-Glass and what Alice found there* [1871], *Alice in Wonderland: Authoritative Texts of Alice's Adventures in Wonderland, Through the Looking-Glass, The Hunting of the Snark,* ed. Donald J. Gray, Norton Critical Edition (New York: W. W. Norton, 1971), p. 115. All subsequent references are to this edition and are cited parenthetically in the text.
2. Henri Bergson, *Time and Free Will: An Essay on the Immediate Data of Consciousness* [1889; 1910], trans. F. L. Pogson (London: George Allen & Company, 1913), pp. 157 f.
3. Bergson, pp. 231, 233.
4. Bruno Bettelheim, *The Uses of Enchantment: The Meaning and Importance of Fairy Tales* (New York: Vintage Books, 1977), p. 36.
5. Vladimir Propp, *Morphology of the Folktale* [1928], trans. Laurence Scott, 2nd ed. (Austin: Univ. of Texas Press, 1968), pp. 79–92.
6. Lewis Carroll, "*Alice* on the Stage," in *The Russian Journal and Other Selections from the Works of Lewis Carroll,* ed. John Francis McDermott (New York: E. P. Dutton, 1935), p. 193.
7. Mikhail Bakhtin, *Problems of Dostoyevsky's Poetics,* trans. R. W. Rotsel (Ann Arbor, Michigan: Ardis, 1973), pp. 87–100.

The Appliances of Art:
The Carroll-Tenniel Collaboration
in *Through the Looking-Glass*

JANIS LULL

Like many nineteenth-century books, Lewis Carroll's *Through the Look-ing-Glass* was written to be illustrated. The pictures in such books are not incidental, but are integral parts of the whole, the best integrations reflecting the most fortunate collaborative relationships between writer and artist. In both the *Alice* books, the Tenniel illustrations are so important that one would expect to find each detail reinforcing the design of the book as a whole. A close analysis of the frontispiece of *Through the Looking-Glass*—the famous picture of Alice and the White Knight (Fig. 1)—demonstrates that the expectation of harmony between illustration and text is fulfilled to a remarkable degree.[1]

Though it was fortunate for art, the relationship between Carroll and Sir John Tenniel was a difficult one. As Carroll's nephew and early biographer Stuart Dodgson Collingwood put it, his uncle was "no easy man to work with."[2] Perhaps partly because it was known that the two men did not get along, many *Alice* commentators have supposed that they didn't understand one another's creative intentions either. In *The White Knight,* A. L. Taylor describes Tenniel's contribution to the *Alice* books as that of an "alien intel-ligence" who "had not the smallest inkling" of Carroll's real purposes.[3] It is true that Carroll was often dissatisfied with Tenniel's first efforts. "Don't give Alice so much crinoline," he wrote to Tenniel, whose original conception of Alice for *Through the Looking-Glass* (see Fig. 2) was more like the other figures in the chess game, with hoop skirts resembling the bases of chess pieces.[4] As the finished engravings show (Fig. 3), Tenniel took out Alice's crinoline. Illustrations were as much a part of the work to Carroll as they later became to his readers, and he often insisted on his conceptions of a scene with minute particularity. Roger Lancelyn Green, in his edition of *The Diaries of Lewis Carroll,* says that Carroll treated his artists "almost as workmen engaged to carry out his own design." [5]

But Carroll was not always dominant in his association with Tenniel. The White Knight, generally thought to be an alter ego of the author, doesn't look anything like Carroll. At one point, Carroll had written to Tenniel that the Knight was not to have whiskers: "He must not be made to look old." (The author was then in his thirties.) But the frontispiece and all the other pictures of the Knight show that Tenniel—and ultimately Carroll—kept the whiskers and the other signs of age. In other instances, as Collingwood notes, Tenniel was even responsible for changes in the text. When advised by his illustrator that representing a wasp in a wig was "beyond the appliances of art," Carroll suppressed the entire section about the Wasp, which had already been set up in galleys.[6]

However trying they found one another, Carroll and Tenniel were obviously capable of the reciprocity that characterizes the interchanges of genuine collaborators. In the case of *Through the Looking-Glass,* they made the portrait of the White Knight—in both words and pictures—function as a subtle emblem of the design of the entire work.

Throughout the text of *Through the Looking-Glass,* there are clues that alert the reader to the nature of the work, which is a complex set of puzzles. (*Alert* is too strong a word. Like the old Sheep, Carroll did not put things into people's hands. The reader has to perceive them on his or her own.) When the White Knight tells Alice that his Punch-and-Judy battle with the Red Knight resulted in a "glorious victory," for instance, one must remember Humpty Dumpty's definition of *glory* ("a nice *knock-down* argument") to understand. This is one of the easier efforts of memory the book requires, because Humpty Dumpty's definition and the White Knight's remark are only two chapters apart.

A less obvious connection can be made between the nature of the White Queen's memory in Chapter 5 and the door Alice enters after she becomes a queen in Chapter 9. In the earlier passage, the Queen explains to Alice that they are living backwards.

> "Living backwards!," Alice repeated in great astonishment. "I never heard of such a thing!"
>
> "—but there's one great advantage in it, that one's memory works both ways."
>
> "I'm sure *mine* only works one way," Alice remarked. "I ca'n't remember things before they happen."
>
> "It's a poor sort of memory that only works backwards," the Queen remarked.
>
> "What sort of things do *you* remember best?" Alice ventured.
>
> "Oh, things that happened the week after next," the Queen replied in a careless tone. (p. 150)

In Chapter 9, many pages after the Queen's careless reply, Alice comes to the door that marks her last transformation. A creature with a long beak puts out its head and says, "No admittance till the week after next!" Nevertheless, Alice is admitted almost at once. The incident will seem just a piece of nonsense unless the reader remembers the earlier remark of the White Queen and realizes that "the week after next" means right away in *Looking-Glass* time.

Figure 1 (*Through the Looking-Glass*, frontispiece)

Figure 2 Tenniel's preliminary drawing

Figure 3 (*Through the Looking-Glass*, Chap. 9)

Such demands on the reader's memory are made often in *Through the Looking-Glass.* In order fully to understand Carroll's design, a reader must collate seemingly "careless" remarks and casual events that are widely separated in both reading time and narrative time. More examples can be discovered once one is aware that the book is as much of a brainteaser as any of Carroll's riddles or logic problems. This is a work that requires a reader's memory to "work both ways," associating dissociated elements to make sense of nonsense. One can never tell when a slightly regarded remark or object from one part of the story may be needed to explain another part. As the White Knight says, "It's as well to be provided for *everything*" (p. 182).

In fact, it is this behavior on the part of the Knight—providing himself with all sorts of eccentric and apparently useless equipment—that suggests most strongly his role as a stand-in for his creator and emblem of the workings of the whole book. Many have seen Lewis Carroll in the Knight. Carroll, too, was an inventor, and the White Knight, alone among the *Looking-Glass* figures, seems to have the kind of sympathetic relationship with Alice that Carroll had with the real Alice Liddell. As Donald J. Gray has observed, "The association between Dodgson and the White Knight is both strengthened and made poignant by the White Knight's departure from Alice, who is going on to become a Queen." [7]

It does seem likely that the mild and kindly Knight was just the sort of person Carroll imagined himself to be, especially with his child-friends. It also seems likely that the poignant parting of the Knight from Alice, described in great detail in the text, was intended as the subject of an illustration.

> Years afterwards she could bring the whole scene back again as if it had been only yesterday—the mild blue eyes and kindly smile of the Knight—the setting sun gleaming through his hair, and shining on his armour in a blaze of light that quite dazzled her—the horse quietly moving about, with the reins hanging loose on his neck, cropping the grass at her feet—and the black shadows of the forest behind—all this she took in like a picture, as, with one hand shading her eyes, she leant against a tree, watching the strange pair, and listening, in a half-dream, to the melancholy music of the song. (p. 187)

But for all the explicitness of this word-picture, none of Tenniel's White Knight illustrations use all the details. The frontispiece does not show the setting sun, nor is Alice leaning against a tree. The figures, including the horse, are in motion—the Knight posting along in his tipsy fashion (no kindly smile), with Alice walking beside. Instead of being on the moment of parting, the emphasis in this picture is on the more general situation of the Knight's escorting Alice through the wood and, significantly, on the odd paraphernalia hanging from the Knight's saddle. Much of this gear is mentioned in the text, but quite a few of the objects seem to have been added by Tenniel.

The differences between Carroll's melancholy word-picture and Tenniel's frontispiece suggest to Taylor that for Tenniel, "The details of the story were less important than the artist's duty to make a good picture at all costs." [8] The same attitude toward the tension between pictures and texts has been expressed more generally, and more elaborately, by J. Hillis Miller. "Illustrations in a work of fiction," Miller wrote, "displace the sign-referent relationship assumed in a mimetic reading and replace it by a complex and problematic reference between two radically different kinds of sign, the linguistic and the graphic." [9]

The evidence in the case of the White Knight pictures indicates, however, that whatever the problems in relating Tenniel's illustrations to Carroll's text, the linguistic and the graphic work together in this book to reinforce the artistic unity of the whole. An analysis of the two different kinds of sign, especially with respect to the objects carried by the Knight, shows that Tenniel's design closely parallels Carroll's. The correspondence between pictures and text is not one-to-one, as might be expected if Tenniel had really functioned as a workman to carry out Carroll's design. Instead, it is a correspondence in spirit, one that reproduces a sense of the intent of the White Knight episodes and of the book as a whole.

The Knight's horse, as described by Carroll, is loaded with unusual equipment. Among the items named by Carroll in the text, Tenniel has represented in his frontispiece a mousetrap (the Victorian kind, looking something like an inverted bowl on the horse's rump), a beehive, a bunch of carrots, a complete set of fire irons, a fighting club, and the spiky anklets on the horse, "to guard against the bites of sharks" (p. 182). Not mentioned in the text are the bell in the horse's halter, the bottle of wine hanging at the animal's side, the turnips, and the wooden sword that the Knight carries. In other illustrations (Figs. 4 and 5), the Knight is also seen to be carrying a bunch of onions, an umbrella, and the horse-head helmet (his own invention) that turns him into an animated chess piece.

The one thing that all the Knight's accessories—both those mentioned in the text and those shown in the pictures—have in common, is that they relate in some way to *other* parts of the story. Most of the objects actually appear elsewhere, either in text or in illustration. The White Knight's wooden sword, for example, also figures in the picture of Tweedledum and Tweedledee as they prepare to fight (Fig. 6). "There's only one sword, you know," Tweedledum tells his brother, "but you can have the umbrella—it's quite as sharp" (p. 148). The umbrella itself turns up in two different pictures of the Tweedles (Figs. 7 and 8), as well as in the frontispiece and one additional picture of the White Knight. The enigmatic curved object in the frontispiece, hanging just in front of the complete set of fire irons, is an oversized version of the very rattle over which Tweedledum and Tweedledee come to blows (Fig. 8). Tenniel had drawn a larger-than-life rattle of this ratchet type before, in a vignette for *Punch* (Fig. 9).[10]

The mousetrap and the beehive are not directly related to any fully realized episode in the story, and perhaps they represent the Knight's readiness for alternate possibilities. ("It's as well to be provided for *everything.*") The beehive might have been useful if Alice had chosen to go toward the elephantine bees she saw from far off at the beginning of her part in the chess game. But she chose another direction, and the beehive remains only potentially a

Figure 4 (*Through the Looking-Glass*, Chap. 8)

Figure 5 (*Through the Looking-Glass*, Chap. 8)

Figure 6 (*Through the Looking-Glass*, Chap. 4)

prop in the story. As for the mousetrap, it may be a reference to the mouse that figured prominently in *Alice in Wonderland,* a tale that was also invented by the White Knight / Carroll. The shark anklets are mysterious but not inappropriate in a place where, as Alice says, "[T]hey're so fond of fishes, all about here" (p. 201).

Because he is ready for everything, the Knight puts the empty plum-cake dish left over from the Lion and Unicorn chapter into his bag. Already in the bag, as he tells Alice, are "many candlesticks." The likely destination of the candlesticks, of course, is the banquet at the end of the book. (Since the reader won't realize this until the book is almost finished, Tenniel's illustration and Carroll's text require a collation backwards in reading time to appreciate the significance of the candlesticks. One must have a memory that

Figure 7 (*Through the Looking-Glass*, Chap. 4)

Figure 9

Figure 8 (*Through the Looking-Glass*, Chap. 4)

Figure 10 (*Through the Looking-Glass*, Chap. 9)

"works both ways.") The candlesticks appear in Tenniel's last illustration for the book (Fig. 10), their candles shooting up to the ceiling. The carrots, onions, and turnips and the wine are presumably bound for the same feast. The satiric representation of a comic knight with a bottle of wine where his pistol case should be was used by other *Punch* cartoonists (see, for example, Fig. 11),[11] although Tenniel himself had drawn the pistol case as a pistol case in *Punch* (Fig. 12), just as it appeared in the standard cavalry equipment of the earlier nineteenth century (Fig. 13).[12] The convention of drawing a wine bottle in its place no doubt comes from the suggestive shape of the case, and perhaps dates back to Falstaff, who carried a bottle of sack in his pistol case in *1 Henry IV*.

The bell that dangles in front of Tenniel's horse is a Victorian doorbell attached to part of its spring. It is the same kind of bell that Alice rings when she comes to the "Queen Alice" door and is admitted "the week after next." And the Knight's clattering fire irons are pieces of furniture inherited from the very beginning of the story, when Alice climbs through the mirror to see whether there is a fire on the other side. It is in the looking-glass room, among the fire implements, that she first sees the White Knight, *"sliding down the poker"* (p. 115) (Fig. 14).

Of all his paraphernalia, only the Knight's fighting club is useful to him

Figure 11

Figure 12

Figure 13. J.F.J. Swebach (Des Fontaines), "Death of General Desaix at the Battle of Marengo, 1800"

Figure 14 (*Through the Looking-Glass*, Chap. 1)

Figure 15 (*Through the Looking-Glass*, Chap. 8)

in his own episode, when he battles the Red Knight (Fig. 15). The rest of his gear belongs to various other parts of the story. The Knight is a sort of propertymaster, whose furniture both recapitulates what has gone before and anticipates what will come. He represents a motive force in the action of the story, though his moves are eccentric and limited, and as Alice notes, he is always falling off his horse—"he balances very badly."

This last remark of Alice's about the Knight's balance is not made when she sees him tumbling off his horse, but much earlier, when she first spots him sliding down the poker. In Chapter 1, the White King tries to make a memorandum as an invisible Alice watches: "Alice looked on with great interest as the King took an enormous memorandum-book out of his pocket, and began writing. A sudden thought struck her, and she took hold of the end of the pencil, which came some way over his shoulder, and began writing for him" (p. 115).

This is what Alice writes for the King: *"The White Knight is sliding down the poker. He balances very badly"* (p. 115). Since there has been no previous mention of the White Knight in the book, this is the moment when he is written into existence, and the writer is Alice. If the Knight manipulates the action in Alice's story by moving the incidental furniture from place to place, Alice is also *his* creator, both as dreamer and as writer.

The relationship between the White Knight and Alice is not the only variation on the creature/creator theme one can find in this very complex book. The question with which the story ends, "Which dreamed it?" refers to the Red King and Alice, but it might also refer to Lewis Carroll and Alice

Liddell, and it certainly calls attention to all the ambiguities within and without the story concerning just whose creation *Through the Looking-Glass* really is. But in the matter of the Tenniel-Carroll collaboration, the White Knight illustrations and the accompanying text show that *Through the Looking-Glass* was a mutual effort and that both creators worked to enhance the book in all its puzzling, even paradoxical, richness.

N O T E S

1. Page references in the text are to *Through the Looking-Glass and what Alice found there* in *Alice in Wonderland,* ed. Donald J. Gray, Norton Critical Edition (New York: W. W. Norton, 1971).
2. Stuart Dodgson Collingwood, *The Life and Letters of Lewis Carroll* (London: T. Fisher Unwin, 1898; New York: The Century Co., 1899), p. 130.
3. Alexander L. Taylor, *The White Knight* (Edinburgh: Oliver and Boyd, 1952), p. 146.
4. Preliminary sketch for *Through the Looking-Glass* reproduced in Frances Sarzano, *Sir John Tenniel,* English Masters of Black-and-White (London: Art and Technics, 1948), p. 68.
5. *The Diaries of Lewis Carroll,* ed. Roger Lancelyn Green, 2 vols. (London: Cassell, 1953; New York: Oxford Univ. Press, 1954), I: 11.
6. The suppressed chapter, lost for over a hundred years, was found in 1974 and published by the Lewis Carroll Society of North America in 1977. That the wasp in a wig was not entirely beyond the appliances of art is demonstrated by the "reconstruction after Tenniel" by Ken Leeder in the British edition, *The Wasp in a Wig* (London: Macmillan, 1977).
7. *Alice,* ed. Gray, p. 181, n. 8.
8. Taylor, p. 146.
9. J. Hillis Miller, *"Sketches by Boz, Oliver Twist,* and Cruikshank's Illustrations," in *Charles Dickens and George Cruikshank* (Los Angeles: William Andrews Clark Memorial Library, 1971), p. 46.
10. From *Punch,* January 19, 1856, p. 27.
11. This cartoon, probably by John Leech, is reproduced in *Mr. Punch's Victorian Era* (London: Bradbury, Agnew, and Co., 1887), I: 125.
12. Tenniel's initial from *Punch* (Fig. 12) is reproduced in Sarzano, p. 94. Figure 13 is J. F. J. Swebach (Des Fontaines), *Death of General Desaix at the Battle of Marengo, 1800,* reproduced in A. E. Haswell Miller and N. P. Dawnay, *Military Drawings and Paintings in the Collection of Her Majesty the Queen* (London: Phaidon Press, 1966), I, Plate 241.

I would like to thank Michael Hancher for inspiration and advice and Dennis Skrade of the University of Minnesota Art Library for help on questions of military equipment and illustration.

The White Knight's Whiskers
and the Wasp's Wig
in *Through the Looking-Glass*

ROBERT DUPREE

I

In *The Life and Letters of Lewis Carroll,* Stuart Dodgson Collingwood speaks of his uncle's instructions to Sir John Tenniel, illustrator of *Through the Looking-Glass:* "Mr. Dodgson was no easy man to work with; no detail was too small for his exact criticism. 'Don't give Alice so much crinoline,' he would write, or 'The White Knight must not have whiskers; he must not be made to look old'—such were the directions he was constantly giving." [1] A glance at Tenniel's final version of the frontispiece for *Looking-Glass* reveals a discrepancy between the author's intentions and the artist's execution, for in it the White Knight is depicted with a long pair of moustaches, whiskers, and a balding pate. The picture could not have been printed without Carroll's approval. What caused him to change his mind?

A canceled section of the book, only recently discovered and published, provides an important clue. Carroll seems to have made a number of changes in the course of shaping the book in collaboration with Tenniel. Yet even Collingwood, who had access to material no longer extant, never saw a missing " 'wasp' chapter" that Tenniel, in another letter, advised the author to omit. In this letter, which the biographer prints in full, Tenniel asserts, "the *'wasp'* chapter doesn't interest me in the least, & I can't see my way to a picture." In still another letter that Collingwood saw, the artist complained that "a *wasp* in a *wig* is altogether beyond the appliances of art." [2] Dodgson must have concurred, for until its surprising recovery, the missing section had been so thoroughly excised that no one could find where it had originally occurred in the text.

There is another instance of the illustrator's prevailing over the author in textual matters. In the same letter that Collingwood prints in facsimile, Tenniel proposes a change in an earlier episode: "I think that when the jump occurs in the railway scene you might very well make Alice lay hold of the goat's *beard* as being the object nearest to hand—instead of the old lady's hair. The jerk would actually throw them together." [3] Carroll adopted both Tenniel's idea and his phrasing; in Chapter 3 of *Through the Looking-Glass,* we read: "In another moment she felt the carriage rise straight up into the air, and in her fright she caught at the thing nearest to her hand, which happened to be the Goat's beard." [4] Though in a man so fastidious this acquiescence may seem surprising,[5] it was not unusual at this time for an author to be advised by his illustrator. In his study *Victorian Novelists and Their Illustrators,* J. R. Harvey describes the intimate collaborations of artists and novelists, such as Phiz and Dickens, and shows that the illustrator often influenced the text in decisive fashion.[6] By Lewis Carroll's time there was certainly a good deal of precedent for such cross-fertilization.

Nevertheless, it is possible to argue that Tenniel's influence may not always have been for the best. If *Through the Looking-Glass* is sheer nonsense and nothing else, then it is irrelevant whether Alice grasps a goat's beard or an old woman's hair. But if these odd gestures emerge as part of a consistent pattern in a book with recognized symbolic dimensions, then the choice becomes more pertinent. Carroll's initial inspiration may have been fresher, more apt. In the remainder of this essay, I wish to explore the meaning of the omitted "wasp" episode in the context of other changes Carroll adopted at Tenniel's suggestion; for if Alice's adventures do have obvious symbolic dimensions—and few would deny that they do—then the relationship of author and illustrator may need reevaluation.

One sees immediately that the four things involved in the conflict between author's and illustrator's conceptions—the old woman's hair, the Goat's beard, the White Knight's whiskers, and the Wasp's wig—are various means of adorning the head. Martin Gardner has already supplied some interesting commentary on this motif: "The White Knight, mounting his horse, steadies himself by holding Alice's hair. The White Queen grabs Alice's hair with both hands in Chapter 9. And, in a reversal of ages when the railway carriage jumps the second brook we know, from Tenniel's letter, that Carroll planned to have Alice seize the hair of an old lady sitting nearby." [7] The "reversal of ages" that Gardner notes but does not explore is significant; for if references to hair throughout the book are examined carefully, one discovers that they form a progression.

Most of the time in *Through the Looking-Glass,* hair is an object of anxiety. Various characters are concerned either with keeping it tidy or with preventing it from falling out. In "The Garden of Live Flowers," for instance, Alice is told that "one can't help one's petals getting a little untidy" (p. 204). Later in the same chapter, Alice runs so fast that the wind is "almost blowing the hair off her head" (p. 209). In Chapter 5 Alice helps the White Queen tidy up her tangled coiffure. In Chapter 8 the White Knight asks Alice if she has her "hair well fastened on" (p. 299) and tells of a plan to keep it from falling off. If the "Wasp in a Wig" episode had been retained, another discussion of hair would have followed in the same chapter. Finally, in Chapter 9 Alice smooths the White Queen's hair and, in turn, has her own hair pulled by the White Queen at the climax of the dream. It is evident that some sort of pattern lies behind these odd events.

II

Hair is an aspect of the human body that serves a distinct cultural and anthropological function. It enables a society to identify and distinguish between the sexes of its members. Unlike dress, however—another means to the same end—bodily hair is a natural sign of one's sex. Men can grow beards; women cannot. Men frequently become bald; women usually do not. Yet unlike other physical indicators, hair can also be a cultural signifier of a person's sex. Women in our society tend to have longer hair than men. Perhaps for this reason, women are more frequently concerned with the appearance of their hair than men. In any case, hair partakes of the nature of both natural and cultural symbols.

If—as part of a system of cultural signs—women are often preoccupied with keeping their hair tidy, men can choose to emphasize their masculinity by growing beards. Although men have no choice in the matter of baldness, they can compensate for the loss of hair on the top of the head by growing a beard (which is unaffected by whatever causes baldness), while women can underline their decreased susceptibility to baldness by letting their hair grow very long. Thus, a man's beard and a woman's hair may be considered as emblematic of something fixed and stable, and to grasp a man's beard or a woman's hair is to hold on to something firmly anchored. In this sense, the goat and the old woman in the railway carriage are interchangeable. Either would offer Alice a grip on something stable while the carriage is leaping through the air.

If we return to Carroll's instructions to Tenniel, we note that he insists on having the whiskers removed from the picture of the White Knight because they make him look old. As Philippe Ariès points out, "The iconography of old age . . . begins with the losing of one's hair and the wearing of a beard." [8] In 1868, the year Carroll began working on *Through the Looking-Glass,* he began to feel the responsibilities and problems of growing older, and the book as a whole seems to be about that very theme. For in that year, Carroll's father died; and while the book was taking shape, he must have felt the burden of caring for others to be especially heavy. Alice points out to Humpty Dumpty that "one can't help growing older," and he replies, "*One* can't, perhaps, . . . but *two* can" (p. 266). Indeed, companionship is essential to growing old gracefully, but Carroll had been estranged from the Liddells for some three years and must have felt his isolation acutely. A melancholy sense of abandonment and impending mortality pervades the prefatory verses of his sequel.

It is probably for these reasons that helping someone grow older or assisting someone who is of advanced age is such a persistent topic in the second *Alice* book. Yet for all the gloom that hovers over it, the book has a delightful vigor that suggests triumph and renewal rather than defeat and decay. Alice has grown from the fairy-child of *Wonderland* to the maturing girl already intent on her role of caring for others in motherhood. Still, before she can care for others, she must learn to take care of herself. As Alice leaves behind the world of the child, in which others care for her, she finds herself increasingly menaced by flux and disorder. The book is a long series of tests and contests—the hostility of adults like the Red Queen or Humpty Dumpty, the violent and petty conflicts between look-alikes such as Tweedledum and Tweedledee or interchangeable figures such as the Lion and the Unicorn, and the condescension that she encounters almost everywhere. As a piece on a chessboard, moving toward queenhood, she must expect to come into conflict with others and to witness struggles around her. As a person who has entered the universe of reflections, she must come to discover who her double in the mirror really is.

Alice must learn to "give . . . sympathize . . . control," as T. S. Eliot puts it in *The Waste Land*. She must recognize that she shares a common vulnerability with flowers, insects, fish, and small animals. In the struggle for survival, man finds himself to be part of a community of victims. In his final confrontation with his own mortality, he is—like the boy who slays the Jabberwock—apt to be all alone. Carroll had originally planned on using Tenniel's Jabberwock as his frontispiece but was afraid that it might frighten his young readers. His decision to use the White Knight instead reflects a shift of emphasis from the self-assured little boy who confronts the monster as David faced Goliath to an eccentric older man who "balances very badly." Carroll clearly meant to imply that man can triumph over the forces that threaten his destruction, but the shift in initial illustrations indicates that he chose mildness and maturity over exuberant and militant youth as the means to achieve this stability of identity.

In the first episodes of her chess game, Alice is quickly made aware of her own fragility. Having lost her familiar orientation in time and space, she too balances very badly. She should be marked "Lass, with care." The Gnat and the other insects she meets after her train ride—a symbol of the rapid changes she is going through as the world shifts around her—remind her that life is very short, but she is too confused to be sympathetic with their plight. She cannot respond properly to the Gnat's overtures because she is afraid of insects, even though her sympathies are briefly engaged by the Bread-and-butter-fly, who always perishes for lack of sustenance. The Gnat's attempt to counter mortality with bad jokes is lost on her. She is still too fearful for herself to care about others—to her, bees look as big and as dangerous as elephants.

Alice comes to achieve her first sympathetic identification with the natural world after encountering plants, insects, and animals; but her mystic experience in the wood of no names cannot last long. Furthermore, she must now come face to face with her own species in the fourth square, where human adolescence greets her in the unpleasant guise of the Tweedle twins. Their story of the rapacious Walrus and Carpenter is a cynical view of human nature that is brought to its conclusion by a silly conflict, itself ending with the appearance of the black crow: that chaos and old night which blots out all identity in death.

It is in the next chapter, "Wool and Water," that the hair motif gets its first full treatment. For once, Alice is allowed to help someone. A strong wind (surely the force of death rather than of life) blows a shawl into her view, then the frightened White Queen. The distracted Queen mutters "bread-and-butter" over and over, reminding us of the unfortunate insect pointed out by the Gnat. Yet she can still get along; it is her recoverable shawl that blows away, not her irreplaceable hair. Her untidy hair, which Alice attempts to fix up, may be tangled, but it manages to stay on. The shawl and the hair are complementary aspects of a woman whose memory works both ways. She can see ahead of and behind herself. She may be disorder and confusion in the present, but she is stable in relation to her past and future.

The opposition between shawl and hair, flux and stability, is reinforced by the White Queen's transformation into the old Sheep. She becomes literally wrapped up in her own hair. Knitting constantly, she is turning her own natural covering into a detachable garment—perhaps a wool shawl. The hair she loses returns to the body in another form. She is transformed from a harried old lady into a kind of Fate, weaving the strand of life into changing forms of birth and death.

Wool is frequently associated with revery and deceit ("wool-gathering," "pulling the wool over one's eyes"), but it can take on palpable shape—unlike its contrary, water, which is the symbol of constant flux. "Things flow about so here!" Alice laments. She is unable to control water the way the old Sheep can knit wool. Nor can she discover what is being woven or who is doing the weaving. At one moment she sees a doll, then a workbox; the human effigy dissolves back into the tools that shaped it. At the end of the episode, Alice pursues living forms all the way back to the egg.

The Sheep warns Alice, but cannot control her illusions. Alice is the real creator of the scene she witnesses, but she mistakes it for something objective and permanent. When she asks the Sheep's permission to collect some of the scented rushes, Alice is told, "I didn't put 'em there, and I'm not going to take 'em away" (p. 256). The Sheep is busy knitting her own reality. Alice must learn to weave her own dreams and to recognize them for what they are. The shop is an externalization of Alice's desires. For that reason, the Sheep refuses to fetch any of the goods for sale in it: "I never put things into people's hands—that would never do—you must get it for yourself" (p. 259).

There is no doubt that the wool in this chapter is to be equated with hair. We are told that the old Sheep sticks "some of the needles into her hair" (p. 255) when they become too numerous to handle. The Sheep has a stability that Alice does not yet possess, but she remains too detached and unsympathetic. Alice could expect no more from a Fate, perhaps, but she does get some valuable guidance in managing a boat. (In the prefatory poem to *Wonderland*, the children row without guiding the boat they are in.) Boating and knitting both involve rowing, but Alice is not yet prepared to sail to her destination. In her quest for a stable form in the shop, she is drawn paradoxically to the egg, a symbol of wholeness that is the fragile vessel for a new beginning.

The egg becomes Humpty Dumpty, that ambiguous figure combining childish petulance with adult sophistication, pride with fragility, the integrity of the egg shape with the incompleteness of his fishing expedition and conversations. His unsatisfactory personality is made definitive in the shattering loss of balance that leaves him permanently fragmented. His fall and the confusion that ensues in Chapter 7 are the violent counterpart to the dreamlike flux of "Wool and Water." Alice is now in a world of Bandersnatch speed where constant disorder is the norm; here she looks like a fabulous monster. Yet all about her—White King, Lion and Unicorn, horses and men—are equally impotent. Having noted how powerless the White King is, Alice is tempted to wake the Red King and find out whether or not he really controls her reality.

It is at this point that the White Knight appears. He contrasts remarkably with Humpty Dumpty; for though the Knight often falls, he always picks himself up. The Knight may be a clumsy visionary, but he is sturdy. He is the only character other than the White Queen and the Wasp for whom Alice shows any concern. Even his pride over his inventions is a mild and harmless kind of conceit—unlike Humpty Dumpty's, which is all ego. Further, Alice's relationship with others changes remarkably in this chapter. It is *her* hair that the White Knight holds onto as he scrambles back into the saddle. She has become a figure of stability, and her hair is now the sign of a balance between fragility and aggressiveness, flux and impassive refusal to act.

The White Knight's peculiar inventiveness must be thought of, not as the result of senility, but as the fruit of an extravagant adult imagination. If, like Humpty Dumpty, he is self-assured, he also has a real heart and youthful vigor. If the Knight is made to look old, then the delicious parody of Wordsworth's "Resolution and Independence" loses its point. The contrast between the vigorous Knight and the indefatigable aged man is important. If the Knight is capable of learning from his experiences, he may acquire the ability to endure his misfortunes with the same absurd inventiveness that the old man deploys so disarmingly. Humpty Dumpty, the White Knight, and the aged aged man are all fence-straddlers who have trouble keeping their balance. The aged aged man seems to fare best of all; the gate he sits on is the threshold between two worlds. Alice glimpsed them both as she sat in the boat and grasped at the scented rushes, weaving her desires into visible forms. The White Knight straddles present and future. His inventions are not so much the ridiculous solutions to projected problems as the projected problems themselves. The aged aged man may have recourse to unusual tactics for staying alive, but he at least lives in the present. The White Knight is fighting against a mortality that he can foresee only as shark bites and puddings that will never be cooked. He is obsessed with an infinity of potentialities and a future that may never come; but his exercises are not, for all that, simply futile. Like a circus acrobat who does outlandish things, he knows he must fall; and, as he tells a concerned Alice, he has had lots of practice. If he survives into old age, he may be as unkillable as the aged aged man.

The best way to understand the White Knight's song is to compare it with its counterpart in *Wonderland,* "You are Old, Father William." Both are parodies of poems by romantic poets and concern a younger man who questions an elderly one with insolent curiosity. The marvelous feats of the elderly men show that they have achieved an equilibrium of sorts. Neither has much dignity, but they both possess some secret to life that the younger men are determined to find out. The young men are obsessed with ways and means (what the Knight's song is called) and not enough with ends. Yet the White Knight learns something that the youthful interlocutor of Old Father William does not. At the end of his song, the Knight speaks of the impact the aged aged man has had on him. When he meets with pain or inconvenience, he recalls the odd figure of the cheerful old man who has triumphed despite his isolation and neglect by the world.

Alice's attitude at the end of this episode has also changed. At the end of her encounter, she is less condescending toward the Knight than she was at the beginning. As she waits on a hilltop to see him off (in both senses), she realizes that "he gets on again pretty easily" (p. 314). He has meant more to her than she has to him, despite her lending her hair at one point for assistance. She is happy to encourage him as he sets out on another quest, and the Knight seems to have adopted her as his lady; but there is little she can do to help him.

III

It is now possible to see precisely how the "Wasp" episode would have entered into the pattern of motifs at this stage of *Looking-Glass.* Alice's reaction to the old insect is quite different from her fear of the Gnat. She has a new compassion for insects. In his Introduction to "The Wasp in a Wig," Gardner notes that male wasps are "amiable, harmless creatures" (pp. 6–7). Perhaps the elimination of the Wasp meant that Carroll had to absorb some of his character into the Knight even if only by allowing Tenniel to keep the balding pate and whiskers in his illustration. In any case, a restoration of the "Wasp" episode helps clarify the meaning of the hair motif and strengthens considerably Alice's search for understanding.

The Wasp's wig is as disorderly as the White Queen's hair; it is "all tangled and tumbled about like a heap of sea-weed" (p. 17). Alice is rebuffed when she suggests tidying it. The Wasp explains that all his troubles are the result of wearing a wig:

> When I was young, my ringlets waved
>   And curled and crinkled on my head:
> And then they said "You should be shaved,
>   And wear a yellow wig instead."

There is a certain poetic logic to this strange action. Carroll once teased Greville MacDonald by urging him to replace his normal head with one of marble, "for then it would never suffer from combing its curls." [9] However, the Wasp soon finds the solution to be worse than the problem. Like the White Knight's plan to keep the hair from falling off by training it to grow up a stick, the wig is neither convenient nor attractive.

> But when I followed their advice,
>   And they had noticed the effect,
> They said I did not look so nice
>   As they had ventured to expect.
>
> They said it did not fit, and so
>   It made me look extremely plain:
> But what was I to do, you know?
>   My ringlets would not grow again.
>
> So now that I am old and gray,
>   And all my hair is nearly gone,
> They take my wig from me and say
>   "How can you put such rubbish on?"
>
> (pp. 18–19)

Fashionable advice is always accepted at one's peril. Whether a wig is meant to save time in tidying one's hair or to disguise the embarrassment of balding, it is an awkward and completely artificial solution to an unavoidable problem. The Wasp has become a social outcast. Lacking the slightest vestige of security, he faces the end of his life in isolation without so much as his own hair to hold on to.

The most poignant and frightening moment in the episode occurs when the Wasp shows Alice that he can remove his wig and then reaches over to grasp her hair. This is the "reversal of ages" that Gardner notes in his comparison with the old woman in the railway carriage. It tells the reader—or would have told him—that Alice has reached a maturity and stability that the poor Wasp has never known. Yet despite the isolation in which he has lived most of his short life, he has not failed to profit by his sufferings. He wears a yellow handkerchief (Gardner notes, p. 17, n. 11, that Carroll associated bright yellow with advanced age) to bind up wig and face as a cure for "conceit." Youthful conceit caused him to listen to bad advice. Now that he is truly old, he will not attempt to be other than what he is.

The Wasp prefers suffering in isolation. Since wasps are social insects, this attitude is out of place; but as Gardner points out, "Except for a few hibernating queens, wasps are summer insects that do not survive the winter" (p. 7). Alice is a "worrity" to him in her solicitude; her first attempts at comforting him are unsuccessful. She reads him a newspaper account of the tragic expedition of some wasps for sugar. In the midst of discovery, the exploring party loses two members in far-off "China," where they are "engulphed" in a lake of treacle. Being swallowed up by sweetness is an unpleasant fate; little wonder that the Wasp does not like the word and tells Alice that it should "stop there." He is warning her not to smother him in sweet attention. Alice wisely changes the subject.

The Wasp's warning against conceit comes at the right moment. Alice is about to become a queen and is in danger of becoming proud, even in her sweetness. The Wasp has been tumbled about in the sea of life, like his wig (p. 17). Caught in the flux of existence, he was drawn into the sweet trap of conceit when he substituted a wig for his yellow curls. Alice may arrange his wig if the comb she uses is full of honey, as he punningly suggests, but she must not overdo it. He distrusts any attempt to make him look younger and warns her, in turn, that she is inadequately equipped for aggression (her jaws are too short) and is limited in vision (her eyes are too close together). Alice's response is commendable. She controls her tongue and helps the old Wasp get settled out of the cold.

> Alice did not like having so many personal remarks made on her, and as the Wasp had quite recovered his spirits, and was getting very talkative, she thought she might safely leave him. "I think I must be going on now," she said. "Good-bye."
>
> "Good-bye, and thank-ye," said the Wasp, and Alice tripped down the hill again, quite pleased that she had gone back and given a few minutes to making the poor old creature comfortable. (p. 21)

Reassured that the Wasp, like the Knight, can get along on his own, Alice leaps over the brook to become a queen.

Without the Wasp, the events of Chapter 9 are slightly diminished in total impact. Alice is confident that she will manage her crown "quite well in time" (p. 317), but it is because she can keep her head from getting too big. She even scolds herself as she had done in *Wonderland.* The arrival of the two queens removes whatever vestiges of conceit might remain, for their hostile remarks and impossible questions test her in good manners and courtesy as well as in self-control and patience. Alice looks at the White Queen and tries to think of something kind, but cannot. Nevertheless, the Red Queen instructs Alice in the proper way of dealing with a colleague: "A little kindness—and putting her hair in papers—would do wonders with her—" (p. 326). Having one's hair done usually improves the spirits, but in the light of what happened to the unfortunate Wasp, this amusing remark takes on a deeper sense. Alice has passed the test. She is gentle and kind after all; and the two queens submit to her with a childlike trust, just as the Wasp finally submitted to Alice's ministrations.

Nevertheless, at the banquet that follows this scene, the two queens treat Alice with precisely the same hostile temper as before. At a dinner where guests and food begin to merge, Alice becomes both vulnerable and a little frightened. But when she rises to speak, she overcomes her fear and pulls the tablecloth off the table, threatening the leg of mutton and the pudding. It is at this point that the last mention of hair occurs. The White Queen seizes Alice's hair with both hands and screams, "Take care of yourself! . . . Something's going to happen!" (p. 335). Alice is at the point of growing up, and the White Queen's alarm seems to be a combination of genuine concern for the new queen and horror at the possibility of being abandoned when Alice grows up. The White Queen is "engulphed" in the soup after trying to cling to the last stable thing—Alice's hair—that she can find at a banquet where everything is in the process of being devoured. Like Carroll, who says in his prefatory poem, "No thought of me shall find a place/In thy young life's hereafter" (p. 173), the White Queen knows that she must face mortality alone. Alice's real triumph is her outgrowing the Red Queen, to whom she is able to give a good shake before the dream is over. The Red Queen turns into the black kitten. Alice has become a mother. Now that she knows herself, her antagonists are simply naughty kittens.

Still, there remains an ambivalence about this last image of maturity; for Dinah, who is licking the fur of the white kitten, is also tidying up the White Queen. Alice lightheartedly warns the mother cat to be more respectful; she and Dinah, it would seem, have changed places. But Dinah may have turned into Humpty Dumpty, that humorless and pedantic adult. In Alice's promise to repeat Humpty Dumpty's poem at her cat's breakfast, there is a paradoxical hint of animal realism that suggests the nightmare banquet. Alice has learned about nature red in tooth and claw. But will she turn into a Humpty Dumpty herself, pompous and oblivious to her own fate? Or will she remain aware of the possibility that she may simply be a figure in the Red King's dream?

One final question remains: Why did Carroll preserve the galleys of the Wasp episode, leaving for us over a hundred years later the pleasure of discovering an unknown corner of his imaginative wit and some important hints about the meaning of his masterpieces? Was it because, as Gardner surmises (p. xi), he had hoped to find some use for them someday? Or was it because he anticipated a time when he might wish to return this passage to its proper place in *Through the Looking-Glass?* Probably, we shall never know, and the book as we have known it has not failed to attract enthusiastic readers without the Wasp. Nevertheless, while I certainly would not want to banish Tenniel's delightful White Knight with whiskers, I would most emphatically welcome the restoration of Carroll's Wasp in a wig.

NOTES

1. Stuart Dodgson Collingwood, *The Life and Letters of Lewis Carroll* (London: T. Fisher Unwin, 1898; New York: The Century Co., 1899), p. 130.
2. Ibid., p. 146.
3. Ibid., pp. 147–49.
4. *Through the Looking-Glass,* in *The Annotated Alice: Alice's Adventures in Wonderland and Through the Looking-Glass,* ed. Martin Gardner (New York: Clarkson N. Potter, 1960), p. 221. Citations from *Looking-Glass* in the text are to this edition.
5. See, for instance, "Alice on the Stage," *The Theatre,* April 1887, rpt. in *The Lewis Carroll Picture Book,* ed. Stuart Dodgson Collingwood (London: Unwin, 1899); rpt. as *Diversions and Digressions of Lewis Carroll* (New York: Dover, 1961), pp.163–174.
6. J. R. Harvey, *Victorian Novelists and Their Illustrators* (New York: New York Univ. Press, 1971).

7. Lewis Carroll, *The Wasp in a Wig: A "Suppressed" Episode of Through the Looking-Glass and what Alice found there,* ed. Martin Gardner (New York: The Lewis Carroll Society of North America, 1977), p. 21, n. 17. All citations are to this edition.

8. Philippe Ariès, *Centuries of Childhood: A Social History of Family Life,* trans. Robert Baldick (New York: Alfred A. Knopf, 1962), p. 31.

9. Cited in Anne Clark, *Lewis Carroll: A Biography* (New York: Schocken Books, 1979), p. 159.

A Time for Humor:
Lewis Carroll, Laughter and Despair,
and *The Hunting of the Snark*

EDWARD GUILIANO

The *Hunting of the Snark* (1876), Lewis Carroll's third and final literary masterpiece, has rested for more than a hundred years in the shadow of *Alice in Wonderland* (1865) and *Through the Looking-Glass* (1871). It is a poem with much of the *Alices* in it, "a kind of *Alice in Wonderland* without Alice," as one commentator has remarked; "it extends and illuminates some of the themes and practices of the two Alice books."[1] Dreams, death, probings into the nature of being, reminders of the inescapability of time, and a quest motif figure in all three works. Moreover, just as one senses terror lurking beneath the surface of the *Alice* books, one senses terror and despair throughout the overtly humorous *Snark*. This tension between the comic tone and the underlying anxieties is perhaps the poem's most distinguishing and fascinating characteristic.

I

In recent years the *Snark* has become "a much more serious piece of humor than it ever was for the Victorians."[2] Intellectuals now find its lurking terrors immediate and compelling. Living at Oxford through mid- and late-Victorian England, C. L. Dodgson's subconscious was surely infused with the anxieties of his age, and a case can be made for reading the poem's subtext as a record of some of the uncertainties that troubled intellectuals of the period, especially the horrors of confronting death and nothingness in a purposeless, post-Darwinian world.[3] But while twentieth-century readers will readily entertain such an assertion, Dodgson and his contemporaries would have dismissed it as ludicrous. For them, *The Hunting of the Snark* was a delirious and harmless flight of imagination very much in one of the mainstreams of Victorian comedy.

The Hunting of the Snark, a heroic nonsense poem in eight episodes, is in the nonsense tradition of Thomas Hood and William Schwenck Gilbert; [4] indeed, Dodgson may well have been influenced when writing the *Snark* by Gilbert's *Bab Ballads* (1869–73). Although *The Hunting of the Snark* is a relatively long comic poem, Victorian readers could regularly find shorter works of its kind in the comic weeklies that flourished in the 1860s and 1870s. One of the reasons the *Snark* continues to amuse adult readers is, according to Donald Gray, that it is a work of a man who "spent a good deal of time watching and practicing the habits of nineteenth-century writers whose profession it was to amuse adults." [5] Even a cursory overview of Dodgson's life reveals how intimate he was with the comic writing and theater of his age. It is not surprising that many of the common techniques and conventions of Victorian comic writing are found in Carroll's works, and that to some extent *The Hunting of the Snark* is, as Gray suggests, an extraordinarily skillful and confident exercise in some of the means by which nineteenth-century writers entertained their contemporaries.

Seen in this context, we can understand that the *Snark*'s initial reviewers were not so much surprised or uncomfortable with the poem's genre as they were puzzled by its nonsense. The first reviews ranged from mixed to bad—frequently finding little of the whimsy and escape of the *Alice*s in it.[6] For the Victorians, at least, it seems there was no tension between the nonsense ballad and the underlying anxieties—but only failed fantasy or delirious nonsense, depending upon the reader's personal taste.

Dodgson himself was at a loss to explain the poem. He admitted this on several occasions. In 1880, for example, when one of his child-friends asked him "why don't you explain the Snark?" he replied " *'because* I *can't.'* Are you able to explain things which you don't yourself understand?" [7] In an often quoted letter to a group of children he wrote: "As to the meaning of the *Snark?* I'm very much afraid I didn't mean anything but nonsense! Still, you know, words mean more than we mean to express when we use them; so a whole book ought to mean a great deal more than the writer meant. So, whatever good meanings are in the book, I'm very glad to accept as the meaning of the book." [8]

We do know something about the poem's genesis. Dodgson recorded an account of a stroll he took on the Surrey Downs on July 18, 1874:

> I was walking on a hillside, alone, one bright summer day, when suddenly there came into my head one line of verse—one solitary line—"For the *Snark* was a Boojum, you see." I knew not what it meant, then: I know not what it means, now; but I wrote it down: and, some time afterwards, the rest of the stanza occurred to me, that being its last line: and so by degrees, at odd moments during the next year or two, the rest of the poem pieced itself together, that being the last stanza.[9]

Morton Cohen has placed this walk in a most revealing context. It was taken when Dodgson was deeply distressed and exhausted. The previous night he had stayed up nursing a dying cousin—his twenty-two-year-old god-child, Charles Wilcox. The walk provided Dodgson with a means of escape from the painful reality he faced at home. His flash of inspiration, his line from the world of nonsense, Cohen believes, can easily be seen as a natural, personal defense. Although there is no outright evidence that Lewis Carroll himself made any connection between the *Snark* and the tragic case of Charles Wilcox, Cohen assures us that there surely is one.[10] The line "For the Snark *was* a Boojum, you see" flowed unquestionably from deep, unsettled springs of imagination. In this line and others in the poem we can see reflected Dodgson's deep personal dreads and anxieties.

The Victorians' attitude toward death and dying was complex and is often different than our own; yet, regardless of context, Dodgson clearly was anxious over and preoccupied with death. One can see some evidence of this even in the "Easter Greeting" he wrote to accompany the first edition of the *Snark,* where we find him electing to write about "when my turn comes to walk through the valley of shadows." Some readers will see more evidence in the understandable but somewhat surprising fact that he regarded his father's death (at age sixty-eight) "the deepest sorrow I have known in life." [11] And before his fifty-second birthday, for a better illustration, he was calling himself an "unconventional old man" on certain points and a "confirmed old bachelor, who is now well over fifty." [12] His concern with death is ever present in the Preface to *Sylvie and Bruno* (1889), and implicit as well as explicit references to death and dying are not infrequent in his letters and diaries. William Empson was the first to point out that both of the *Alice* books "keep to the topic of death." [13]

Although the death jokes that pervade the *Alice*s do not contribute to the progress of the story, their striking frequency causes the reader to maintain a subtle awareness of the topic throughout the stories. No doubt intimations of death were never far from the consciousness of the author while he was writing; they were at least active in his subconscious. Elizabeth Sewell has pointed out that nonsense holds a fear of nothingness quite as great as its fear of everythingness. She suggests that it is perhaps simpler to think of the fear of death (which she agrees is a crucial topic of both the *Alice* books) as a fear of nothingness.[14] Consider in the Tweedledum and Tweedledee chapter of *Through the Looking-Glass* that the twins challenge Alice with the most horrifying suggestions regarding existence and the nature of nonexistence. They tell her she is just a character in the sleeping Red King's dream, and if he were to awake, " 'you'd go out—bang!—just like a candle! . . . You know very well you're not real.' 'I *am* real!' said Alice, and began to cry" (p.145). How similar going out like a candle is to softly and suddenly vanishing away at the sight of a Boojum.

This positing of existence (being) as life in a dream occurs repeatedly in the *Alice* books. Dreams figure prominently in the *Snark* as well. The Snark—or a snark—exists, being clearly defined in the Barrister's dream. A snark (another snark?) exists for the Baker—every night he engages "in a dreamy delirious fight" with it. For the Baker, at least, life and dream become fused.

Not surprisingly, Dodgson—acutely aware of death and fascinated by states of being (which include not only dying but dreaming and even spiritualism)—was also more than normally frustrated by the limits real time presents. In *Alice in Wonderland,* for example, the familiar White Rabbit, always late, always checking his watch, is Carroll's comic expression of his own, and others', anxious preoccupation with the passage of time. In 1881 Dodgson resigned his Mathematical Lectureship to have more time to devote to writing and other projects. Within a few years he had "retired from society," since he resented the time "lost" on social affairs. Still in his fifties he would write, "Friends wonder sometimes at my refusing all social invitations now, and taking no holidays. But when old age has begun, and the remaining years are *certainly* not many, and the work one wishes to do, before the end comes, is *almost* certainly more than there is time for, I think one cares less for so-called 'pass-times.' I want the time to go more *slowly,* not more *quickly!*" [15] Here one is reminded of the Red Queen's famous dictum, "it takes all the running *you* can do, to keep in the same place" (p. 127). Throughout his life, in his letters and in his diary, Dodgson expresses his distress over unfulfilled expectations and about opportunities lost in the continued lapse of moments. Consider this diary entry:

> Dec: 31.   (Th.). 1863   Here, at the close of another year, how much of neglect, carelessness, and sin have I to remember! I had hoped, during the year, to have made a beginning in parochial work, to have thrown off habits of evil, to have advanced in my work at Christ Church. How little, next to nothing, has been done of all this! Now I have a fresh year before me: once more let me set myself to do something worthy of life 'before I go hence, and be no more seen.' . . .[16]

Here is Dodgson bemoaning his unfulfilled plans. The year is ended, another year has passed, a year gone forever—the time before his death is dwindling. But the thirty-one-year-old clergyman does not call it death. His dread is apparent, and what he dreads, in his own words, is going hence and being no more seen. Being no more? Being seen no more? How, too, like a confrontation with a Boojum.

II

In the *Snark* the Bellman is a constant reminder of time. Curiously, the Bellman is a character almost totally neglected by modern critics of *The Hunting of the Snark.* For the Bellman is, after all, the central character in the poem. A figure of power and authority, he organizes the expedition and remains in charge of it and of the ship. He knows how to hunt a snark and is able to define its five qualities. Despite his questionable ability to handle the voyage, he sees the hunt through to success: They do find a snark. The Bellman is the central character also in that he is the character most often present in the narrative, and when he is present he is always in possession of his bell. In all of Henry Holiday's approved illustrations of the poem, the Bellman is shown holding the bell—often ringing, tingling it. (For an example, see the reproduction of the frontispiece to the *Snark* that accompanies this essay.)

The Bellman's bell is an ordinary school bell, which is struck to mark off time. *Bellman* is, of course, another term for town crier. On a ship, a bell is rung at half-hour intervals to mark off the time in a watch. The bells of a school, too, mark time. And church bells not only mark off time, they also announce death. The Bellman and his bell are both symbolic and real reminders of time—its steady passage and its inevitability. The pulsating repetitions of the bell's ringing signal to the reader the regular and perpetual movement of time. Holiday's illustrations of the Bellman even suggest a wise Father Time figure. Another interesting aspect of the approved illustrations is that all but one contain the figure of the Bellman and his bell—haunting reminders of the inescapability of time. An image of this haunting temporality occurs when the Barrister falls into a dreamful sleep in the sixth fit. It is the sound of the Bellman's bell in his ear that awakens him and cuts short his dreams. The Bellman's centrality as a character indicates the centrality of time in the poem.

Martin Gardner interprets *The Hunting of the Snark* as being:

> . . . a poem about being and nonbeing, an existential poem, a poem of existential agony. The Bellman's map is the map that charts the course of humanity; blank because we possess no information about where we are or whither we drift. . . .
> The Snark is, in Paul Tillich's fashionable phrase, every man's ultimate concern. This is the great search motif of the poem, the quest for an ultimate good. But

Henry Holiday's frontispiece to *The Hunting of the Snark*, showing the Bellman this motif is submerged in a stronger motif, the dread, the agonizing dread, of ultimate failure. The Boojum is more than death. It is the end of all searching. It is final, absolute extinction.[17]

Naturally, the Snark can represent different things to different people; the Barrister sees it one way, the Baker perhaps another. The ending can also be read differently; it can be equated by some with a conventional, even Christian, death or by others with an existential nothingness. I agree that the Boojum can be viewed as an existential horror. It seems to be an expression of Dodgson's dread, his nightmare, his anxiety toward facing the end of his being. The equation of the ending with absolute extinction expresses a powerful anti-Christian, anti-Protestant belief, something Dodgson would never consciously confess. In the pessimism of the *Alice* books, and in the horror of the *Snark,* there is no evidence for Christian hope of salvation. (The figure of Hope does appear in the *Snark* as part of Henry Holiday's iconography, but not in the text—she is rendered in the illustration to the fourth fit, paradoxically carrying the ship's anchor on this ill-fated voyage. Her image may at first function traditionally, suggesting hope and virtue, but for me she provides no affirmation of Christian values. On the contrary, her image is ultimately an inverted image, an emblem of virtue failed, of despair and frustration.)

In the third fit of the *Snark,* the Baker, a character sometimes viewed as Dodgson's satirical self-portrait,[18] expresses his dread of the Boojum. He explains his emotional response to his uncle's warning to "Beware of the day, if your snark be a Boojum!"

> It is this, it is this that oppresses my soul,
>   When I think of my uncle's last words:
> And my heart is like nothing so much as a bowl
>   Brimming over with quivering curds!
>
> (p. 221)

It is easy and justifiable to equate this reaction with a state of acute existential nausea, which Gardner suggests. The Baker also describes what can be viewed as a state of existential dread:

> I engage with the Snark—every night after dark—
>   In a dreamy delirious fight:
> I serve it with greens in those shadowy scenes,
>   And I use it for striking a light.
>
> (pp. 221–22)

This stanza provides an excellent illustration of the tension that exists between the comic tone and the underlying terror that characterizes the poem for readers today. It also provides us with a glimpse at the nature of Carroll's artistic temperament. The first two lines, "I engage with the Snark—every night after dark—/In a dreamy delirious fight:" can be read as a statement that parallels Dodgson's own experience. He was an insomniac kept awake at least partially by haunting and troubling thoughts. In fact, he published a book of puzzles devised to help ease the pain of his sleeplessness—

some mental work to help free his mind of its troubling thoughts, thoughts that surely occurred to many of his contemporaries as well. In the Preface to that book, *Pillow Problems* (1893), he writes of the realization that: "There are skeptical thoughts, which seem for the moment to uproot the firmest faith; there are blasphemous souls; there are unholy thoughts, which torture with their hateful presence, the fancy that would fain be pure."

But although we can find suggestions of Dodgson's anxieties in the Baker's dread, in the closing lines, "I serve it with greens in those shadowy scenes,/And I use it for striking a light," we find only whimsy and nonsense. They change the tone completely.

If we view the stanza's opening lines as being somewhat autobiographical, and if we view certain critical lines, such as the paramount "The Snark *was* a Boojum, you see," as springing up as raw psychic impulses from Dodgson's troubled unconscious, then we might view much of the poem's humor as springing up in Dodgson's self-defense and its laughter as liberating, tension-relieving. These impulses would insulate and isolate the moments of despair and would prevent them from spreading—which is consistent with Bergson's and Freud's beliefs that comedy enables us to assert a degree of control (mastery) over fears, or threats, by removing them from our conscious and immediate world and setting them off at a comfortable distance.

But let us not forget that Carroll's literary works were composed as entertainments. They were his hobby, his own entertainment as much as an entertainment for others—principally his child-friends. Initially they grew from spontaneous impulses, and later they were crafted into highly wrought stories and poems. As a hobby, writing provided Dodgson with a diversion, an escape, really, from his sober and demanding duties as a mathematics don and as a clergyman, as well as from his responsibilities as the head of a large family. By discussing some of Dodgson's apparent anxieties, I do not want to suggest that he was a deeply troubled man; on the contrary, by all accounts he seems to have been in reasonably sound mental and physical health. If he was a bit eccentric and perhaps even suspect on some grounds, he appeared happy and tolerably well adjusted. I have been suggesting in fact that his "entertainments" and his humor helped him to cope with the anxieties of his own life and those of his age. When he relaxed and let his mind soar without restraint, it is not unnatural that a few deep-seated dreads were in evidence. (Need I even suggest the techniques of psychoanalysis?) It is also not surprising that when these anxieties emerged, they were accompanied by laughter; indeed, such a response is natural and healthy. At times he was able to defeat pain, to achieve escape from the troubling problems common to his age through laughter; it denied pain its province. Sometimes his humor is like that of Freud's prisoner, who remarks, on his way to the gallows: "Well, this is a good beginning to the week." [19] It is a rebellious assertion by the ego that in the face of inevitable extinction, it is somehow invulnerable.

At other times Carroll's humor is (as I have suggested earlier) conscious and skillful craftsmanship in the Victorian comic tradition. This humor is often the reshaping of the gifts of his comic muse. Whether the humor in

Carroll's writings is the result of a spontaneous or a willed activity, it can be viewed as a means for Dodgson to control his world. Humor was a means for him to order his experience. In his life and in his art Dodgson continually sought refuge, temporary escape, from life's exigencies through order and reason. This is evidenced in both his books and his personal habits. Witness his *Pillow Problems* as one example. Even witness Dodgson's playful battle with his unconscious in the Preface he wrote to the *Snark*. Unable to comprehend the nonsense "Then the bowsprit got mixed with the rudder sometimes," he invents a ludicrous explanation. In doing so, he asserts control. The gaining of control through order is even evidenced in the structural integrity of his literary works—the *Snark* tightly organized in a poetic ballad form, the *Alices* each carefully written in twelve chapters—in the prosody of his poems, in the logic of his dialogues, his puns, his narrative structures. *The Hunting of the Snark* is, as Michael Holquist has justly pointed out, the most nonsensical nonsense that Carroll created, and it best exemplifies what his career and all his books sought to do: achieve pure order.[20]

On the thin line separating laughter from despair in Lewis Carroll's writings there is an anxiety-ridden outlook that is rooted in Dodgson's life. From the child's dreamworld of *Alice in Wonderland* with its strange and comical characters—a world in which escape really seems possible—to *Through the Looking-Glass*, pessimism is readily evidenced. Escape is not possible in the later book. The fears over existence and time are bound up into a metaphor of life as a chessboard and all its people as but pawns and pieces. In this game, this book, there is a determinism, a fatalism, that taints much of the mirth and depressingly eliminates individual possibilities. *The Hunting of the Snark* can be read as a statement of despair over the state of being—Dodgson's despair over the threat of nonexistence and the inescapability of time. This poem, which on the literal level has so many humorous moments, turns out to be the saddest of Carroll's writings. The ending is not at all funny. One character vanishes, and another, the Bellman, remains a grave and depressing figure. He has, after all, but one notion of navigation, and that is to toll his bell.

NOTES

1. *Alice in Wonderland: Authoritative Texts of Alice's Adventures in Wonderland, Through the Looking-Glass, The Hunting of the Snark,* ed. Donald J. Gray, Norton Critical Edition (New York: W. W. Norton, 1971), p. xi. Citations given in the text for quotations from the *Alices* and the *Snark* are to this edition.
2. Robert Martin Adams, *Nil: Episodes in the Literary Conquests of Void During the Nineteenth Century* (New York: Oxford Univ. Press, 1966), p. 96.
3. Late Victorian England was, of course, an age troubled by uncertainties: about the nature and origins of man; about the authority of reason and scriptural revelation; about the established church; about the long-held belief that the

universe was purposive; and about the changes that were being made in the fabric of society, especially changes in the political and educational systems brought about by the emerging middle class.

4. See Roger B. Henkle, "Spitting Blood and Writing Comic: Mid-Century British Humor," *Mosaic,* 4 (1976), 77–90; and Henkle's *Comedy and Culture: England, 1820–1900* (Princeton, New Jersey: Princeton Univ. Press, 1980), 185–237.

5. *Alice,* ed. Gray, p. viii. As an adult, Dodgson, it will be remembered, regularly attended theatrical burlesques and pantomimes, and he sent ideas for jokes and cartoons to *Punch.* Earlier, as a boy, he had edited a series of illustrated family magazines that were imitations of the popular comic weeklies and monthlies. And beginning as a young man he had contributed verse and prose sketches to these comic journals. And Gray reminds us that "the use of parody, for example, and of puns, dialect, and other plays on the sound of words, was frequent in comic journalism and in theatrical burlesque and pantomime. So was the creation of a fanciful grotesquerie—in the cartoons of comic periodicals, for example, and in the plots and staging of burlesque and pantomime—in which ordinary objects and contemporary people and events were jumbled together with talking animals, animated playing cards, and creatures from fairy tale, folklore, and the legendary past of a child's history" (p. viii).

6. Early reviews of the *Snark* are reprinted in Morton N. Cohen's "Hark the Snark," in *Lewis Carroll Observed: A Collection of Unpublished Photographs, Drawings, Poetry, and New Essays,* ed. Edward Guiliano (New York: Clarkson N. Potter, 1976), pp. 95–110.

7. *The Letters of Lewis Carroll,* ed. Morton N. Cohen with the assistance of Roger Lancelyn Green, 2 vols. (London: Macmillan; New York: Oxford Univ. Press, 1978), I:374.

8. Ibid., I:548.

9. "Alice on the Stage," *The Theatre,* April 1887, rpt. in *The Lewis Carroll Picture Book,* ed. Stuart Dodgson Collingwood (London: Unwin, 1899); rpt. as *Diversions and Digressions of Lewis Carroll* (New York: Dover, 1961), p. 165.

10. Cohen, "Hark the Snark," p. 95.

11. Quoted by Stuart Dodgson Collingwood in *The Life and Letters of Lewis Carroll* (London: T. Fisher Unwin, 1898; New York: The Century Co., 1899), p. 131.

12. *Letters of Lewis Carroll,* ed. Cohen, I:523.

13. William Empson, "The Child as Swain," in *Some Versions of Pastoral* (1935; rpt. New York: New Directions, 1960); rpt. in Gray, ed., *Alice in Wonderland,* p. 347.

14. Elizabeth Sewell, *The Field of Nonsense* (London: Chatto and Windus, 1952), p. 124.

15. *Letters of Lewis Carroll,* ed. Cohen: II:759–60.

16. *The Diaries of Lewis Carroll,* ed. Roger Lancelyn Green, 2 vols. (London: Cassell, 1953; New York: Oxford Univ. Press, 1954), I:230.

17. *The Annotated Snark,* ed. Martin Gardner (New York, 1962; rpt. Harmondsworth, England: Penguin, 1967), p. 28.

18. Ibid., p. 63, n. 29.

19. Sigmund Freud, "Humor," *International Journal of Psychoanalysis,* 9 (1928), 1.

20. Michael Holquist, "What is a Boojum? Nonsense and Modernism," *Yale French Studies,* 43 (1969), pp. 145–64; rpt. in Gray, ed., *Alice in Wonderland,* see p. 407. Holquist—and Donald Rackin, in his essay in this volume—view Carroll's quest for order as, in part, an organizing principle in his life and art.

Lewis Carroll the Surrealist

J E F F R E Y   S T E R N

> ". . . living backwards . . . always makes one a little giddy at
> first. . . . but there's one great advantage in it, that one's mem-
> ory works both ways."
>
> The White Queen, *Through the Looking-Glass*

Giddiness is a small price to pay for a memory that works both ways,
yet it will be a necessary hazard here in looking at a phenomenon from both
directions simultaneously. In short, what follows will be an examination of
what is Carrollian about surrealism and what is surrealist about Carroll.
With a critical memory that "works both ways" the "great advantage" here
will be in the demonstration that it took the surrealists to understand and to
elaborate an essential element of Carroll's genius—using it also in their own
work. Similarly, it is through understanding *their* understanding of Carroll
that we can more readily approach the work of the surrealists.

In choosing this approach we must, however, beware of falling into the
obvious trap of oversimplification, and from the outset the point must be
made that it is necessary not to overstate the case in order to relate Carroll's
work to the surrealist movement. It would be equally wrong to claim either
that Carroll was exclusively surrealist or that the movement could not have
existed without the knowledge of his work. Nevertheless, we can find a starting point in André Breton's pamphlet *What Is Surrealism?* which was
"specially prepared for the occasion of the first International Surrealist Exhibition to be held in London" in 1936. Here he lists the movement's "sponsors" and in addition to

> Swift is Surrealist in malice,
> Sade is Surrealist in sadism,
> Poe is Surrealist in adventure,
> Baudelaire is Surrealist in morality,
> Rimbaud is Surrealist in the way he lived, and elsewhere,
> Jarry is Surrealist in absinthe.

we find that:

> Carroll is Surrealist in nonsense.[1]

Although there is an element here of self-parody (where is Rimbaud's "elsewhere"?), there is nevertheless an awareness by the surrealists of their bloodline and a keenness to recognize it. This was not simply a case of intellectual fireworks, but was also a typical surrealist paradox—for while they were, as surrealists, dedicatedly calling the rational world into doubt, they gained reassurance from finding a rationale for this in chosen elements within the work of certain artistic ancestors.

I

In their *Surrealism, Permanent Revelation,* Cardinal and Short make the point that these ancestors "had all, in their ways, been rebels." In his own gentle way, this was certainly true of Carroll, whose rebellious framework is obvious—nonsense against sense, the dream against the mundane, Wonderland against Victorian England, and so on. Cardinal and Short further generalize that the "sponsors" of surrealism "had rebelled against a hyperlogical view of the world, against the railings put up by convention to fence in desire, against mechanical conceptions of time and space expressed in chronological description or perspective, and against the classical idea that art's task is to imitate or interpret exterior reality. In so far as they anticipated or registered the discredit of commonsense reality, they had all sought to enable a liberated imagination to benefit from this."[2]

Rebellion and reaction against the approved status quo has, of course, often been an important source of artistic energy, but the significant point here is that the surrealists and Carroll reacted in similar ways to similar things. For clearly Wonderland and the world through the looking-glass are, even in their names, both vitally concerned with breaking down fences of convention ("I've tried to say *'How doth the little busy bee,'* but it all came different! . . ."[3]), and even ideas of space (" 'Now, *here,* you see, it takes all the running *you* can do, to keep in the same place' " [p. 210]) and time (" 'If you knew Time as well as I do,' " said the Hatter, "you wouldn't talk about wasting *it.* It's *him* . . .' " [p. 97]). Indeed Alice's problem is that there is no stable so-called reality, and Carroll's standard joke that punctuates virtually every page of her adventures is that whenever she challenges anything, it nearly always retreats into an unexpected second or third meaning—usually by breaking the accepted idiom, (" 'I see nobody on the road' said Alice. 'I only wish *I* had such eyes,' the King remarked . . .' " [p. 279]) or by punning ("'it isn't etiquette to cut any one you've been introduced to. Remove the joint!'" [p. 331]). With this in mind, it would have been uncharacteristically ill-informed of the surrealists to have missed the connection between their work and Carroll's. Some of these connections have been noted before; as Paul C. Ray observes in *The Surrealist Movement in England:*

> The surrealist program to discredit conventional reality included an attack on the object, the basic irreducible component of that reality. The first and easiest step in this procedure is to remove the object from its habitual surroundings, or simply to change the angle from which it is customarily perceived. Lewis Carroll in a mild way was doing precisely that in the following: "I like very much a little mustard with a bit of beef spread evenly under it; and I like brown sugar —only it should have some apple pudding mixed with it to keep it from being too sweet. I also like pins, only they should always have a cushion put around to keep them warm." Marcel Duchamp went several steps further than Carroll by violently wrenching real objects from their normal contexts and claiming that he was raising them to the level of works of art simply by the act of choosing them. In 1914 Duchamp signed an ordinary bottle rack made of galvanized iron. Three years later, he submitted a urinal standing on its side, signed "R. Mutt" and titled "Fountain," to the Salon des Independants in New York. . . . [As he said,] he took an ordinary article of life, placed it so that its usual significance disappeared under the new title and point of view and created a new thought for the object.
>
> The banal object deliberately and systematically torn from its realistic context and put to an unbecoming use becomes a source of radiating energy. Duchamp's signed urinal, elevated to the status of a work of art, comments eloquently on the sentimental and cosmetic role usually assigned to art in a bourgeois society. From the surrealist point of view it goes a long way towards achieving the shock to "normal" categories essential to the achievement of the "alienation of sensations" on which the surrealist revolution is predicated.[4]

Ray's choice of an example from Carroll, though apposite, is almost the mildest he could have found and looks almost insipid and whimsical in comparison with "R. Mutt's" work. But in fact it could rightly be said that the very practice of wrenching Alice herself from her ordinary and realistic context to place her in an environment where everything is alien and nothing is normal and expected—and where even she does not seem to stay the same size or retain her name—actually radiates more provocative and sustained energy than Duchamp's misplaced urinal. The only reason for there seeming to be a difference in effective power between them is that Carroll's work was never outrageous in an obvious way and he used the authorized license of the children's fairy tale to slip past the censorship of adult reason. Consequently, the revolutionary spirit that his work contains has not often been recognized. The surrealists found that to achieve a similar result, they had to deliberately court and provoke outrage, so that they might, in theory at least, stimulate the individual spectator to discovery. As Cardinal and Short explain: "At all times the surrealist artist works with a view to provoking images that will work upon the mind in a way that bypasses reason. The more disturbing an image, the more likely it will be to produce a numbing of the rational faculties, whereby the unconscious is directly contacted. The criterion of good surrealist art is its effectiveness in this special sense." [5]

Though Carroll's work is not in this sense deliberately out to shock the reader, nevertheless to numb and thereby qualify her "good sense" is precisely his aim with Alice. He provokes her (or rather the good sense that she has learned from her teachers), shows her an environment where reason will not work, and disturbs her equanimity and confidence whenever he can—as, for example, in the exchange in *Through the Looking-Glass* where the Red Queen carefully demolishes Alice's security (and ours) about terms of comparison and measurement, about gardens and hills: "The Red Queen shook her head. 'You may call it "nonsense" if you like,' she said, 'but *I've* heard nonsense, compared with which that would be as sensible as a dictionary!' " (p. 207).

But this kind of nullification is still mild when we compare it with some of Carroll's questioning directed toward Alice: "Who are *You?*" for example (asked by the Caterpillar, p. 67), and "Where do you come from. . . . And where are you going?" (asked by the Red Queen, p. 206). Such metaphysical taunting is of the most considerable kind and is both frightening and exhilarating if taken (as it surely was intended to be) as seriously as the surrealist readers did. At its most profound, then, the garden glimpsed by Alice is no less than the strange garden of the unconscious. The surrealists—sure (perhaps oversure) of what Freud had meant—were anxious to use his discoveries in their own work, and to demonstrate again something that was akin to "what Alice found there" decades earlier: that is, that there are levels of life and thought that are often tantalizingly out of the reach of reason and yet still extremely worthy of exploration and eternally beguiling. Though it cannot be claimed that Carroll formulated his own theories of the unconscious, it is not difficult to argue that he was himself aware of this "other life" to which a key should be able to be found: "How Alice longed to get out of that dark hall, and wander about among those beds of bright flowers and those cool fountains. . . ." (p. 31).

II

The surrealists' method of effecting the transition between the two worlds was hardly as simple as Carroll's, yet they effectively arrived at three solutions similar to his. These were: first, to pay full attention to what the phenomenon of the dream had to offer; second, to explore the idea of inspirational creation that bypasses the censoring reason of consciousness; and finally, to question the validity of so-called reality through probing the nature of language, space, and time. The surrealists learned to do the first—that is, to listen to the dream—again as a direct result of Freud's influence. As Breton says in the *First Manifesto:* "Freud very rightly brought his critical faculties to bear upon the dream. It is, in fact, inadmissible that this considerable portion of psychic activity . . . has still today been so grossly neglected. I have always been amazed at the way an ordinary observer lends so much more credence and attaches so much more importance to waking events than to those occurring in dreams." [6]

Breton was exaggerating the level of "gross neglect" shown by the art of the past to the phenomena of the dream; nevertheless, the fact that all of Carroll's major work takes place in a dream state is of great importance. Carroll recognized that the dream's additional dimension by which to understand so-called reality demonstrated two important things: first, that consciousness was more complex than might at first be apparent ("Who in the world am I?" [p. 37]) and, second, that such consciousness was, in any case, a limited mode of exploration, since, where logic or sense (as opposed to nonsense) are the only permitted tools of expression and communication, then there are whole realms that cannot ever be experienced. The supreme value of the dream for both Carroll and the surrealists was that it was a constant demonstration that absolutes—distinctions and oppositions that seem to be totally proven—can nevertheless be shown as false because they can be regrouped and even reconciled. Thus a fish, a bird, and a bowler-hatted man stand posed side by side and are all the same height in Magritte's painting *Presence of Mind* (1958); thus flowers can talk, and Rocking-horse flies (made entirely of wood and living on sap and sawdust) get about by swinging from branch to branch in the world through the looking-glass. For the surrealists in particular, the world of dreams was of fundamental importance since in it there is nothing real to contrast with the imaginary; no license or restriction; no morality or immorality; indeed, nothing that can hold as constant or coherent and that might not find itself in a new combination or reconciliation. It does not seem coincidental therefore to find that despite the differences in tone, vocabulary, and confidence, Carroll and Breton both questioned the nature of reality and sanity in similar ways. For example, here is a passage from Carroll's diary for February 9, 1856:

> Query: when we are dreaming and, as often happens, have a dim consciousness of the fact and try to wake, do we not say and do things which in waking life would be insane? May we not then sometimes define insanity as an inability to distinguish which is the waking and which the sleeping life? We often dream without the least suspicion of unreality: "Sleep hath its own world," and it is often as lifelike as the other.[7]

Compare this with a passage from Breton's *Second Surrealist Manifesto:*

> From an intellectual point of view, it was and still is necessary to expose by every available means the fictitious character of the old contradictions hypocritically calculated to hinder every unusual agitation on the part of man, and to force its recognition at all costs, if only to give mankind some faint idea of its abilities and to challenge it to escape its universal shackles to some meaningful extent. The bugbear of death, the music-halls of the beyond, the shipwreck of the future, the towers of Babel, the mirrors of inconsistency, the insurmountable silver-splashed wall of the brain—all of these striking images of human catastrophe are perhaps nothing but images. There is every reason to believe that there exists a certain point in the mind at which life and death, real and imaginary,

Figure 1. (*A*) Tenniel, *Alice in Wonderland* (Chap. 4); (*B*) Magritte, "Les idées de l'acrobate," 1927 or 1928, oil, 45⅜″ by 31⅛″ (*Urvater Collection, Belgium*); (*C* and *D*) Tenniel, *Through the Looking-Glass* (Chaps. 3, 4); (*E*) Tenniel, *Alice in Wonderland* (Chap. 8)

past and future, communicable and incommunicable, high and low, cease to be perceived in terms of contradiction. Surrealist activity would be searched in vain for a motive other than the hope to determine this point.[8]

For Carroll the implications of his dreams and the concomitant complexity of then defining reality are also a root cause for his own constant curiosity, which in turn informed the creation of Wonderland. For in Wonderland he could experiment with Alice, changing the rules just at the moment when she begins to win, just like unconsciousness does in the dream—in order, in Breton's words, "to challenge it to escape its universal shackles"; "For, you see, so many out-of-the-way things had happened lately that Alice had begun to think that very few things indeed were really impossible" (p. 30). There are many moments of real tension in Carroll's work when these complex questions come close to the surface (just as the dream becomes real); when, for example, Tweedledee tells Alice "Why, you're only a sort of thing in [the Red King's] dream," to which his brother adds "If that there King was to wake, you'd go out—bang!—just like a candle" (p. 238). The play here is obviously beyond the realm of the nursery and has all of the metaphysical implications of surrealist questioning about the nature of reality.

The next stage in such an inquiry, where sane perimeters are abandoned and the irrational deliberately embraced, leads to an eventual appreciation of actual madness as a state of insight rather than a malady. Certainly the surrealists flirted with that idea—though in reality they went no farther than an evocation of the "fool-as-seer" tradition that extends throughout the history of literature. Charcot's and Janet's studies were current, however, and the surrealists cruelly produced photographs of imbeciles in their periodicals (e.g., *La Revolution Surrealist,* No. 11, March 15, 1928), claiming that hysteria was "the greatest poetic discovery of the late nineteenth century . . . [which can] from every point of view, be considered as a supreme form of expression."[9] In more recent years R. D. Laing has upheld similar views, though the fashion has turned against them, doubtless for the same reasons that Rousseau's noble savage ideal could only be appreciated by those who were the exact opposite of the savage. To be insane is similarly only a desirable theoretic concept to sane intellectuals. Nevertheless there are obvious—if over-romantic—links between childlikeness, childishness, the infantile, and the genius and the madness coming from unrestrained enthusiasm. Certainly, and most importantly, all these states are also in Carroll's world and are vital to it (a mad tea-party, a mad hatter, a grinning cat, et al.), and Alice's protest to the Cheshire Cat, "But I don't want to go among mad people" only brings the rejoinder "Oh you can't help that, . . . we're all mad here. I'm mad. You're mad . . . you must be . . . or you wouldn't have come here" (p. 89).

III

The second way in which Carroll anticipated the surrealists was in a method of creative writing that they came to call "automatism." Paul C. Ray again relates the history of this idea.

Andre Breton, the founder and principal theoretician of surrealism, in [his

First Surrealist Manifesto, 1924] recounts how, just before falling asleep one evening, he heard a sentence that had nothing to do with his preoccupations of the
moment: "There is a man cut in two by the window." This sentence was accompanied by a weak visual image of a man bisected by a window perpendicular to
the axis of his body. Other sentences, equally gratuitous, followed the first. He
concluded from the experience that any control he thought he exercised over his
mental process was entirely illusionary. These imaged sentences struck him as
being valuable poetic elements; and the subsequent attempt to produce them
led him, together with Philippe Soupault, to the discovery of automatic writing
and the production of the first book written automatically, *Les Champs Magnet-
iques* (1919).

   . . . The important discovery of surrealism is that there is a continuous discourse going on below the level of consciousness to which one needs only to pay
attention in order to register it; equally important is the surrealist insistence that
this discourse deserves the most intense attention, even when it seems discordant
or incoherent. Automatism, shortly after Breton's discovery, became the very
basis of surrealism, and Breton's first definition of surrealism is really a definition
of automatic writing:

   "SURREALISM, n.m: Pure psychicautomatism by which it is intended to
express, verbally, in writing, or by any other means, the real process of thought,
without any control exercised by reason, outside of all aesthetic or moral
preoccupations." [10]

Through using methods akin to those used by spiritualists and mediums,
automatic writing, drawing, and painting were meant to liberate the unconscious and to allow it a tangible expression other than the always fugitive
natural expression of the dream. In this way the artist was to be the agent of
the unconscious. Because it had no part to play, repressive reasoning would
not be able to interfere with or to censor this creativity. The result, since it
would be absurd, would bypass the spectator's consciousness to penetrate and
communicate to the unconscious. This quite special approach made by the
surrealists meant that the art medium (words, images) was to regain fluidity,
to expand in its own way and with almost its own life to find a new integrity
in strange combinations and juxtapositions. The results were not, in the
event, to be wholly arbitrary, since the conscious and unconscious are obviously related in the individual personality.

As a philosophy of art the complete concept of surrealist automatism was
more complex than has been suggested here, and it changed significantly as
the movement grew. There is scarcely space here to elaborate beyond this
outline, however, and in any case J. H. Matthews's *An Introduction to Surreal-
isms* [11] and Paul C. Ray's opening chapter ("Definitions") in *The Surrealist
Movement in England* make another rehearsal of the history redundant. But
even at the most basic level, it is remarkable how Carroll's own methods of
working anticipated something of the surrealist concept of automatism as a
creative method. We find, for example, his confession that he wrote *Alice in
Wonderland* in the first instance with no real concentration of conscious
effort—the Liddell sisters, to use his words, "goaded" his "jaded Muse into
action [which] plodded meekly on, more because she had to say something
than she had something to say," or else, again without deliberation, "fancies

unsought came crowding thick" upon him.[12] This is confirmed by Robinson Duckworth (at that time a fellow of Trinity) who rowed stroke to Carroll's bow on that "golden afternoon" when *Alice's Adventures Under Ground* was first told. He testified that it "was actually composed and spoken *over my shoulder* for the benefit of Alice Liddell, who was acting as 'cox' of our gig. I remember turning round and saying 'Dodgson, is this an ex tempore romance of yours?' and he replied, 'Yes, I'm inventing as we go along.' "[13] We might compare this with what Breton in the *First Surrealist Manifesto,* under the subheading "Secrets of the Magical Surrealist Art," gives as the conditions necessary for successful automatic writing:

> . . . Put yourself in as passive, or perceptive, a state of mind as you can. Forget about your genius, your talents, and the talents of everyone else. . . . Write quickly, without any preconceived subject, fast enough so that you'll not remember what you're writing and be tempted to re-read what you had written. The first sentence will come spontaneously, so compelling is the truth that with every passing second there is a sentence unknown to our consciousness which is only crying out to be heard. It is somewhat of a problem to form an opinion about the next sentence; it doubtless partakes both of our conscious activity and of the other, if one agrees that the fact of having written the first entails a minimum of perception. . . . Go on as long as you like. Put your trust in the inexhaustible nature of the murmur. If silence threatens to settle in, if you should ever happen to make a mistake, . . . break off without hesitation with an overly clear line. Following a word the origin of which seems suspicious to you, place any letter whatsoever, the letter "L" for example, always the letter "L" and bring the arbitrary back by making this letter the first of the following word.[14]

The relaxed unforced conditions necessary for automatic writing, with no real thought of "genius" or "talent," prestige or permanent result, were almost exactly the conditions under which Carroll's first *Alice* story was written. As Carroll has said, none of these "extemporised" tales told to Alice and her sisters on the river were written down: "they lived and died, like summer midges, each in its own golden afternoon until there came a day when, as it chanced, one of my little listeners petitioned that the tale might be written out for her. That was many a year ago, but I distinctly remember now as I write, how, in a desperate attempt to strike out some new line of fairy-lore, I had sent my heroine straight down a rabbit-hole, to begin with, without the least idea what was to happen afterwards."[15]

Again, despite differences in tone, what Carroll says here can effectively be compared with what the surrealists said about their own working methods—for example, this from Joan Miró:

> Rather than setting out to paint something. . . . I begin painting and as I paint the picture begins to assert itself under my brush, or suggest itself under my brush. The form becomes a sign for a woman or a bird as I work. . . . The first stage is free, unconscious.[16]

—or this from André Masson:

> Often I feel I have no need of images. I have only to let my brush run. . . . But

when the image appears I do not chase it away, I accept it, I even multiply it.[17]

—or even this from Dali:

> The fact that I myself, at the moment of painting, do not understand the significance of my pictures cannot mean that my pictures have no meaning; on the contrary their meaning is so profound, complex, coherent, involuntary, that it escapes mere analysis of any logical intuition.[18]

When Carroll's comment about the meaning of the Snark is remembered: "I'm very much afraid I didn't mean anything but nonsense! Still, you know, words mean more than we mean to express when we use them; so a whole book ought to mean a great deal more than the writer meant" (see n. 8 and accompanying text from preceding essay), then Dali's remark in particular seems uncannily close to some of Carroll's ideas. Moreover, such was the element of chance and lack of conscious effort (both factors essential to automatism), that Carroll's stories were, by definition, potentially more naturally surreal than even the productions of concentrated lack of concentration as practiced by the surrealists could be. For he had even been able to avoid one of the greatest pitfalls that threatened the success of automatic writing: the self-conscious control that intruded because of the writer's awareness of the possibility of publication.[19] Of course, when such a possibility presented itself, Carroll did consciously intrude into his stories, but—according to his own account—unpredictably, very little. About writing *Alice's Adventures Under Ground* out, he says:

> I added many fresh ideas, which seemed to grow of themselves upon the original stock; and many more added themselves when, years afterwards, I wrote it all over again for publication: but (this may interest some readers of "Alice" to know) every such idea and nearly every word of the dialogue, *came of itself.* Sometimes an idea comes at night, when I have had to get up and strike a light to note it down—sometimes when out on a lonely winter walk, when I have had to stop, and with half frozen fingers jot down a few words which should keep the newborn idea from perishing—but whenever or however it comes, it *comes of itself.* I cannot set invention going like a clock, by any voluntary winding up: nor do I believe that any *original* writing . . . was ever so produced. . . . "Alice" and the "Looking Glass" are made up almost wholly of bits and scraps, single ideas which came of themselves.[20]

Carroll here is talking partly of what has always been recognized as a virtually essential element for successful art—nothing less than inspiration; but he implies the presence of more than just that. For he, like the surrealists, had not only a belief in inspiration but also a total trust in it and listened to and valued its findings whether they were coherent or not. Therefore, just as Breton found poetic value in the sentence "There is a man cut in two by the window," so also did Carroll in the line "For the Snark *was* a Boojum, you see"—as he explained in relating how *The Hunting of the Snark* was composed (see n. 9 and accompanying text in the preceding essay). And in that familiar account he explains that for all quotations about possible meanings of the *Snark* he had "but one answer, 'I don't know!'"

Carroll does not say that the *Snark* is without meaning; it has meanings, although some of these meanings he himself recognized would be difficult to understand. Each individual should properly bring his own ideas to bear on the poem, which are as valid or invalid as any others; one should not be able, as he himself put it, "to explain things which you don't yourself understand" (see n. 7 and accompanying text in preceding essay). Again, this approach was one that the surrealists also adopted, each picture and poem being for them a deliberate journey into the unknown, like a Snark hunt, where conclusions are irrelevant to the value of the actual exploration itself. The vocabulary that the surrealists used differs from Carroll's—but not their purpose; Eluard's revolutionary comment that "poems always have big margins, big white margins of silence in which ardent memory is consumed to re-create a delirium that has no past . . . their principal quality is not to evoke but to inspire," [21] is essentially no more revolutionary than the Bellman's map: a perfect and absolute blank!

Breton's remark that lucidity was "the great enemy of revelation" or Humpty Dumpty's "Impenetrability! That's what *I* say!" are more than revelations here, and also seem to reflect at least a large part of Carroll's purpose. Certainly, as we have seen earlier, he regarded the *Snark* as an exercise in reader revelation rather than as having any single solution; he wrote to one child-friend, for example, shortly after the poem appeared: "When you have read the Snark, I hope you will write me a little note and tell me how you like it, and if you can *quite* understand it. Some children are puzzled with it. Of course you know what a Snark is? If you do please tell *me:* for I haven't an idea what it is like." [22]

In order to ensure that the *Snark* especially was generative rather than explicative, Carroll even achieved arbitrariness in a thoroughly Bretonian surrealist way. For whereas Breton advocated the letter *L* as the first letter "to bring the arbitrary back" when self-consciousness intruded in automatic writing, Carroll seems to have anticipated him in the way in which he chose the Snark hunters themselves, since their names (actually their professions) all begin with the letter *B* (Bellman, Boots, Bonnet-maker, Barrister, Broker, Billiard-maker, Banker, Beaver, Baker, and Butcher). When asked by Henry Holiday (who did the illustrations for the poem—which incidentally, are not without surreal qualities themselves) "why he made all the members of the crew have occupations beginning with B, he replied, 'Why not?' " [23] Though obviously more intense, and often with a specific revolutionary or political end in view, the surrealists, like Carroll, defied explication and championed intuition from a standpoint similar to his. For them, as at times for him, such an assertion of freedom to choose was perhaps in reaction to the periods in which they each lived, and it is attractive to suppose that Carroll was positively protesting about some of the difficulties of living in Victorian England. Certainly the surrealists reacted strongly against the restrictions of a period of world war, believing that: "In our period, only the imagination can restore to menaced man the feeling of being free." [24] Such freedom could be achieved by breaking other accepted codes too, and importantly, as Ray has shown, language itself heads the list of culpable restrictive forces: "one of the steps in freeing man from the mediocrity of the universe is to dissolve the forced marriage between words and their meanings. Words, for the surrealists, exist outside of their common denotive or connotive functions. Words have a far more active life than any dictionary or etymology can guess; for . . . associations of sounds, ideas, even of the shapes of words play their part." [25]

Carroll's nonsense world also gives words an extradictionary life, and at the same time it demonstrates how inaccurate, but nevertheless evocative, words can be. Continually in the *Alices*, as Robert D. Sutherland exhaustively shows in his *Language and Lewis Carroll* (The Hague: Mouton, 1970), Carroll is both exhilarated and disturbed by the ambiguity of words. His understanding of the "forced marriage" between them and their meanings, which tries to prevent their "active life," is nowhere more apparent than in the philosophy of Humpty Dumpty, whose way with language seems to be effectively akin to Duchamp's with a urinal: A Machiavellian determination decides the meaning and context—so that, " 'When *I* use a word,' Humpty Dumpty said, '. . . it means just what I choose it to mean—neither more nor less. . . . The question is . . . which is to be master—that's all' " (p. 269). But even more significant than Humpty Dumpty's new definitions is the way in which verbal freedom brings imaginative and perceptual freedom, so that distinctions and oppositions become "artificial fabrications of the rational man" [26] that prevent the occurrence of the marvelous or the wonderful. Once such distinctions disappear, analogies are also abolished, and every combination of thought and image becomes a possibility. Moreover, the resultant image, word, or idea becomes far more powerful than the sum of its parts, and—theoretically at least—artistic creation is infinite: as in Humpty Dumpty's interpretation of "Jabberwocky" (pp. 270–271).

The surrealist's attempts at what Max Ernst has called "verbal collage," though less memorable and perhaps less successfully evocative, clearly owe their origin to Carroll's portmanteau words, as here from Ernst: "What is a phallustrade: It is an alchemical product composed of the following elements: the autostrade, the balustrade and a certain quantity of phallus. A phallustrade is a verbal collage. One might define collage as an alchemy resulting from the unexpected meeting of two or more heterogeneous elements provoked either by a will which—from a love of clairvoyance—is directed towards systematical confusion of all the senses (Rimbaud), or by chance, or by a will favourable to chance." [27]

In the same way, many surrealists like Paul Delvaux, Giorgio de Chirico, and Dali used just this collage or portmanteau technique in their mock storytelling paintings to provoke confusion or elation (or both), and Magritte, the most literary of the surrealist painters, executed a whole series of canvases that were concerned with exposing the categories that we use to tie down what we see and to defuse the impact of the image. Paintings such as *Homage to Alphonse Allais,* 1964 (a fish that has become a burning cigar by the time we come to look at its tail, or vice versa); *The Red Model,* 1935 (shoes that have

Figure 2. (*A*) Magritte, "La chambre d'écoute," 1952, oil, 17¾ by 21¾ *(Collection Philippa de Menil, Houston, Texas);* (*B, C, D*) Tenniel, *Alice in Wonderland* (Chaps. 4, 1, and 2)

A

B

C

D

become feet or feet that have become shoes); *The Explanation,* 1952 (a wine bottle that has become a carrot, or vice versa); *Collective Invention,* 1935 (a nude woman lying on a beach who has become a fish, or vice versa); *Acrobatic Ideas,* 1927; and *The Listening Room,* 1952 (Fig. 2)—all these are as "curious-looking," in a similar way and for similar reasons, as those images that Humpty Dumpty describes and Alice discovers (see Figs. 1 and 2). In addition to this series about the ambiguity of images, Magritte painted another series of related pictures that were concerned with exposing the ambiguities of words and their fragile relationship with the object to which they are supposed to be eternally attached. As a surrealist, he could not trust the semantic conventions if their only truths were in the fact that they were established. Therefore, in paintings such as *The Use of Speech,* 1928; *Person Walking Towards the Horizon,* 1928–29; *The Empty Mask,* 1928; *The Air and the Song,* 1928–29; *The Key of Dreams,* 1936; *The Proper Meaning IV,* 1928–29; *The Two Mysteries,* 1966; and *The Use of Words I,* 1928–29 (all of which are concerned with labels that ostensibly do not relate to the objects to which they are attached), Magritte enjoyed dismantling ideas about the fixed nature of language. The naming word is seen in this light as a symbol with its own substance and vitality, and consequently can be exchanged with another image or subject: As Magritte says in *Les Mots et les Images,* "an object is not so possessed of its name that one cannot find for it another which suits it better,"—a proposition that brings us back to:

> "... but tell me your name and your business."
> "My *name* is Alice, but—"
> "It's a stupid name enough!" Humpty Dumpty interrupted impatiently. "What does it mean?"
> *"Must* a name mean something?" Alice asked doubtfully.
> "Of course it must," Humpty Dumpty said with a short laugh: *"my* name means the shape I am—and a good handsome shape I am—and a good handsome shape it is, too. With a name like yours, you might be any shape, almost.' "
> (p. 263)

Humpty Dumpty does not mean "egg-shaped," of course, except to those intent on believing it; equally, *Alice* does not mean "little English girl," and logically she could have any name (just as a certain chief of an African tribe was actually called Oxford University Press, and some girls in Nyasaland were named Frigidaire). The central issue for Magritte in particular and for the surrealists in general was (as Gablik points out in her book on Magritte) that:

> ... non-paradoxical statements about reality are merely selective conclusions attempting to proclaim that the universe is *only* this or *only* that. ... What appears inevitably true in one sense, because it has been endorsed by reason, is an oversimplified and limited notion of the possibilities of experience, since it does not take into account the ambivalent, paradoxical nature of reality. In Magritte's paintings, everything is directed towards a specific crisis in consciousness, through which the limited evidence of the commonsense world can be transcended.[28]

Though Carroll's work cannot be said to be entirely directed toward this crisis, it is, nevertheless, one of his central concerns. Moreover, his sense that what is often accepted as truth in a world where to call in doubt, to change, or to revise anything is sinful can be merely a matter of chance rather than of investigation gives an exchange such as the one that follows its point.

> "What is the cause of lightning?"
>
> "The cause of lightning," Alice said very decidedly, for she felt quite certain about this, "is the thunder—no, no!" she hastily corrected herself. "I meant the other way."
>
> "It's too late to correct it," said the Red Queen: "when you've once said a thing, that fixes it, and you must take the consequences." (p. 323)

One of the central surrealist ideas developed as a reaction against this sense that difficult consequences are inevitable with change (so that, indeed, changes of all kinds were part of the point, and therefore no opinion or idea was considered stable or fixed), and this conception made them seek ways in which to celebrate the "ambivalent, paradoxical nature of reality." Again, like Carroll, early on in their experiments they saw that the most potent and provocative method by which to attack the common-sense world and "selective conclusions attempting to proclaim that the universe is *only* this or *only* that" was to deliberately juxtapose alien elements—as they are, for example, in "Jabberwocky" or in Magritte's paintings. In this way the resultant energy was often more effective (in being nonsense and surrealist) than sense and reality could be. An important factor in the effectiveness of this was to be found in the super-reality of the elements involved—thus Alice has to be very "normal" in her reactions and Magritte has to paint in an academic style in order for the energy to be released. Similarly, according to Simon Wilson, only when his paintings were "hand-done colour photography . . . hyper-normal and sickly images of concrete irrationality" would Dali be satisfied with his work. The classic example of such alien juxtaposition of otherwise "normal" images and virtually the model for nearly every subsequent surreal work was the poet Lautréamont's image of the fortuitous encounter of an umbrella with a sewing machine on a dissecting table, which Max Ernst analyzed in 1927 as follows:

> Let a ready-made reality with a naive purpose apparently settled once for all (i.e., an umbrella) be suddenly juxtaposed to another and no less ridiculous reality (i.e., a sewing machine) in a place where both must be felt as *out of place* (i.e., on a dissecting table), and precisely thereby it will be robbed of its naive purpose and its identity; through a relativity it will pass from its false to a novel absoluteness, at once true and poetic: umbrella and sewing-machine will make love. This very simple example seems to me to reveal the mechanism of the process. Complete transmutation followed by a pure act such as the act of love must necessarily occur every time the two given facts make conditions favourable: the pairing of two realities which apparently cannot be paired on a plane not suited to them.[29]

This one definition remained a firm principle of surrealism because it incorporated much of the basic ingredient of its magic. For in addition to including the movement's theory of the juxtaposition of alien elements, it also pinpointed its inherent throwaway wit (so often used to exasperate the bourgeoisie), and the deliberate avoidance by the movement of "art subjects" and its love of the ephemeral and the unheroic. Partially these ideas were dadaist, but partially also they were inherited from less strident precursors like Carroll, who also delighted in "pairing the unpairable" as in

> He thought he saw an Elephant,
> That practised on a fife:
> He looked again, and found it was
> A letter from his wife.
> "At length I realise," he said,
> "The bitterness of Life." [30]

IV

Not only was Carroll's work known to the surrealists but they were actively involved in publicizing it and translating it. Louis Aragon translated *The Hunting of the Snark* into French in 1929 and wrote an article about Carroll in the magazine *Le Surrealism au service de la revolution* in 1931 (no. 3, pp. 25–26). This essay was rather wild and often inaccurate—for example, it opens with the sentence: "Almost nothing is said about Lewis Carroll, who was a professor and wore a fair pointed beard and lived towards the middle of Victoria's reign." [31] Despite its factual inaccuracies, Aragon's essay is not without interest, in that it was one of the earliest attempts to draw the surrealists' attention to Carroll and what he had to offer them. Its major purpose was to recommend his work because "The success of *Alice* is perhaps the greatest of modern times from the poetic point of view. . . . The works of Lewis Carroll, via childhood, are presented for the admiration of men. . . ." Aragon accordingly suggests editions, complains of abridged French versions and poor translations of Carroll's work, and especially recommends the nonsense poetry. He also enjoys the parodies of the pious poems of the bourgeoisie and the fact that Alice's adventures all take place during an escape from the restrictive parental or adult Victorian world and that the schoolroom is mocked. Such a recommendation to potential French readers was necessary, according to Aragon, because "it goes without saying that it is in France, the country of self-complaisant ignorance, that *Alice* has been less read [than elsewhere]." Most importantly, however, and for the first time, Aragon also saw Alice in a kind of English Joan-of-Arc role, delivering the innocent from the horrors of contemporary hypocrisy in a very positive way.

> In those shameful days of massacres in Ireland, of nameless oppression in the mills—where was now established the ironic compatibility of pleasure and pain advocated by Bentham—when, from Manchester there rose like a challenge, the theory of *free*-trade, what became of human liberty? It lay wholly in the frail hands of Alice where it had been placed by this curious man Carroll whom no-one mistrusted because he had never said anything irreverent except about chess queens, and because he showed to children the absurdity of a world which exists only on the other side of the looking glass.

Aragon's rhetoric is overambitious here, and he implies incorrectly that Carroll wrote to a formulated political thesis. Even at the time, Aragon was seen as being too stridently committed in his view of Carroll, and in his introduction to an extract from *Alice in Wonderland* in the *Anthologie de l'humour noir* (1939), Breton himself questioned Aragon's insistence on a simple political motive on Carroll's part, preferring a less defined interpretation.

> It seems no less abusive a distortion to present Lewis Carroll as a "political" rebel than to give his work specific satirical targets. It is pure and simple fraud to insinuate that the substitution of one regime for another might bring to an end such a resistance that the child will always oppose to those who are inclined to form him and consequently reduce him in order to more or less arbitrarily limit his magnificent field of experience. All those who preserve their sense of revolt will recognize in Lewis Carroll the first teacher of how to play truant. [32]

This sense of "basic resistance"—rather than a particularized aim and a clear plan of attack—that was detected by Breton here was in itself attractive to the surrealists. For the lack of a system (where such a system would necessarily mean the censorship of conflicting notions and the rejection out of hand of other possibilities of approach) was, on its own account, a championed surrealist cause. For if formulae are abandoned, then the whole experience of life can be seen as having value if viewed by unconditioned eyes (one of the effective points of Duchamp's urinal—which, out of context, we are forced to reconsider as a work of art). Nothing, according to the early surrealists, was to be relegated below the level of significance; and nothing was seen as being above reproach and questioning (thus the *Mona Lisa* earns a moustache). "The marvellous," wrote Aragon in his *Challenge to Painting* "is opposed to the mechanical, to that which is so good that it is no longer noticeable, and thus it is generally believed that the marvellous is the negation of reality. This rather summary view is conditionally acceptable; certainly the marvellous is born of the refusal of *one* reality [only], but also of the development of a new relationship, a new reality liberated by that refusal." [33]

It follows from this that, like Carroll, the surrealists saw that the experience of childhood—a time when there is no innate or automatic acceptance or refusal of anything that any experience has to offer, because no such conditioned response has been inherently instilled—was a period of life to be remembered, and even relived in certain aspects. In short, the surrealist movement almost aimed at the reinstatement of something near to child-vision in adulthood. Breton, for example, in the *First Manifesto*, claimed that:

> The mind which plunges into surrealism re-lives with glowing excitement the best part of its childhood. For such a mind, it is similar to the certainty with which a person who is drowning reviews once more, in the space of less than a second, all the insurmountable moments of his life. Some may say to me that the parallel is not very encouraging. But I have no intention of encouraging those who tell me that. From childhood memories, and from a few others, there emanates a feeling of being unintegrated, and then later of *having gone astray*, which I

hold to be the most fertile that exists. It is perhaps childhood that comes closest to one's "real life." Childhood, beyond which man has at his disposal, aside from his laissez-passer, only a few complimentary tickets; childhood, where everything nevertheless conspires to bring about the effective, risk-free possession of oneself. Thanks to Surrealism, it seems that opportunity knocks a second time.[34]

The "fertile feeling" of being "unintegrated" and of "having gone astray" is precisely what happens to Alice as she goes through her adventures in Wonderland and through the looking-glass. She is continually challenged by the marvelous, and she adjusts to retain her balance and self-possession—usually while accommodating, not rejecting, what she sees around her. To choose just one brilliant example: Alice finds herself in an extremely unstable situation (as unintegrated as anything in a surreal painting's landscape or in Ionesco, Beckett, or Genet) when the White Queen perplexes her by turning into a sheep in charge of a "little dark shop," a fact that Alice is forced to accept ("was it really a *sheep* sitting on the other side of the counter?"). Accordingly, she tries to do what is ordinarily done in shops, to buy something, in order to restore equilibrium. This Carroll prevents, first by making the goods unstable, then by thwarting her plan to "follow [the article] up to the very ceiling," and then by conjuring the whole shop into a rowing boat and the Sheep's knitting needles into oars, with Alice using them.

> The shop seemed to be full of all manner of curious things—but the oddest part of it all was that, whenever she looked hard at any shelf, to make out exactly what it had on it, that particular shelf was always quite empty; though the others round it were crowded as full as they could hold.
>
> "Things flow about so here!" she said at last in a plaintive tone. . . .
>
> "Can you row?" the Sheep asked, handing her a pair of knitting-needles as she spoke.
>
> "Yes a little—but not on land—and not with needles—" Alice was beginning to say, when suddenly the needles turned into oars in her hands, and she found they were in a little boat, gliding along between banks: so there was nothing for it but to do her best. (pp. 253–54)

The giddiness here is not only the Sheep's but also must be shared by the reader, especially since the boat subsequently metamorphoses back again into the little shop, in which Alice tried to buy an egg, which itself eventually turns into Humpty Dumpty. If surrealism can be broadly defined as the reconciliation of distant realities on a new and unexpected plane, then—as such sustained bewilderment as we have seen here is just a sample from Carroll—it is scarcely surprising that the *Alice*s were a favorite surrealist text and that Alice herself was a special talisman that often featured in their own work. Thus, she is a presiding spirit over most of Breton's last large oeuvre, *Arcane 17* (transported into the *femme-fée* Melusine); she is found throughout surrealist painting in her role as spectator of marvels in the work of Leonor Fini, Hans Bellmer, Leonora Carrington, Toyen, Dorothea Tanning, and others; she (or someone very like her) features in many of Buñuel's films (especially *Viridiana*), and she—or a first cousin—is also to be found in absurd and surreal drama.

Max Ernst was another who was typical of those surrealists who actively responded to Carroll's work and he paid direct homage both in particular paintings such as *Pour les amis d'Alice* (1957) and *Alice envoie un message aux poissons* (1964) and in illustrations to editions of Carroll's work. He illustrated *The Hunting of the Snark* in 1950 and 1968 (see Fig. 3), *Logique sans peine* in 1966, and an anthology of Carroll pieces chosen by him and Werner Spies, which was called *Lewis Carroll's Wunderhorn,* in 1970. This last is in many ways the most interesting, since it largely concentrates on collecting up many of Carroll's examples used to illustrate logical (and illogical) arguments from *Symbolic Logic,* and representing them as poetry. Spies wrote an illuminating Afterword to this volume, concluding that: "Concentration on the fixed logical mechanisms sets the great liberties of Carroll's world free. That it was for him, the Oxford mathematics don, not just an amusing paradoxical game is made clear by a glance at the hundreds and hundreds of pages in which Carroll grimly rattles at the bars of thinking . . ." (my translation).

The final piece of direct documentation linking surrealism with Carroll that needs mention here is Salvador Dali's fine illustrated edition of *Alice in Wonderland* published in 1969 (see Fig 4). In what is undoubtedly the only version of *Alice* illustrated by an important artist of world class, this edition is also one of the most elaborate ever produced. In one important way Dali's work is an act of double homage—not merely to Carroll but also to the grand progenitor of surrealistic painting, de Chirico. This is achieved by directly using de Chirico's image of innocence—a girl skipping through a menacing cityscape—as his image of Alice herself (see, for example, *Melancholy and Mystery of a Street,* 1914). Throughout the series of Dali's illustrations, a silhouetted Alice with a jump rope similarly plays in alien landscapes, an obviously fragile figure in a curious world. This link to de Chirico documents yet again Carroll's place at the heart of the surrealist movement; as we might expect, this edition is an important (and beautiful) work of homage.

By way of conclusion it might be rightly said that, though heterogeneous, the ideas of the surrealists enumerated in this essay have affinities with some of Carroll's—their mutual use of the dream; their employment of "automatism" as a mode of creation; their exploration of reality by questioning the status quo through challenging the established ideas of language, logic, time, and space; their admiration of childhood and the child's capacity to perceive new relationships between things and details that escape the flawed adult eye. A fundamental shared conviction central to the ideas of both Carroll and the surrealists was that thoughts, ideas, and feelings do not have to be totally comprehensible consciously, rationally, or logically in order to be communicated.

The danger of this kind of art is clear, and cries of "Emperor's new clothes" have always been voiced by detractors. For the lack of adequate (i.e., conscious, provable) ways in which to judge either nonsense or surrealism has meant that critics have always justifiably been at a loss finally to analyze either. This is because, as we have seen, to compromise and even to destroy

Figure 3. Max Ernst, *The Hunting of the Snark*, 1968

Figure 4. Salvador Dali, *Alice in Wonderland*, 1969, etching in brown and white. (*Courtesy Random House, Inc.*)

the weapons of rational certainty have been fundamental preoccupations for both movements: the loss of reference that critics feel has always been part of the point. But to demonstrate also that things are not always just what they seem largely because they are not adequately observed or experienced (since presumption and prejudice is an adult habit) is as much the valid point of a bottle marked "DRINK ME," the contents of which we find taste of "cherry-tart, custard, pineapple, roast turkey, toffy, and hot buttered toast" (p. 31) as it is of a cup, saucer, and spoon that we find covered in fur (a "ready-made" with additions, by Oppenheim of 1936), or a typewriter that has become a *Soft Typewriter* (by Oldenburg, 1963–64) and is made, not of metal, but of vinyl. Expectation is foiled in order to kick awake slumbering imagination and to demonstrate that classification of the world is not as easy as it is assumed to be, and that the sense of the possible and the impossible is often arbitrarily determined by those who have gone before us rather than by our own eyes and experience ("What-is-this?" [said the Unicorn] . . . "It's as large as life, and twice as natural!") (p. 287). Whether oiling watches with butter or painting them to look as if they are made of it (as Dali did)—both methods effectively put paid to time, and they mock all who force themselves to be ruled by the clock. The general effect of these ideas was summed up by Magritte in the final number of the surrealist magazine *VVV* (1944): "The principal value of Surrealism seems to me to be that it has re-introduced the marvellous into everyday possibilities. It has taught that if reality seemed baleful and flat it is because man did not know how to see, his glance was limited by an education deliberately intended to blind him and by an aesthetic censor inherited from past ages." [35]

The idea that the marvelous is always at hand if only our delimiting expectations can be foiled or our perception increased by stimulating the natural (but usually repressed) sense of curiosity is one that surrealists like Magritte obviously have in common with Carroll.

> Alice laughed. "There's no use trying," she said: "one *can't* believe impossible things."
>
> "I daresay you haven't had much practice," said the Queen. "When I was your age, I always did it for half-an-hour a day. Why, sometimes I've believed as many as six impossible things before breakfast." (p. 251)

A dialogue such as this has prepared us for "ready-made" sculptures like Duchamp's *Why Not Sneeze* (a bird cage containing lumps of marble cut to resemble sugar cubes, which we are invited to lift and find surprisingly heavy). Similarly, we are also prepared to wait for Godot and countless other similar surrealist and postsurrealist works that are designed to delight, surprise, and perplex us. We are prompted to be wary of our facts and curious about things that are not necessarily what they seem and that only remain true because unquestioned, while at the same time we are warned to be alive to unforeseen possibilities; *the* great Carrollian and surrealist ideal is to induce in the reader a feeling like Alice's after she has read "Jabberwocky": ". . . it's *rather* hard to understand! . . . Somehow it seems to fill my head with ideas—only I don't exactly know what they are!" (p. 197).

NOTES

1. André Breton, *What is Surrealism?*, trans. David Gascoyne (London: Faber, 1936), p. 61.
2. Roger Cardinal and Robert Stuart Short, *Surrealism, Permanent Revelation* (London: Studio Vista; New York: Dutton, 1970), p. 12.
3. *The Annotated Alice: Alice's Adventures in Wonderland and Through the Looking-Glass*, ed. Martin Gardner (New York: Clarkson N. Potter, 1960), p. 36; subsequent references to the *Alices* are to this edition and are given parenthetically in the text.
4. Paul C. Ray, *The Surrealist Movement in England* (Ithaca, N.Y.: Cornell Univ. Press, 1971), pp. 28–30.
5. Cardinal and Short, pp. 33–34.
6. *Surrealists on Art*, ed. L. R. Lippard (New York: Prentice-Hall, 1970), pp. 12–13.

7. *The Diaries of Lewis Carroll,* ed. Roger Lancelyn Green, 2 vols. (London: Cassell, 1953; New York: Oxford Univ. Press, 1954), I:76.

8. *Surrealists on Art*, ed. Lippard, p. 28.

9. Quoted by Dawn Ades in *Dada and Surrealism Reviewed* (London: Arts Council of Britain, 1978), p. 183.

10. Ray, pp. 2–3.

11. J. H. Matthews, *An Introduction to Surrealism* (College Park: Pennsylvania State Univ. Press, 1965).

12. "Alice on the Stage," *The Theatre,* April 1887, rpt. in *The Lewis Carroll Picture Book,* ed. Stuart Dodgson Collingwood (London: Unwin, 1899), rpt. as *Diversions and Digressions of Lewis Carroll* (New York: Dover, 1961), p. 165.

13. Quoted in Derek Hudson, *Lewis Carroll* (London: Constable, 1954), p. 128.

14. *Surrealists on Art*, ed. Lippard, pp. 21–22.

15. "Alice on the Stage," p. 165.

16. Quoted in William S. Rubin, *Dada, Surrealism, and Their Heritage* (New York: Museum of Modern Art, 1968), p. 68.

17. Quoted in Matthews, p. 91.

18. Quoted in ibid., p. 124.

19. See Ray, p. 9.

20. "Alice on the Stage," pp. 196–97.

21. Quoted in Matthews, pp. 93–94.

22. Quoted in *The Annotated Snark,* ed. Martin Gardner (New York, 1962; rpt. Harmondsworth, England: Penguin, 1967), p. 21.

23. Ibid., p. 53.

24. Matthews, p. 77 (quoting from the "Catalogue of the International Surrealist Exhibition," Amsterdam, 1938).

25. Ray, p. 45.

26. Ibid., p. 12.

27. *Surrealists on Art*, ed. Lippard, p. 130.

28. Suzi Gablik, *Magritte* (London: Thames and Hudson, 1971), p. 126.

29. Max Ernst, "Inspiration to Order," rpt. in *Beyond Painting* (1948). Translation by L. R. Lippard.

30. From "The Mad Gardener's Song" in *Sylvie and Bruno* (London: Macmillan, 1889), p. 65.

31. Unfortunately, however, such mistakes have prejudiced English critics' attention to the relationship between the surrealists and Carroll, the only work of any substance on the subject having been intent mostly on laughing at the blunders. This article, Philip Thody's "Lewis Carroll and the Surrealists," *Twentieth Century,* 163 (May 1958), 427–34, begins from the unworthy premise that "what is astounding is the ability of the French to build up intellectual theories about those figures in English literature who seem to us to be the least suitable to such treatment. A particular example of this is the case of Lewis Carroll . . ." (p. 427).

32. André Breton, *L'Anthologie de l'humour noir* (1939; rpt. Paris: Pauvert, 1966), p. 184.

33. *Surrealists on Art*, ed. Lippard, pp. 36–37.

34. Ibid., p. 25.

35. Quoted in Matthews, p. 144.

Lewis Carroll in
Finnegans Wake

A N N   M c G A R R I T Y   B U K I

> A spitter that can be depended on. Though
> Wonderlawn's lost us for ever. Alis, alas,
> she broke the glass! Liddell lokker through
> the leafery, ours is mistery of pain.
> > James Joyce, *Finnegans Wake*

The Reverend Charles Lutwidge Dodgson and his characters inhabit *Finnegans Wake* in a variety of ways. Echoes in sound and sense from the *Alice* books appear throughout *Finnegans Wake,* and there are similarities in theme and character in Carroll's novels and in Joyce's. The Carroll-Joyce connection has long been recognized and sometimes analyzed, most notably by James Atherton.[1] A careful look at Carroll and the *Alice*s in *Finnegans Wake* demonstrates how pervasive Carrollian elements became in the texture of Joyce's novel and thus how Carroll is anchored in modern literature. The many similarities between Carroll's and Joyce's works help illustrate both writers' interests and techniques and show in just what ways Carroll was one of Joyce's predecessors along an important road in literary history.

Joyce supposedly came late to Carroll; he claimed not to have read him until 1927,[2] but the "bits and scraps" that Joyce had heard may have been more substantial than he was willing to concede. It has been demonstrated, for example, that there is an allusion to Carroll's parody of the Thomas Moore poem "Lalla Rookh" ("I never loved a dear Gazelle") in *Ulysses* (written from 1914 to 1921).[3] It seems unlikely that the author who parodied styles of writing from all of English literary history in the "Oxen of the Sun" chapter of *Ulysses* would have been unaware of Lewis Carroll's writing. Whatever Joyce's misgivings were about Carroll's influence on his work, he assured the continuation of that influence in the literary tradition by placing him in the ultimate modernist text that is *Finnegans Wake*.

I

The portrait of Carroll that Joyce gives us is complex, because Carroll is mirrored in nearly every character in *Finnegans Wake*. Aspects of his appearance and personality are manifest in each of the seven members of the family. Martin Gardner describes Carroll: "He was of moderate height, thin, carrying himself stiffly erect and walking with a peculiar jerky gait. He was afflicted with one deaf ear and a stammer that trembled his upper lip."[4] H.C.E. (Humphrey or Harold Chimpden Earwicker), the father in *Finnegans Wake*, shares Carroll's odd walk ("his rather strange walk,"[5]) and stutter ("stutters fore he falls," 139:9). Both Carroll and H.C.E. admired young girls; Joyce thought them both to be "grisly old Sykos who have done our unsmiling bit on 'alices, when they were yung and easily freudened" (115:21–23). Old Joe, the family handyman, who is an older manifestation of H.C.E., is called a "lewd man of the method of godliness" (141:16–17); this continues

Carroll/Joyce (*Courtesy Mark Burstein*)

Joyce's unpleasant insinuation that Carroll used his position as a deacon in the Anglican church to veil his intentions with " 'alices."

Shem and Shaun, the twin sons in *Finnegans Wake,* also have elements of Lewis Carroll. Shem is described as having "the wrong shoulder higher than the right" (169:14–15); Gardner's description points out that "[i]n appearance Carroll was handsome and asymmetric. . . . One shoulder was higher than the other." [6] Further, Shem the Penman's anxiety over the originality of his writing was shared by Lewis Carroll, who wrote: "Perhaps the hardest thing in all literature—at least *I* have found it so: by no voluntary effort can I accomplish it: I have to take it as it comes—is to write anything *original.*" [7] Similarities with Shaun are also evident; he has poor hearing and good sight ("The Mookse had a sound eyes right but he could not all hear," 158:12–13). Lewis Carroll was deaf in one ear, and proof of his excellent sight exists in the photographs that he took of Alice Liddell and others. Shaun, too, likes little girls, and in his double-entendre speech to his sister Issy and her schoolmates he mentions "Mary Liddlelambe's flitsy tales" (440:18). Shaun is a postman; Lewis Carroll was the inventor of "The Wonderland Postage Stamp Case" and author of its accompanying pamphlet, entitled *Eight or Nine Wise Words About Letter Writing* (1890).

Through Alice, Lewis Carroll's presence is also felt in the three major female characters of *Finnegans Wake.* The mother, Anna Livia Plurabelle, shares her initials with Alice Pleasance Liddell. A.L.P.'s tea-stained letter from Boston, Mass. (the site of a famous tea party) connects her with Alice and "A Mad Tea-Party." A.L.P. is the River Liffey ("Alicious, twinstreams twinestraines, through alluring glass or alas in jumboland?" 528:17–18); Alice swims in a pool of her own tears. A.L.P.'s daughter, Issy, is known for "kissing and looking into a mirror" (618:19); Alice went through the looking-glass. Issy's name also refers to Isa Bowman, the actress child-friend of Lewis Carroll who wrote a memoir about him and played Alice in the stage version of *Alice in Wonderland:* "Poor Isa . . . Hey, lass! . . . Her beauman's gone of a cool" (226:4–7). The old woman, Kate, uses the word "madrashattaras" (10:16) in her guided tour of the "Willingdone Museyroom" (8:10), an important passage in the first chapter of *Finnegans Wake.* Later, Kate is called upon to testify at the trial of H.C.E., as Alice was at the trial of the Knave of Hearts, and she alludes to Lewis Carroll during her testimony by the words *duck* and *dodo* (531:6–7).

As James Atherton has pointed out, the facts of Carroll's life were known to Joyce through Collingwood's *Life and Letters of Lewis Carroll,* and he was working on *Finnegans Wake* both during the centenary of Carroll's birth in 1932, and at the time of Alice Hargreaves's death in 1934. The details about Lewis Carroll with which he filled *Finnegans Wake* could have been taken from the "unusually large number of articles about Carroll in magazines—of which Joyce was a great reader . . ." [8] published during those years. The evidence that some aspect of Lewis Carroll is reflected in the character of each family member demonstrates that he was of primary importance to

Joyce; but *Finnegans Wake* is further strewn with clusters of clues that point to Lewis Carroll as an inspiration for the book as a whole.

II

Aside from a recognition of their similar pursuits, the incorporation of Lewis Carroll into *Finnegans Wake* might have come from a kinship Joyce felt with him. Joyce was amused by coincidence and must have noticed that July 4 was the day of "the Duck and the Dodo" and the three Liddell sisters' expedition on the Thames. Joyce's father was born on July 4, and Joyce married Nora Barnacle on that day in 1931.[9] Lewis Carroll kept a careful record of his days in a diary, marking the days when he met or visited a child-friend "with a white stone";[10] Joyce echoes this Carrollian augury early in *Finnegans Wake:* "whitestone" (5:17). It is not surprising that further parallels exist between Wakean characters and those from Wonderland and the looking-glass world.

The March Hare and the Mad Hatter in *Alice's Adventures in Wonderland* are types of Shem and Shaun. The Mad Hatter's watch is "Two days wrong! . . . It tells the day of the month, and doesn't tell what o'clock it is!" (p. 69). He has no sense of time because of a disagreement he had with that dimension: " 'We quarrelled last March—just before *he* went mad, you know—' (pointing with his teaspoon at the March Hare)" (p. 71). Shaun is likewise blindly space-oriented and oblivious to time. His spokesman, Professor Jones, attacks the time-oriented brother Shem in a verbose tirade that includes the fables of "The Mookse and the Gripes" and "Burrus and Caseous." Shem defends himself in the poem that ends the fable of "The Ondt and the Gracehoper" and despairingly asks of Shaun, "Why can't you beat time?" (419:8). The Mad Hatter's offense, for which he suffers the punishment of a perpetual teatime, is similar. Speaking of a concert at which he had performed, the Hatter says: "Well, I'd hardly finished the first verse . . . when the Queen bawled out 'He's murdering the time! Off with his head!' " (p. 71). Shaun is ironically trapped, as is the Hatter, by the dimension whose existence he wishes to deny.

Since Shaun is the Mad Hatter, Shem must be the March Hare; the two are paired in both *Alice* books (they reappear in *Through the Looking-Glass* as Hatta and Haigha, the Anglo-Saxon messengers) and in *Finnegans Wake:* "it's hatter's hares, mon, for me" (83:1) and "hitter's hairs" (84:23). Shaun (as Justius) says to Shem: "Do you see your dial in the rockingglass? . . . You are mad!" (193:16, 28), but the same accusation could be made of him. The Cheshire Cat's words describing the Hatter and the Hare to Alice could apply to Shem and Shaun as well: "Visit either you like: they're both mad" (p. 65).

A pair of characters from *Through the Looking-Glass* also resemble the twins of *Finnegans Wake*. They are identical twins, mirror images of one another, whom Alice can tell apart only "because one of them had 'DUM' embroidered on his collar, and the other 'DEE' " (p. 147). The two are mentioned in *Finnegans Wake:* "from tweedledeedumms down to twiddledeedees" (258:23–

24), and the battle that they agree to have in the nursery rhyme completes their identification with Shem and Shaun, because those "sonnies had a scrap" (194:24) as well.

Tweedledum and Tweedledee are easily interchangeable because they are so much alike; Shem and Shaun (as Tristopher and Hilary) were exchanged in their cradles by the Prankquean. Shem and Shaun are in continuous conflict because they are polar opposites whose union would form a complete person. The incomplete halves' opposition to one another is simultaneously a magnetic and a repellent force; A.L.P. rightly calls them "Two bredder as doffered as nors in soun" (620:16). As Tweedledum could not be without Tweedledee (the signs to their homes point in the same direction, but one says "TO TWEEDLEDUM'S HOUSE," and the other "TO THE HOUSE OF TWEEDLE- DEE," p. 146), neither Shem nor Shaun could exist without the other as his opposite but complementary half.

Tweedledum speaks to Alice first, ending his sentence with "Nohow"; and Tweedledee, beginning his sentence with "Contrariwise" (p. 147), gives the opposing point of view. When A.L.P. says of her sons, "Them boys is so contrairy" (620:12), she not only means that they are quarrelsome; her state- ment incorporates the theory of Giordano Bruno that a thing must know its opposite in order to understand itself. This is a recurrent theme in *Finnegans Wake,* and what Alice saw in Tweedledum and Tweedledee was a notable precedent for A.L.P.'s understanding of Shem and Shaun.

Both sets of twins realize that they are too similar to harm one another but too different to resolve the conflicts estranging them. Shem realizes that he and Shaun need each other, and he expresses his desire for reconciliation in "The Ondt and the Gracehoper": 'I forgive you, grondt Ondt,' said the Gracehoper, weeping,/For their sukes of the sakes you are safe in whose keeping" (418:13–14). He recognizes that they are responsible for one an- other in spite of their differences and pleads for a reunion: "Can castwhores pulladeftkiss if oldpollocks forsake 'em . . . ?" (418:23). The names of Castor and Pollux, combined with brotherly love, express metaphorically Shem's understanding of the need that he and Shaun have for one another.

Tweedledum and Tweedledee also share brotherly love and hate, and the resolution of their battle comes from outside; the "monstrous crow" provides their excuse not to fight at all. At the sight of it, "the two brothers took to their heels and were out of sight in a moment" (p. 159), and Alice is left behind. There is a similar scene in *Finnegans Wake;* the discussion of "the Mookse and the Gripes" is ended by nightfall: "It was so duusk that the tears of night began to fall . . ." (158:20–21) and "Nuvoletta, a lass" (159:5) is left behind. In the unresolved conflicts of Shem and Shaun and Tweedledum and Tweedledee, Joyce saw a symbol of the necessarily conflicting movement of nature expressed in the Blakean proverb: "Without Contraries is no pro- gression."

Humpty Dumpty, the troublesome egg whom Alice encounters in *Through the Looking-Glass,* appears throughout *Finnegans Wake,* and his ubiquitous pres- ence is Joyce's most overt acknowledgment of his debt to Lewis Carroll.

James Atherton has enumerated Humpty Dumpty's many functions in *Finnegans Wake,* among them his role as an aspect of H.C.E.[11] He is incorporated into the name and character of H.C.E.; the name "Humphrey" has the echo of "Humpty," and like Humpty Dumpty, H.C.E. falls and is broken. There are further similarities between the characters, and these parallels demonstrate the common pursuits of their creators.

Joyce paid much attention to the name of H.C.E.; his initials are repeated throughout *Finnegans Wake,* and at each appearance another aspect of his character is emphasized. Book I, Chapter 2, of *Finnegans Wake* concerns "the genesis of Harold or Humphrey Chimpden's occupational agnomen" (30:2–3); the name "Earwicker" is derived from his pastime of "cotchin on thon bluggy earwuggers" (31:10–11). Humpty Dumpty is also concerned with a name's appropriateness to its bearer. He proudly asserts that he is more than he appears to be: "It's *very* provoking . . . to be called an egg—*very!*" (p. 170). When Alice asks him: *"Must* a name mean something?" he replies, "Of course it must, *my* name means the shape I am—and a good handsome shape it is, too" (p. 171).

The fall of H.C.E. occurs early in *Finnegans Wake,* and during that scene H.C.E. needlessly defends himself to "the cad," because he suspects that the latter has heard rumors about him. Humpty Dumpty is likewise suspicious of Alice, and accuses her of "listening at doors—and behind trees—and down chimneys" because she knows about the king's promise to "send all his horses and all his men" (p. 171) if Humpty Dumpty should fall. Both H.C.E. and Humpty Dumpty indicate their guilt by jumping at an apparently innocent questioner.

When H.C.E. breaks, A.L.P. gathers up his pieces, and his life is rebuilt through Shem and Shaun. Humpty Dumpty is mentioned on the first and last pages of *Finnegans Wake,*[12] and he can be reassembled by turning from the final page back to the beginning, where he will be found again. James Joyce uses Humpty Dumpty, as does Lewis Carroll, to suit his own purposes in *Finnegans Wake,* and completes the job that "all the king's horses and all the king's men" couldn't accomplish.

By using Humpty Dumpty, the March Hare and the Mad Hatter, and Tweedledum and Tweedledee in *Finnegans Wake,* Joyce acknowledged that Lewis Carroll and he trod common ground. As we look further into their use of language, we shall see that these Carrollian creatures were well placed in a book so thoroughly dreamlike as *Finnegans Wake.*

III

Humpty Dumpty is one of many vehicles through which Carroll and Joyce displayed their shared interest in verbal gymnastics. Lewis Carroll was able to abuse and twist the laws of logic and mathematics so amusingly because he was an expert in those fields. Joyce had at his command a thorough knowledge of several languages and a smattering of many others, and could handle them skillfully enough to deviate deliberately from their normal patterns. Both writers knew the importance of the sounds and rhythms of words;

"Jabberwocky" ("Tis jest jibberweek's joke," 565:14) delights the ear because the nonsense words sound so thoroughly Anglo-Saxon. Likewise, during the mad tea-party, Alice is puzzled by the Mad Hatter's disregard of logic and lack of sense: "The Hatter's remark seemed to her to have no sort of meaning in it, and yet it was certainly English" (p. 69). Joyce's language in *Finnegans Wake* is the opposite of this; the words themselves may sound non-English and even nonsensical, but upon closer inspection, they are seen to be overloaded with layers of sense. "The Ondt and the Gracehoper," for instance, ends with a singsong rhyme packed with portmanteau words that contain both obvious and oblique references to the warring brothers whose problems it explores.

Carroll punned on Alice's name throughout his books—e.g., "alas for poor Alice!" (p. 27)—and Joyce followed his cue in *Finnegans Wake*: "A liss in hunterland" (p. 276, n. 7). Carroll and Joyce also shared a love of parody. Joyce converted Tennyson's refrain "Ring out the old, ring in the new" from *In Memoriam* to a washerwoman's command: "Wring out the clothes! Wring in the dew!" (213:19–20). From "The Charge of the Light Brigade" Joyce took "Cannon to the right of them/Cannon to the left of them,/Cannon behind them," combined it with a section of St. Patrick's prayer, "Christ to the right, Christ to the left of me," and made: "(plunders to night of you, blunders what's left of you, flash as flash can!)" (188:12–13). He echoed the rhythms of various songs, poems, and nursery rhymes, including "Humpty Dumpty" ("Nor for all our wild dances in all their wild din," 627:26–27), thereby setting the original in contrast to his version of it.[13] He twisted common expressions and clichés for his own use, e.g., "the eye of a noodle" (143:9), "the sowiveall of the prettiest" (145:27), "is as quiet as a mursque but can be as noisy as a sonogog" (135:36–136:1), "Spitz on the iern while it's hot" (207:21–22).

Carroll converted the didactic verse that Victorian children were made to memorize, such as Isaac Watt's "How doth the little busy bee," into nonsense. The most acclaimed of his parodies victimizes Wordsworth's "Resolution and Independence." In the original, the poet finds comfort in his despair at the thought of the "old leech-gatherer"; a very different occasion prompts the narrator of the White Knight's poem to think of his "aged aged man":

> And now, if e'er by chance I put
> My fingers into glue,
> Or madly squeeze a right-hand foot
> Into a left-hand shoe,
> Or if I drop upon my toe
> A very heavy weight . . .
>
> (pp. 199–200)

Carroll reduces the egotistical sublime of Wordsworth to nonsense.

Carroll played with the names of insects in *Through the Looking-Glass*, calling them the "Rocking-horse-fly," "Snap-dragon-fly," and "Bread-and-butter-fly" (pp. 142–43). H.C.E. is himself a kind of insect, and at his pub, his ear "buzzes with the annoying roar of insect—or earwig-like (Earwicker) customers." [14] The manner in which they pursue the possibilities of the meanings of words differs, but both Carroll and Joyce give the words a life of their own.

There are themes connected with the use of language that are common to *Alice's Adventures in Wonderland* and *Finnegans Wake*. The theme of forgery runs throughout *Finnegans Wake;* the often-repeated misspelled word "hesitency" (in which Atherton finds Carroll's presence because of his "stammer, which is described as a 'hesitancy' of speech" [15]) refers to an infamous forgery in Irish history [16] and to the stutter of H.C.E. It also alludes to Shem the Penman, who is described as having studied "with stolen fruit how cutely to copy all their various styles of signature so as one day to utter an epical forged cheque on the public for his own private profit" (181:14–17) and as writing "penmarks used out in sinscript with such hesitancy" (421:18–19). Forgery is an issue at the Knave of Hearts' ("knives of hearts," 405:29) trial in *Alice's Adventures in Wonderland;* the King accuses the hapless Knave of forging the letter/verses that are the main piece of evidence at the trial: " 'He must have imitated somebody else's hand,' said the King. . . . 'If you didn't sign it,' said the King, 'that only makes the matter worse. You *must* have meant some mischief, or else you'd have signed your name like an honest man' " (p. 105).

Both *Alice's Adventures in Wonderland* and *Finnegans Wake* leave riddles unanswered. The Mad Hatter asks Alice: "Why is a raven like a writing-desk?" but when she gives up and asks for an answer, Alice gets little satisfaction from either the Hatter: "I haven't the slightest idea" or the Hare: "Nor I" (pp. 68–70). Some of the riddles in *Finnegans Wake* are unanswered; "The Prankquean's 'why do I am alook alike a poss of porterpease?'(21:18), . . . the heliotrope riddle of the game of colors in II.1, and the question 'where was a hovel not a havel' (231:1)" are all left unresolved.[17]

Carroll and Joyce's common aim in leaving unsolved riddles, and in using puns, parody, and apparent nonsense, was to represent the dreaming mind; further exploration will demonstrate that language was one among many devices that each used to create his "nightynovel" (54:21).

IV

Alice's Adventures in Wonderland, Through the Looking-Glass, and *Finnegans Wake* are all books of the night; Joyce followed Carroll in founding an entire dreamworld with similar freedoms of movement, association, and metamorphosis. Lewis Carroll's creative process had its foundation in dreams and dreamlike states. Consider his account of how *The Hunting of the Snark* grew from the final line, which came to him suddenly while out walking. (Cited in context by Edward Guiliano in his preceding essay on the *Snark.*) Joyce characterized his book of the night as having been written for "that ideal reader suffering from an ideal insomnia" (120:13–14); it is perhaps "the Strangest Dream that was ever Halfdreamt" (307:12).

Alice's Adventures in Wonderland ends with her sister saying: "Wake up, Alice dear! . . . Why, what a long sleep you've had!" (p. 109). The ending of *Through the Looking-Glass* is more ambiguous; its final chapter is entitled

"Which Dreamed It?" *Finnegans Wake* records the dream universe of characters aware of themselves as dreamers ("You mean to see we have been hadding a sound night's sleep?" 597:1–2), thus making it a dream within a dream. Likewise, in *Through the Looking-Glass,* Tweedledum and Tweedledee tell Alice that they are all only parts of the Red King's dream, and "if that there King was to wake . . . you'd go out—bang!—just like a candle!" (p. 155).

There is a blurring of reality in *Alice* akin to that in *Finnegans Wake;* sleeping and waking states are confused and are often used interchangeably. The dimensions of time and space, discussed frequently in *Finnegans Wake* in connection with the warring brothers Shem and Shaun, are rendered useless in the *Alice* books by a total disregard of their laws. The perpetual "Mad Tea-Party" shows the results of time suspended, and Alice's frequent changes in size defy the space to which she should be confined. Joyce shows the necessity for a sense of each without the other; Lewis Carroll does the same by showing the chaos that results when either is ignored.

The diffusion of reality through dreams often results in a loss or a confusion of one's identity. In both *Alice's Adventures in Wonderland* and *Through the Looking-Glass,* Alice is uncertain of her identity. She wonders, " 'Who in the world am I?' Ah, *that's* the great puzzle!" (p. 30). When the Caterpillar demands, "Who are you?" Alice can only stutter: "I—I hardly know, Sir, just at present—at least I know who I *was* when I got up this morning, but I think I must have been changed several times since then" (p. 50). Her problem, in the language of *Finnegans Wake,* is how to "isolate i from my multiple Mes" (410:12).[18] When the Fawn asks Alice, "What do you call yourself?" she is bewildered: " 'I wish I knew!' thought poor Alice. She answered, rather sadly, 'Nothing just now' " (p. 145).

The identities of the characters in *Finnegans Wake* are continually in flux. The three women are actually the same woman at different stages of her life, and Shem and Shaun are incomplete halves whose union forms H.C.E. As in the doctrine of the Trinity (referred to as "Dodgfather, Dodgson and Coo," at one point in *Finnegans Wake* [482:1]), each of the three persons is separate, yet when united they form a complete being. The members of "the Doodles family" (p. 299, n. 4) merge into one another and then split into an infinity of particles. Their transformation from one form to another is sometimes reminiscent of the confusion of the roles of the characters and the food that closes the "Queen Alice" chapter of *Through the Looking-Glass.* Each family member displays a characteristic of Lewis Carroll or Alice, and his or her identity is both distinct from and intermingled with Carroll's and Alice's. In Alice's dreams she loses her identity; in the dream that is *Finnegans Wake* the characters are surrealistically dissociated from themselves. One becomes part of another to dissolve back into itself, thus: "Wakean figures are interchangeable because characters in dreams are fictions created by the dreamer—including fictions of himself." [19] Alice's loss of identity stems from her own confusion, from the changes in her size, and from the illogical world in which she finds herself. The flux of identities in *Finnegans Wake* comes from within each of the characters, and the resultant confusion is cosmic because they represent all of humanity.

The movement, both in Carroll's *Alice*s and in *Finnegans Wake,* is cyclical. *Alice's Adventures in Wonderland* begins with Alice falling asleep and ends at her waking. In *Through the Looking-Glass,* Alice begins to "pretend the glass has got all soft like gauze, so that we can get through" (p. 120), and her wish is immediately fulfilled. The book ends in a similar fashion as Alice grabs the Red Queen and threatens her: " 'I'll shake you into a kitten, that I will!' . . . and it really *was* a kitten, after all" (pp. 214–16). The transition from dream to reality is further softened by the story's final line: "Which do *you* think it was?" (p. 218).

The interplay of death and rebirth themes constitutes the movement of *Finnegans Wake*; its progression is from the darkness of night in which the dreamer sleeps to the light that awakens him at dawn. In *Alice's Adventures in Wonderland, Through the Looking-Glass,* and *Finnegans Wake,* the elements of illusion and reality are so thoroughly intermingled that "Which Dreamed It?" could be asked about each.

V

Lewis Carroll wrote of the passing of time in *Alice's Adventures in Wonderland* and *Through the Looking-Glass,* and Joyce considered the attitude expressed there, as well as the events of Carroll's life, when re-creating him in *Finnegans Wake. Alice's Adventures in Wonderland* ends with Alice's sister reflecting "how this same little sister of hers would, in the after-time, be herself a grown woman . . . and how she would gather about her other little children . . . remembering her own child-life, and the happy summer days" (p. 110). An admirer of little girls, whom he saw as symbols of innocence and beauty, Lewis Carroll felt sadness at their growing up. He was most at ease with them, and lost his stutter in their presence.[20]

Throughout his life, Carroll continually sought replacements for Alice Liddell in other little girls—who inevitably grew up also. He wrote of the separation by age, and of his search for another Alice, in the poems that open and close *Through the Looking-Glass:* "Though time be fleet, and I and thou / Are half a life asunder" (p. 113), "Still she haunts me, phantomwise. / Alice moving under skies / Never seen by waking eyes" (p. 219). Joyce saw Lewis Carroll as a man who was unable to accept the fact that "soft youthful bright matchless girls" will "bosom into fine silkclad blooming young women" (134:23–24) and thought that Carroll's refusal to acknowledge sexuality was a denial of life. Joyce felt that "Lewd's carol" (501:35) was selfish not to let his " 'alices" grow up, and ironically identifies him with H.C.E., whose alleged indiscretion with two young girls is the cause of his downfall.

However irreverently Joyce treated Carroll's attitude toward the passing of time, there are nonetheless common elements between the treatments it is given in *Finnegans Wake* and *Through the Looking-Glass.* Time is the dominant element in *Finnegans Wake,* and it is one for whose sake the reader must suspend disbelief. The action of the book covers one day and one night, but the span of time incorporated within it is infinitely greater. The scope of *Finnegans Wake* includes all of human history—past, present, and future ("Anna was, Livia is, Plurabelle's to be," 215:24)—and the movement from one era to another is continual.

Similar to this way of presenting time is that of the looking-glass country, where everything lives backwards. The White Queen tells Alice: "—but there's one great advantage in it, that one's memory works both ways" (p. 161). So it is with Joyce in *Finnegans Wake:* His memory extends from man's prehistory—"riverrun, past Eve and Adam's" (3:1)—to his future: "The silent cock shall crow at last. The west shall shake the east awake" (473:22–23). Time is extended indefinitely for the convenience of the looking-glass world's inhabitants:

> ". . . last Tuesday—I mean one of the last set of Tuesdays, you know."
>   Alice was puzzled. "In *our* country," she remarked, "there's only one day at a time."
>   The Red Queen said, "That's a poor thin way of doing things. Now *here*, we mostly have days and nights two or three at a time, and sometimes in the winter we take as many as five nights together—for warmth, you know." (p. 205)

Each book of *Finnegans Wake* covers a Viconian cycle of human existence, yet within each, all eras are simultaneously contained. This total action takes place in a dream of one day and night that is an eternal "set" of days and nights; the novel "moves in vicous cycles yet remews the same" (134:16–17). As with other Carrollian elements in *Finnegans Wake,* Joyce treated time with the variations he saw worked out in Carroll's life and writing.

VI

We have seen how Carroll is presented to the reader in *Finnegans Wake,* and that his appearance there is the result of themes and techniques that he and Joyce shared. A final similarity exists between their theories of writing.

Lewis Carroll modestly assumed that there was more in his writing than he intended at the time of its composition: "Still, you know, words mean more than we mean to express when we use them; so a whole book ought to mean a great deal more than the writer means." [21] He denied himself full credit for the meanings of his words or of his works.

Although he may have considered this another of "old Dadgerson's dodges" (374:1–2), James Joyce also strove to put himself at a distance from his art. Stephen Dedalus explained in *A Portrait of the Artist as a Young Man:* "The artist, like the God of the creation, remains within or behind or beyond or above his handiwork, invisible, refined out of existence, indifferent, paring his fingernails." [22]

The "grin without the cat" of *Alice's Adventures in Wonderland* could serve as a symbol for both Carroll's and Joyce's endeavors, because each sought in his own way to eliminate traces of himself from his writing and to leave the words to speak for themselves. Despite the unanswered riddles left in their wake, the words in *Alice's Adventures in Wonderland, Through the Looking-Glass,* and *Finnegans Wake* do succeed on their own.

NOTES

1. James S. Atherton, *The Books at the Wake: A Study of Literary Allusions in James Joyce's "Finnegans Wake"* (New York: Viking, 1960), pp. 124–36; Stuart Gilbert, "Prolegomena to Work in Progress," in *Our Exagmination Round His Factification for Incamination of Work in Progress,* eds. Samuel Beckett et al. (Paris, 1929; rpt. New York: New Directions, 1972), pp. 58–59; Adaline Glasheen, *A Third Census of "Finnegans Wake": An Index of the Characters and Their Roles* (Berkeley: Univ. of California Press, 1977); Hugh Kenner, *Dublin's Joyce* (Bloomington: Indiana Univ. Press, 1956), pp. 276–300; Robert M. Polhemus, *Comic Faith: The Great Tradition from Austen to Joyce* (Chicago: Univ. of Chicago Press, 1980), pp. 245–337.

2. Joyce wrote to Harriet Weaver, May 31, 1927: "I never read him till Mrs. Nutting gave me a book, not *Alice,* a few weeks ago—though, of course, I heard bits and scraps." Atherton, p. 127.

3. John A. Rea, "A Bit of Lewis Carroll in *Ulysses,*" *James Joyce Quarterly,* 15 (1977), 86–88.

4. *The Annotated Alice: Alice's Adventures in Wonderland and Through the Looking-Glass,* ed. Martin Gardner (New York: Clarkson N. Potter, 1960), p. 10.

5. James Joyce, *Finnegans Wake* (New York: Viking, 1958), p. 131:29. All subsequent references to page and line in this work appear in the text.

6. *The Annotated Alice,* ed. Gardner, p. 10.

7. "Preface to *Sylvie and Bruno,*" in *The Works of Lewis Carroll,* ed. Roger Lancelyn Green (London: Hamlyn, 1965), p. 380. All subsequent references to *The Works* appear in the text.

8. Atherton, p. 136.

9. Richard Ellmann, *James Joyce* (London: Oxford Univ. Press, 1959), pp. 12, 537, 650.

10. *The Annotated Alice,* ed. Gardner, p. 11.

11. Atherton, pp. 126–27.

12. Glasheen, p. 133.

13. M.J.C. Hodgart and Mabel P. Worthington, *Song in the Works of James Joyce* (New York: Columbia Univ. Press, 1959), p. 21.

14. Margot Norris, *The Decentered Universe of* Finnegans Wake: *A Structuralist Analysis* (Baltimore: Johns Hopkins Univ. Press, 1974), p. 75.

15. Atherton, p. 136.

16. Glasheen, p. 234.

17. Norris, pp. 91–92.

18. For a discussion of Issy's multiple personalities in *Finnegans Wake,* see Adaline Glasheen, "*Finnegans Wake* and the Girls from Boston, Mass.," *Hudson Review,* 7 (1954), 89–96.

19. Norris, p. 8.

20. Florence Becker Lennon, *The Life of Lewis Carroll (Victoria Through the Looking-Glass),* 3rd ed. (1945; rpt. New York: Dover, 1972), p. 108.

21. Stuart Dodgson Collingwood, *The Life and Letters of Lewis Carroll* (London: T. Fisher Unwin, 1898; New York: The Century Co., 1899), p. 173.

22. James Joyce, *A Portrait of the Artist as a Young Man*, in *The Portable James Joyce*, ed. Harry Levin, 2nd ed. (New York: Viking, 1966), p. 483.

I would like to thank J. Mitchell Morse for his assistance in revising this essay, and to acknowledge the late Mabel Worthington who first encouraged me to study Joyce and Carroll.

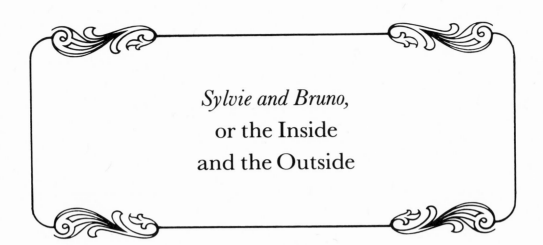

Sylvie and Bruno,
or the Inside
and the Outside

JEAN GATTÉGNO

We don't understand why the best critics of Carroll, especially the French, express so much reserve and shallow criticism about *Sylvie and Bruno,* a masterpiece which shows entirely new techniques compared to *Alice* and *Through the Looking-Glass."* [1] When the distinguished critic Gilles Deleuze wrote this, only specialists could take his word for it, but now there is evidence to support his judgment. Interest in this work published just under a century ago was not significant for much of this century: It was rarely reprinted, and few commented on it. This attitude has changed; over the past decade or so, *Sylvie and Bruno* has been reprinted in several English editions, and we now have for the first time translations into French, German, Spanish, and Japanese.[2] Still, readers who are just getting to know *Alice in Wonderland* and *Through the Looking-Glass* will be surprised and even disconcerted by the *Sylvie and Bruno* books.

The adventures of Sylvie and Bruno do not follow on from those of Alice. In his Preface to *Sylvie and Bruno,* there is no rest for Carroll until he has convinced his readers of the difference. For one who reads that Preface through, there can be no doubt. For this Preface—with its moving commitment not to be repetitive and its desire, both expressed and fulfilled, "to strike out yet another new path" where others could follow, as they followed *Alice*—is innovatory, going as it does behind Carroll's book, laying bare the seams, showing us the reverse side. Now, if this outside refers to an inside, this book can't be *Alice.*

Sylvie and Bruno (SB) was started in 1867 (between *Alice in Wonderland* and *Through the Looking-Glass),* but there are only slight affinities between the two chapters that are said to have formed the core of the book (*SB,* Chaps. 14 and

15) and the *Alice* cycle. The Preface to *Sylvie and Bruno,* however, underlines many minor similarities. First, it is worth mentioning what Carroll tells us about the construction of this book. The core, which gradually expands and crystallizes, is not like that of *The Snark,* which originated entirely (Carroll says) from the last line: "For the Snark *was* a Boojum, you see." The point of arrival was then the starting point, and there was movement from one point to another and progressive development. *Sylvie and Bruno* was constructed differently, however. What is essential and new is to be found in the author's assertion that a work of literature is fundamentally heterogenous—not a whole that has been fragmented and subsequently reconstituted, but an aggregate of fragments that may never make a whole. In this respect, what Carroll wrote about some species of literature containing "padding" (none in *Sylvie and Bruno,* he avowed) gives food for thought: When he wrote those lines, the memory of Fielding and Sterne and their debunking of the organic novel had faded away; Victorian novels would never dream of describing themselves in this ironic and even sacrilegious way. Carroll's remarks about the literary mode of production (commonplace remarks coming after scores of novels already published in serial form) strike home less than his few sentences hitting out at the myth of the artist-writer and preventing the sacrosanct relation between the reader and the work. This cheapening of writing, much more explicit than in the realistic novel of the time, is accompanied by punning that—coming as early as 1889 and under the pen of Carroll—may surprise those ready to believe that it was invented by Joyce, if not by J. Lacan;[3] Carroll, carefully underlining a spelling mistake, applies to the bits of text already piled up the word *litter-ature,* where *litter* can already be made out under *letter.*

The work of literature, as an artifact, is cheapened: There is nothing left of the grand inspiration (the Spirit's breath, or the unconscious) or of the novel seen as a harmonious unity. We shall see this in the case of both plots— the real world and dream world stories—but it is already very daring, for the times, to open the first chapter with a dash followed by the conjunction "and"—which is not conjunctive at all, as nothing comes before. Victorian writers are unfamiliar with that kind of opening, in medias res, which here is also reinforced by doubts cast on the narrative sentence and hence on programming. In the same way (and this was just as new at the time), the concept of "characters" comes under attack as early as the Preface. Twenty years before, George Eliot wrote with emotion of two of her characters (in the last chapter of *Middlemarch*): "All who have cared for Fred Vincy and Mary Garth will like to know that these two made no such failure, but achieved a solid mutual happiness." This shows a wonderfully clear conscience—which Carroll explicitly rejects (and not only in his letters, as others do) when he says of "Arthur" (the quotation marks are Carroll's) that he has lent him this or that phrase. Characters are flattened out—something *Alice* worked toward either metaphorically with characters that are playing cards, or in a literary fashion by reducing them to some phrase that creates and defines them (a good example here is Humpty Dumpty).[4] We shall see that the flattening out in the *Alice*s takes on a precise and new dimension in the *Sylvie and Bruno* books.

I

In *Alice* the push of the dreams gave a definitive direction to the literary form—for instance, to characterization. Alice's dream followed laws that Carroll wanted to be seen as characterizing dreams in general, and the narrative relied more on juxtaposition or contiguity than on causality—unless it be the causality of desire. In *Sylvie and Bruno* dreams are constantly coupled with reality, and the narrative is grounded in the coupling of the two. First, the main objective, for the narrator, is to go beyond reality into dreamland. Second, dreams are constantly presented by the narrator as the "other side" of reality, perceived and conceived as such; his aim is to make dream and reality coincide. In this regard, perfection obtains when, in Chapter 7 of *Sylvie and Bruno Concluded* (*SBC*), the narrator sees one of the characters of his dream step into "real" life and become visible to Lady Muriel, and he asks himself: "What was to be done? Had fairy life been merged into the real life?" [5] For from then on, the characters of both "worlds" will be traveling, without any problem for most of them, from one world into the other.

But this is not the main point. We have to go back to the difference between the *Sylvie and Bruno* books on the one hand, and *Alice in Wonderland* or *Through the Looking-Glass* on the other. In the two earlier tales, dream relied directly on desire—with the latter not necessarily clearly formulated, in spite of peremptory assertions such as: "I want to be Queen." The underlying structure was still obscured, even if the phrasing enabled the reader to find it easily. But at the end of the dream, it was Alice, who stood for her creator (Carroll) or her referential model (little girls, the Child), upon whom the dream threw light. Indeed, the famous conversation between Alice and the twins, Tweedledum and Tweedledee (*Looking-Glass,* Chap. 4),[6] and especially the final question in *Looking-Glass*—Who has been dreaming?—were questions addressed to the dream, no longer to the dreamer. But in the *Sylvie and Bruno* books, on the contrary, fiction disintegrates a little further, desire becomes intellectual or hides behind an urge for knowledge, and the dream becomes science and invites theorizing. For Carroll's aim, both within the text itself and outside of it (in his Preface to *SBC*), is to bring dreaming to the very heart of reality seen as an object of study and experimentation. This accounts for the duplication or doubling effect (as when Sylvie doubles Lady Muriel, or Mein Herr the Professor), which is to be connected to Carroll's remark in his diary: "Last night I had a dream which I record as a curiosity, as containing *the same person at two different periods of life,* a feature entirely unique, so far as I know, in the literature of dreams . . .";[7] and this remark by the same narrator coming out of one of his dreams is even clearer: " 'And all of that strange adventure,' I thought, 'has occupied the space of a single comma in Lady Muriel's speech! A single comma which grammarians tell us to 'count one!' " (*SB,* p. 463).[8] In a more general way, the ever-stressed link between dreams and language (speech and discourse) has the same theorizing value.

This is why we *understand* that dreams occur more easily in the context of "absurd" discourse (see, for example, the transition in *SB*, Chap. 2, from waking to dreaming); or, with the occurrence of a single word that acts as a detonator (as *potato,* at the end of *SB*), reinforced sometimes by the use of homophony *(weight* and *wait,* at the end of *SB*, Chap. 21). In other cases grammar comes into play: "The Gardener's Song" (*SB*, Chap. 5) comes out of the conjugation of two verbs. To sum up, Carroll's theorizing effort, which the Preface to *Sylvie and Bruno Concluded* sets forth, helps disintegrate what could be taken (as in *Alice*) as a homogenous fabric, a seamless garment: And it does so by falling back upon the text and questioning its surface structure.

II

To an even greater extent than dreams, language is Carroll's object of study par excellence. The way in which language works, to which the *Alice*s had already constantly emphasized, is clarified even more vividly as dreams are shown to be connected to language (language or a manifestation of language? Carroll does not decide), and in this regard, the character Bruno plays a most important part. A naive listener and speaker, he ends up having to stress at every opportunity the arbitrary aspect of signs. (When a female speaker blames him for saying "a mile or *three,*" commenting: "It isn't usual to say 'a mile or *three,*'" Bruno retorts: "it would become usual if we said it" p. 60.) Hence, an accumulation of puns, of words formed by condensation etc. But in this connection Bruno and Alice (or the characters she meets) have different approaches: Alice is often described as "puzzled" by sentences that look like good English, but are void of meaning. Bruno deliberately plays with signifiers, in order to bring forth their autonomy in relation to the signified. In *Alice* the Duchess declares: "Take care of the sense, the sounds will take care of themselves." The formula is now applied literally: While sounds look after themselves, one has to take heed of the meaning. Signifiers need neither sounds nor sense to come into play together or to work. Language, taken in its social functioning, goes wrong when it claims to set up as semantic (or syntagmatic) rules that are only the practices of a given social group. This is shown by the example given above. *Or* in "a mile or *three*" can have no other value than to separate terms that are mutually exclusive: Disjunction is its specific function; but nothing requires—apart from the social character of language, and especially in the phrase used above—that *one* be opposed to *two* rather than *one* to *three,* which are just as mutually exclusive. Choice is limited by social practice, not by language itself. The mistake made by Bruno's partners in conversation, throughout the book, is to mix up such practice with the very structure of language, to mix up semantics and syntax.

Underlying Bruno's endless games with signifiers, there is the theme of duality—or is it doubling?—of language. In *Alice*, the *other* language (the one that takes heed of meaning) is associated with the characters Alice meets, thus acquiring a nonsensical value that might depreciate it. Here, however, it comes out as Bruno's privilege (his sister Sylvie is already past that stage, and ejaculates "Oh! Bruno!" each time he throws off balance one of his partners in conversation). Thus it demands to be seen as being, at a certain level, children's language. This is a new theme for Carroll, which goes beyond the child obsession that runs through all his writings. Indeed, what matters is that Bruno, for example, sets up as a *system* the principle of condensation (saying "river-edge" for "revenge" (p. 393), and "bone-disease" for "bonhommie"), thus explicitly connecting (for present-day readers, of course, but it holds true for readers in 1889 as well) his language to the language of dreams. Bruno's language—as distinct from the adults'—may well be the language of dreams, of freedom, as opposed to the censored language of adults. Is it only a matter of chance that the Gardener—whose madness is just as clearly evidenced as the Hatter's or the March Hare's in *Alice*—follows along the same pattern as Bruno, transforming, among all possible words, *parents* into *payrints* (*SB*, p. 328)?

So we have two languages—whose description is of course unequal: One, which is natural, or given, and which does not rely upon our social logic for its functioning, can be found in privileged situations (childhood, dreams, madness, all conditions in which censorship does not apply); another, which we misshape through our practice, through arbitrary conventions specific to a given social group, and above all to the group of adults, from which children are excluded. (For this opposition between nature and nurture conveys also—although it goes much beyond it—the opposition inherited from English Romanticism between the natural world of children and the artificial one of adults.) And in a way, the effort in *Sylvie and Bruno* is geared toward the raising up of the bar that divides these two languages.

III

Two characters are mentioned in the title; there are two plots in the "story"; an anonymous narrator organizes the whole thing and furthermore merges with the author of the Preface in a nonspecified "I." Both plots run simultaneously, one in the "real" world around the narrator and his friends (Lady Muriel and her father, Arthur Forester, and Eric Lindon), the other in a "dream" world, around Sylvie, Bruno, and their friends (their father, who is the Governor; the latter's brother, his wife and their son; the Professor; and the Gardener). This second plot is set out as a traditional folktale; the hero (the Governor) leaves; while he is away, others take up his place (Sibimet and his wife), to the detriment of his two children; but the hero comes back, puts everything back in order, forgives, and goes away again, taking his children with him. The first plot is related to the equally traditional love story; the hero (Arthur) is in love with a young woman whom a rival (Eric) just about manages to snatch away from him; he defeats his rival, but he must go away; he is believed to be dead, but comes back and ends up happy. The structure is the same, with the same simplicity in the linking up of dramatic functions, reduced in fact to a single one: The hero meets an obstacle and overcomes it.

What is interesting of course is, not the plots in themselves, but their juxtaposition and that they relate to distinct "universes" (in the sense logicians speak of "universes of discourse")—"reality" and "dreams." So, at first glance, one could believe that they are opposed, but, in fact, they are not. The Preface to *Sylvie and Bruno Concluded*, along with the introductory poem in *Sylvie and Bruno*, underlines the fact that the disjunction is a mere hypothesis: "Is all our Life, then, a dream?" (p. 275). And Chapter 2 of *Sylvie and Bruno* brings back the same question: "Is Life itself only a dream, I wonder?" (p. 296). The characters in both universes, even then, are to join up together, since the "unknown friend" (Muriel) has the same face as Sylvie; in Chapter 19, when Sylvie and Bruno step into the "real" world, the narrator puts forth his question again: "Is this a *dream?*" (p. 439). What must be noticed here, is not so much the coincidence of both worlds (and both plots), as the solution, from the beginning of the book, of the disjunction set up right at the beginning. From this point of view, the programming is perfect; the last pages say nothing more than the first ones: "All that I had so fervently longed for, prayed for, seemed to have now come to pass" (*SBC,* p. 747). For the solution, in Carroll's eyes, is not to unite "dream" and "reality" but to bring the two worlds into contact, in a vision of mystical quality (words such as *bewitching* or *strange* are given here as a sort of caution) as Sylvie—who still remains Sylvie—becomes an "angel."

But this rhetorical signified coincides thus with the logical one (the "message") insofar as the aim put forth by the author in his Preface to *Sylvie and Bruno Concluded* is clearly to build his story upon a *theory,* which the story will illustrate and prove true all in one. So his effort is directed at folding the narrative signifier (the "story") back upon the narrative signified (the "message"). The other characteristic of *Sylvie and Bruno* is now apparent: It is a generalized attempt to reshape an initial multiplicity into a unity.

Such nondisjunction as the novel reveals is also carried through characterization in two converging ways. First, the *conversion* theme is central to both plots; villains (Sibimet and Eric) both change for the better. One asks to be forgiven by his brother; the other accepts Christian faith. Here, no doubt, we have a familiar device of fairy (or epic) tale, but the way it is put to use here is significant. Second, the "double" system applies to all characters: Muriel corresponds to Sylvie, Mein Herr to the Professor (who, in turn, relates to the Other Professor), the Governor to the narrator (or to Arthur, but the latter is also an avatar of the narrator), Eric to Sibimet. (I shall come back later to the triangle Bruno-Uggug-Gardener.) This marks the passage from a non-novel-like literature (fairy- or epic-tales)—in a way, a literature for consumers would not be different—to the novel proper; thus, above all, Carroll is seen to show us the other side of the setting, the seams in his piece of work, ignoring the so-called motivation of the realistic novel, choosing instead to transform what others call psychological depths into a contact between two surfaces. Here again, Carroll's endeavor is interesting more because he lays bare the falsely disjunctive structure than because he takes up the epic or the fairy tale.

IV

This is, in fact, an approach that gives a direction to the whole book, as expressed through signifiers and signified. Three striking examples of the approach can be found at the level of the signified: the principle of dichotomy (*SBC,* Chap. 13); Fortunatus's purse (*SBC,* Chap. 7); and the wonderful Jewel (*SBC,* Chap. 25). The principle of political dichotomy, as exposed by Mein Herr, helps him describe the English political system, i.e., the shifting of power between Whigs and Tories—the ones being the exact mirror image of the others. The "absurdity" of such a system is proved by its extension to all aspects of social life, and the conclusion Mein Herr draws out of it is that the concept of dichotomy itself is to be banned (this can be connected to Bruno's peremptory reaction: "Well, I'm glad I is a singular boy! . . . It would be horrid to be 2 or 3 boys!" [p. 643]).

Fortunatus's purse makes the idea more precise, but in a special form. It is a version of Moebius's ring, which Mein Herr reveals to Lady Muriel. In the same way as Moebius's ring (a strip of paper twisted in a particular way) has but one surface and one side, Fortunatus's purse (made out of two handkerchiefs also sewn in a particular way) proves to have but one opening, instead of the two that could logically be supposed to exist. There can be no better way of saying that the inside is also the outside and that multiplicity is unity.

The theme of the wonderful Jewel comes as a conclusion to Sylvie and Bruno's adventures. In *Sylvie and Bruno,* Chapter 6, we had two jewels, a red one and a blue one, bearing two opposite inscriptions ("All—will—love—Sylvie" and "Sylvie—will—love—all"); Sylvie had chosen the red one ("Sylvie—will—love—all"). Now, the end of the book reveals that the red one was *also* the blue one, that Sylvie had made but a pseudo choice and that the two inscriptions are not opposite after all. Here again, duality was but an illusion.

This insistent repetition of the fact that there is no disjunction, but always nondisjunction, can be expressed through another metaphor: the coincidence of two surfaces (or of two dimensions). Thus, the geographical map (*SBC,* Chap. 11) that Mein Herr advertises would have exactly the same dimensions as the piece of land it claims to represent, so that the representation of an object could be made to coincide exactly with the object itself. The whole structure of the novel operates as just such a coincidence: Like a series of playing cards, dream coincides with reality, the former plot folds back upon the latter, characters fold back upon one another, the signifier folds back upon the signified. And this generalized coincidence is expressed, in its turn, in the small tale that the Professor narrates, whose hero is a coincidence (*SBC,* Chap. 23).

V

An addition-reduction should be no problem and should leave no reminder. In other words, if our hypothesis of a generalized reduction of multiplicity to unity is faultless, we should be able to solve the problem raised by three characters and one concept, the Gardener, Uggug, Bruno, and love. There is nowhere a replica or a paradigm of the Gardener; he may well echo other creations by Carroll, being a monstrous hybrid between the Mock Turtle in *Alice* and the White Knight in *Through the Looking-Glass*. But his specificity is essentially his madness, and this accounts for his isolation. His madness is described as soon as he appears in the book (*SB,* Chap. 5) and is recalled whenever he appears subsequently, with the same term, *wild*—always a mark for some kind of generally physiological aberration that characterizes his madness. This has led the author of the only psychoanalytical study of Carroll [9] to see in the Gardener a picture of an old man caught by young Carroll in a state of sexual arousement. The song he keeps humming whenever he appears is no decisive ground for such an assumption, however, although we can at least reasonably emphasize the fact that *declared* madness (as distinct from the folly we are free to attribute to the Professor) puts the Gardener beyond the norm. And his disappearing after the metamorphosis that befalls Uggug could be understood more easily by his being so carefully out of the norm.

Uggug, the usurper's younger son, is a case more easily dealt with. Throughout the book he is shown as Bruno's antithesis: Wicked, ugly, vulgar, and stupid, he piles up faults. I have said elsewhere [10] that we find in Uggug Carroll's deeply rooted hostility toward little boys. But what matters most is that we regard him as Bruno's contrary, not his paradigm. There is no doubt that he stands for bare, brutish sex. The metamorphosis he undergoes is clear enough: He is changed into a porcupine (Harry Furniss's drawing is frightening, as Uggug in it looks like one of Goya's, or even Bosch's, monsters). The word *porcupine* and its sonorities are repeated six times as such, and are taken up in two more words in which the same sounds come into play: *portcullis* (the gate) and *preoccupied,* which Bruno had first misheard for *porcupine.* Considering that a porcupine's specificity is to be prickly, and that *prickly* is based upon *prick*—a word commonly, if vulgarly, used to mean "penis"—the game with signifiers and even letters (p, r, and the k phoneme) can hardly pass as neutral. If doubts remained (but is it possible after you have read the description of the animal?—*SBC,* Chap. 24), the epitaph Sylvie and Bruno's father comes up with when it dies, and Bruno's answer to it, would not allow them to persist: "You see what befalls a loveless one!"—with Bruno replying: "I always loved Sylvie, so I'll never get prickly like that!" (p. 739).

The radical opposition, the unresolved disjunction, lies between love and sex. Love—to which Sylvie and Bruno sing eternal praise, and which is taken up as the last discourse in the book—must obviously be understood in the Christian sense, synonymous (but stronger than) charity. It has nothing to do with carnal love, of course. It is possible to reverse the formula "Sylvie will love all" into "All will love Sylvie" ($a\,b\,c = c\,b\,a$), since only the position of the elements changes, but since sex cannot be substituted for love no equation of that type can be set up. Nothing comes to fold back upon "love," which is the apex of the monument patiently built up by Carroll.

Still . . . all solution centers on this unity built up around Love (the capital L is a must). Sylvie and Bruno are "concluded"—a word that must be interpreted as "included one in the other," with the original dyad here again vanishing—but something remains outside the reach of this unifying law, something *escapes.* When the Professor carries out his great scientific experiment (*SBC,* Chap. 21), the flea he magnifies through his megaloscope (it reaches the size of a horse, *equus communis*)—now a monster—comes out of its cage by mishap. When Uggug becomes a porcupine, the new monster is finally trapped in a cage that Providence has put in the way ("curiously enough, there happened to be one standing in the gallery," Carroll writes). The Gardener's harmless madness, Uggug the porcupine's murderous fury, must be locked in, since they can't be reduced. Erring sex falls under common law, for it alone comes out of the Law.

NOTES

1. Gilles Deleuze, *Logique du sens* (Paris: Editions de Minuit, 1969), p. 58; I am indebted to Deleuze's ideas, though somewhat metamorphosed, in many parts of this essay.
2. This essay is based on my preface to the first French translation of *Sylvie and Bruno* (Paris: Seuil, 1972), pp. 9–19. For complete publication information on recent editions and translations of *Sylvie and Bruno,* see Edward Guiliano's *Lewis Carroll: An Annotated International Bibliography, 1960–77* (Charlottesville: Univ. Press of Virginia, 1980), pp. 248–49.
3. See J. Lacan, "Lituraterre," *Littérature,* 3 (October 1971), p. 3.
4. Here and in other instances, I take the liberty of referring the reader to my *Lewis Carroll* (Paris: José Corti, 1970), Part 1.
5. See Gattégno, *Lewis Carroll,* p. 307 ff.
6. See Hélène Cixous's Preface to *Through the Looking-Glass,* trans. Henri Parisot (Paris: Aubier-Flammarion, 1971), especially pp. 33–34.
7. *The Diaries of Lewis Carroll,* ed. Roger Lancelyn Green, 2 vols. (London: Cassell, 1953; New York: Oxford Univ. Press, 1954), II:379.
8. All citations given in the text from *Sylvie and Bruno (SB)* and *Sylvie and Bruno Concluded (SBC)* are from the one-volume edition, *The Complete Works of Lewis Carroll* (New York: Random House/Modern Library; London: Nonesuch Press, 1939).
9. Phyllis Greenacre, *Swift and Carroll: A Psychoanalytic Study of Two Lives* (New York: International Universities Press, 1955).
10. Gattégno, *Lewis Carroll,* pp. 163–64.

Lewis Carroll, the *Sylvie and Bruno* Books, and the Nineties: The Tyranny of Textuality

JAN B. GORDON

I really didn't want to send it across the Atlantic—
the whales are so inconsiderate.
    Isa Bowman, *Lewis Carroll as I Knew Him,* p. 86

I

Lewis Carroll's *Sylvie and Bruno,* and its sequel, *Sylvie and Bruno Concluded,* have traveled no better among contemporary readers than it apparently did in that stormy winter of 1889 when its author postponed sending a copy to its intended dedicatee in America. His hesitation is all the more unusual, since Dodgson habitually struck up friendships with his numerous prepubescent companions by sending them a volume of one of his works as a sort of authorial foreplay. It is ironic that a more formal and sentimental occasion, the publication of a text that had occupied his mind for over twenty years, should produce that characteristic interstice that exemplified so much of the man's life and work. The long pauses; prolonged tea parties; commas that produce a mouse's tail as well as a tale; even, alas, the chronic stutter of the boring don that, in pronouncing his own name, provides us with the Do-do— all serve to remind the reader of the ways in which Dodgson's texts call attention to themselves, not merely by language but by the persistent absence of language.

Perhaps in this instance, America competed with all the other "new" worlds that are continually created in the *Sylvie and Bruno* volumes—that assortment of Outlands, Faery Lands, and ivory-guarded gates. For, it must be remembered, nineteenth-century America seemed exiled from the evolution of a distinctive literature for children that swept England: the *Phantastes* of George MacDonald; the Mowgli books of Kipling; Robert Louis Stevenson's *A Child's Garden of Verses;* the tiny, concentrated miniatures of Beatrix Potter, where the text itself is reduced to the dimensions of a typographic childhood. So fashionable had the fiction of childhood become by the nineties that even that eternal child Oscar Wilde created his own fairy kingdom, complete with fishermen, mermaids, phallic rocket ships, and chronologically arrested males. But alas, no whales!

The story of the inconsiderate whale, America's archetypal adolescent romance, reminds us that American literature lagged behind England in the creation of a distinctive, autonomous literature for children, perhaps because the classics of our adult literature are filled with those who die and are reborn, one way or another, or with those who otherwise carry the ontogenetic primitivity of childhood with them into middle age, so as to avoid growing up: Huck Finn, Isabel Archer, Jay Gatsby, Catherine Berkeley, Benjy Compson, Holden Caulfield, Norman Mailer's D.J., John Barth's spermatazoic narrator of *Chimaera*. If Henry James had to move Isabel Archer to Europe in order that she might grow up—and hence into a perception of the nature of evil—so John Lennon stylized "Starting Over" in the country where it is done so effortlessly. The awful truth is that America has shown the same disaffection for a literature of aging—an authentic *texte du senex*—as it has legislatively for its senior citizens. All the more reason why the achievement of Lewis Carroll's late years should have remained so elusive, for the *Sylvie and Bruno* books are to the *Alice* books what the literature of aging is to the fairy tale of growth.

Above all, the *Alice* books were Victorian in both structure and meaning—embodying the paradigms of a Fall; a zoological version of something like the Circumlocution Office with its dizzying loss of perspective and incredible delays; and the judgment and trial scene with which so many Victorian novels affirmed the ubiquitous General Moral Will. But we often forget that little Alice commences her descent into the underworld by an act of rebellion—taking flight from a book! And Wonderland, as Donald Rackin has suggested,[1] is a kind of counter-kingdom, not merely, I would argue, to above-ground systems of order but to the whole question of textuality, in which its creator—the obsessive correspondent of nearly twenty-thousand letters and the creator of games, children's verse, abridgments, schemes for children's bibles, verbal puzzles, and inventions—lived. Dodgson's entire world—as curate, don, author, letter writer, inscriber of gift volumes, and even photographer—is revealed, finally, as (to borrow from Derrida) one more *scène de l'écriture*.[2] *Alice in Wonderland* and *Through the Looking-Glass* collectively represent that transformation from Bildungsroman to *Künstlerroman* that I have discussed elsewhere.[3] Alice rejects the book offered her by a guardian sister for a flight of fancy into Wonderland that reaches its conclusion when the object of development becomes a necessary narrative subject:

> Lastly, she pictured to herself how this same little sister of hers would, in the after-time, be herself a grown woman; and how she would keep, through all her riper years, the simple and loving heart of her childhood; and how she would gather about her little children, and make their eyes bright and eager with many a strange tale, perhaps even with the dream of Wonderland of long ago; and

how she would feel with all their simple sorrows, and find a pleasure in all their simple joys, remembering her own child-life, and the happy summer days.

(p. 110) [4]

The last paragraph of *Alice in Wonderland* is the collective dream of the guardian sister who now imagines little Alice as the narrator of her own adventures, with her proximate family of children (either literal or figurative) as the audience. *Alice in Wonderland* hence begins and ends with a book, the first of which is the occasion of a rebellion and the latter, the symbolic bond of a community that includes Alice and her family. *Through the Looking-Glass,* the necessarily disappointing sequel, is surely Alice's adventures *retold,* as it were, and hence self-reflexively aware of itself as narrative. It lacks the spontaneity of the first volume precisely because it is supposed to. Whereas *Wonderland* begins with a real beginning ("Alice was beginning to get very tired . . ."), *Through the Looking-Glass* commences with the discontinuity of narrative absence, the Lacanian ex nihilo (". . . the white kitten had had nothing to do with it"). But it is important to note that the transformation of the *Adventures in Wonderland* into the self-conscious narrative of the *Looking-Glass* world is possible only after Alice becomes a figurative parent to her children, much as the sister reading to her had been a figurative parent against whom Alice herself had rebelled. Thus, Alice is able to assume narrative author(ity) only after she has imagined or projected the more tangible authority of symbolic or real parenthood. Although victimized by the arbitrary demands and organization of Wonderland, Alice begins her sequential narrative with the equally arbitrary: "Kitty, dear, let's pretend—" (p. 119). The cause of her victimization in Wonderland, the ability of its inhabitants to pretend at will, is, paradoxically, a first condition of her constituted role as a narrator. Crucial here is an unstated relationship between an arbitrary narrative authority and a familial authority.

The very displacement from a sense of historical continuity emblemized by the ever-present orphan figure of nineteenth-century fiction doubtlessly gave its literature a structure analogous to that of the fairy tale. The child of the Victorian novel must either locate his missing legitimate parents (Arthur Clennam in *Little Dorrit*) or accommodate himself to a surrogate parent by recognizing a kinship stronger than kinship (Pip and Magwitch in *Great Expectations*)—or, alternatively, by becoming a parent himself in fathering forth either a biological or a verbal progeny (Stephen Daedalus in *Portrait of an Artist as a Young Man*). The crisis of the antecedent can be remedied only by reconstituting a fictional "beginning" in place of an absent origin.[5] The establishment of a demonstrable lineage that might lend a given family a sense of history, and hence legitimize inheritance, was as important to Darwin as it was to Cardinal Newman's apostolic succession to the compilers of the *Oxford English Dictionary* or to the drunken John Durbeyfield—who dispatches his daughter to claim her rightful lineage from the "noble" Alec d'Urberville. The pattern is remarkably parallel to that of so many fairy tales where, typically, a victimized child escapes from a constraining, "false" family (so often headed by an evil father or a wicked stepmother) in order to establish his own genuine family that lives happily ever after. In order to escape the confines of some highly endogamous family, the child must solve a riddle—must reverse or otherwise overturn a prescriptive text that had kept him in a figurative prison. Solving the riddle of a given textual injunction is a first step toward becoming the author of your own family/text.

This pattern is shared by works as different as the *Alice* books, the *Autobiography* of John Stuart Mill, and, say, *David Copperfield.* In the latter, for example, David grows up by moving through a series of successive "texts," each of which imprisons: the pasteboard placard that Mr. Mell puts on David's back as a label; Mr. Dick's kite with its laboriously written, minute biography; Micawber's increasingly apocalyptic epistles; Em'ly's confession; the work on Dr. Strong's Dictionary; the epistolary courtship with Dora. But the author is able to escape imprisonment at the hands of all these "private" manuscripts only when he comes to write his own public story as the one and "Eminent Author" of the novel's last page. The growth from victimized orphan to the head of your own household precisely parallels the gradual assumption of narrative authority as legitimate inheritance: The novel that we read by Charles Dickens is *David Copperfield* through a self-consciously narrative looking-glass. D.C. and C.D. are interchangeable in the same way that Haighta and Hatta of *Through the Looking-Glass* are versions of the Hare and the Hatter in *Wonderland.* The movement from a private textual enclosure that tyrannizes the author to a publicly perceived act of self-consciousness involves a collateral shift from the orphaned child's temporal discontinuity to an authorial patriarchy such that familial political authority is equated with narrative authority. One comes into his own, restores the kingdom, or at least creates an exogamous realm by telling one's own riddle!

II

Sylvie and Bruno commences, as do so many fairy tales, with an act of rebellion or subterfuge that denies apparently innocent children a legitimate inheritance. Although the rebellion has a possible cause in the confused demands of the mob beneath the window, the actual coup itself is not merely bloodless, but is in fact, a textual revolution. The usurpers alter the conditions of the inheritance—surely one of the primary fantasies of all those Victorian prodigal sons—resulting in the reconstruction of the ruling family. It is quite literally a revolution caused by a floating signifier that does not descend from the empyrean, but rather ascends from the floor: "And he picked up from the floor a wandering scrap of manuscript, on which I just caught the words, 'after which Election duly holden the said Sibimet and Tabikat his wife may at their pleasure assume Imperial—' " (*SB,* p. 400). The Warden, about to go into exile with his two children, Sylvie and Bruno, is at pains to show the great zero at the core of meaning. Words function much as do the people who frequent the superficial social gatherings that characterize ruling-class life, insofar as they have only an operative value as placeholders. The social and the linguistic civil servant share the same existential space.

He unrolled a large parchment scroll, and read aloud the words, *"item,* that we will be kind to the poor. The Chancellor worded it for me," he added, glancing at that great Functionary. "I suppose, now, that word *item* has some deep legal meaning?"

"Undoubtedly!" replied the Chancellor, as articulately as he could with a pen between his lips. He was nervously rolling and unrolling several other scrolls, and making room among them for the one the Warden had just handed to him.

(*SB,* p. 402)

Conspiracy and revolution commence with a multiplication of textuality, each of which strives to preserve its own space. Language itself—as well as the politics whose contours it shapes and defines—appears devoid of all meaning. Whatever meanings accrue from linguistic utterance have their origins in operations rather than some a priori value. Meaning comes to in here, as it often does in Carroll's works, in commas and semicolons: in the spaces between words, rather than in the denotative function of words.

This practice, which *Sylvie and Bruno* shares with the *Alice* books, serves to convert these various "texts" into a game, in the ontological sense, much in the manner that the Chancellor recognizes when he greets the conspiracy with the phrase "What a game, oh, what a game!" (*SB,* p. 403). In the *Alice* books, games tend to supplant ritual very quickly, and Alice's helplessness is largely the result of a change in the way in which Alice comes to regard her own development. The ritual fall down the rabbit-hole and the ritual wandering in the labyrinth of linguistic meaning is very quickly transformed into the more defensive experience of the world as a game: croquet games, social occasions as a game (the mad tea-party), chess games, card games. The conversion of all experience into one game or another tends to reduce meaning to a question of learning operational rules, of course. Alice continues to lose, because she has not learned the rules! But the experience of meaning as a function of learning to play some game obviously has a deeper cultural significance, both for Alice and for the rest of us. The ritual fall into experience in *Alice in Wonderland* can end only when she realizes that all the participants are a pack of cards. That recognition amounts to her conquest of the kingdom of meaning, i.e., she becomes the Queen. After the coronation, she becomes the authoress of her own text: She has earned the right to say, "let's pretend." *Sylvie and Bruno,* by contrast, commences with the disjunction—the revolutionary game that has primarily a textual existence. Sibimet, Tabikat, and Uggug are "winners" of Outland. The remainder of the two-book work is an elaborate attempt to restore prelinguistic ritual to a world increasingly imprisoned by textuality.

The spiritual occasion—an octagenarian afflicted by a vaguely defined "illness of the heart"—suggests that narratively *Sylvie and Bruno* begins where *Alice in Wonderland* concludes. For it is written from the perspective of an old man (like Carroll himself), immersed in textuality, who in the curious Preface to the first volume establishes a twilight setting for an author who, "perhaps for the last time," speaks to an audience. That Preface both describes how the *Sylvie and Bruno* volumes came to be written (the past) and indicates

Dodgson's plans for the future. He speaks of the "huge unwieldy mass of literature" that only needed "stringing together upon the thread of a story" in order to constitute the book, of his awareness of the chaos that constantly threatened to engulf the project, characterized as it was by random jottings, notes, and ideas: "for the story had to grow out of the incidents, not the incidents out of the story" (*SB*, p. 380). But throughout that Preface, Dodgson is at great pains to talk of the story's *genesis,* of a near obsession with ensuring its *originality,* especially in the light of all the imitations of the *Alice* books. Yet the obsession with originality is balanced, later in the Preface, by his list of future projects, almost all of which are adaptations of other works: a child's Bible; a collection of passages from books other than the Bible; an edition of Shakespeare for girls between the ages of ten and seventeen. And all of these texts are characterized by censorship. None of these works, for Dodgson, are sufficiently reduced to be committed to memory, nor are they sufficiently expurgated to be suitable for children. On the one hand, he establishes originality as a criterion, while simultaneously, in his future projects, he desires to "omit . . . all that seems too difficult" (*SB*, p. 382) in adaptations of classic texts. The desire to reduce any text to bare essentials may be, in fact, a cultural impulse of the nineties. These contradictory, or binary, attributes of textuality are embraced in the same Preface, a document whose authorship was interrupted by a telegram announcing the death of a dear friend.

III

To all of the moral tests ever devised for literature, from Matthew Arnold to Leavis, perhaps the most striking is that of Lewis Carroll in the conclusion of the Preface to *Sylvie and Bruno:* "the possibility of death—if calmly realized, and steadily faced—would be one of the best possible tests as to our going to any scene of amusement being right or wrong." For the aging don, the moral test of good drama is "that we should not dare to live in any scene in which we dare not die" (*SB*, p. 384). Which would suggest, of course, that every individual has a different aesthetic morality, dependent largely upon his ability to project his own death into a given scene. And the threat of death looms large over *Sylvie and Bruno* and *Sylvie and Bruno Concluded* not merely at the level of the plot, with its anxious brooding over Arthur's possible demise, and in the aesthetic considerations of the Preface, but perhaps most importantly in the narrator's "condition." As the story commences, the narrator, who defines himself as "one of those subordinate characters that only turn up when needed for the development of his destiny" (*SB*, p. 391), is en route to seek a cure. His journey will be, like so many pilgrimages, a journey in search of health, as the *voyage imaginaire* of the *Alice* books is replaced by the *voyage de la mal;* the birthday party of children's literature, with its promise of periodic renewal and growth, is replaced by the threat of death as a moral test of life. Arthur Forester, the jaded (and soon to be jilted) physician, begins his course of gerontic therapy at Elveston for the narrator-patient at the same time that the faerie children, Sylvie and Bruno, are dispossessed of Outland. These books are about the difficulties of restoration—to health and to childhood, respectively—and as such they are much more akin to the literature of illness, like *The Magic Mountain,* than they are to Carroll's other achievements.

The narrator and Lady Muriel Orme, Sylvie's counterpart in the real world, first meet in the railway carriage, that mode of conveyance so important to the development of a middle-class reading public—and with it, of the novel. And their initial conversation is, quite literally, over a *book*. She is curious about the relative dispensation of knowledge, wondering whether books or minds contain the greatest quantity of scientific knowledge. "If you mean living minds, I don't think its possible to decide. There is so much written science that no living person has ever *read:* and there is so much *thought-out* Science that hasn't yet been *written*. But, if you mean the whole human race, then I think the *minds* have it: everything recorded in *books,* must have once been in some *mind,* you know" (*SB,* p. 393). It is an argument designed to minimize the importance of the book, just as the discoveries on the narrator's recuperative journey serve to discount the findings of that volume, *Diseases of the Heart,* that we first see him reading. Lady Muriel wishes to mathematically reduce linguistic utterance by a complicated process of *écrasure,* so that the least common multiple of all the minds in the universe contains all the books and the least common denominator of all the books contains all the minds. The result would be the cancellation of every recorded thought, except in the sentence where it is expressed with the greatest intensity, which could thence be committed to memory. It is the textual equivalent of one of Lewis Carroll's own zany inventions, the Nyctograph, né Typhlograph—a device that consisted of a grating of sixteen squares, cut in a card, and of an alphabet of which each letter could be made by drawing lines along the edges of the squares and dots at the corners. The Nyctograph was devised to spare the writer the task of getting out of bed and lighting a lamp when he wanted to commit an idea to paper, but it obviously involved as much labor to shed any light on the subject using the Nyctograph as lighting the lamp did. As Lewis Carroll tried to reduce night thoughts to a coded memory reenforcer, so Lady Muriel desires to reduce all language to a binary system of ratios. The result would be George Steiner's hell and IBM's heaven—the end of the library:

> "Some books would be reduced to blank paper, I'm afraid!" she said.
> "They would. Most libraries would be terribly diminished in *bulk*. But just think what they would gain in *quality.*"
>
> (*SB,* p. 393)

That opening journey by rail to Elveston repeatedly reveals the inadequacy of books either to entertain or to explain. The satire on "railway ghosts" in Chapter 5, "A Beggar's Palace," is a case in point. Lady Muriel carries a book of domestic cookery, yet another one of those increasingly popular late-Victorian instructional manuals, perhaps yet another attempt (punning on the title of a popular late-nineteenth-century cookbook, *The Way to a Man's Heart)* to remedy illnesses of the heart. But Lady Muriel, like Sylvie, her counterpart in "eerie," wants to be entertained, not instructed.

And the conversation quickly turns to the colorless railway ghosts that stalk the popular fiction read by commuters: books wherein "the Murder, comes at page fifteen, and the Wedding, at page forty" (*SB*, p. 408), a vogue that she attributes to steam. Continuing her logic (which in Carroll's oeuvre is usually extended when a pun is misunderstood), the narrator advances the radical idea that improvements in technology in fact constitute a threat to the book. " 'And when we travel by Electricity—if I may venture to develop your theory—we shall have leaflets instead of booklets, and the Murder and the Wedding will come on the same page' " (*SB*, p. 408). Long before Marshall McLuhan or Denys Thompson, the narrator is, of course, elaborating a relationship between the speed of conveyance, the reading public, and an incipient threat to the book. As communication media increase their efficiency with respect to speed, the quantum of leisure time—in whose lacunae we read—is progressively lessened. Textuality becomes increasingly shortened, so that thought and image occur simultaneously; the lineality of the book gives way to the abbreviated simultaneity of the pamphlet. The book is made progressively obsolete, not merely by virtue of "colorless ghosts" but in terms of the very limits of textuality.

Those affected most by the tyranny of the text in the *Sylvie and Bruno* books are the various academics whom we meet: the Professor and his double, "His Adiposity the Baron Doppelgeist," both of whom use texts to evaluate growth. And of course the doctor, Arthur Forester—who, at least at the outset, uses texts to prescribe a cure, until finally experience of the world forces him to recognize that "his only books [are] woman's looks" (*SB*, p. 469). In the foreground of Dodgson's satire on the academic life is surely consciousness of his own pedagogic limitations: the boring don whose students drew cartoons to amuse themselves during his lectures. But lurking in the background is the subtle awareness of the metaphoric Teuton—the Red Baron of education, and perhaps of politics as well. The immediate target of the satire may well be the child educationalist Friedrich Froebel, who opened his first kindergarten at Blankenburg in the Thuringian Forest in 1837 and ran it according to rather vague philosophical and religious principles that probably owe something to Rousseau. The most important of these seems to have been a belief that little children already possessed innately ideas and skills that it was the function of education to develop by creating an environment such that the flower of childhood might bloom naturally and spontaneously. Because Froebel also was convinced that all living matter shared a unity, the development of the child was to take place in an environment harmonius with nature.[7] The principle of *mens sana in corpore sano* meant that physical growth and mental growth were to take place in synchrony, with an ensuing emphasis upon, say, archery that we see as a feature of Outland. Given the utilitarian bent of British theories of childhood education, Froebel's ideas could be satirized in the way Summerhill might now be satirized.

Surely, Carroll's portrait of the teaching methods at the court of Outland is topical in the extreme: crazy (Outlandish) watches; horizontal barometers that convert the weather to a "readable" text; and the emphasis upon sports.

Professors dwell in a pedagogic garden that they cannot leave.

> So we went into the garden, and soon found the window of the Other Pro-
> fessor's room. It was a ground-floor window, and stood invitingly open: the
> Professor first lifted the two children in, and then he and I climbed in after
> them.
>
> The Other Professor was seated at a table, with a large book open before him,
> on which his forehead was resting: he had clasped his arms round the book, and
> was snoring heavily. "He usually reads like that," the Professor remarked,
> "when the book's very interesting: and then sometimes it's very difficult to
> attend!"
>
> (*SB,* p. 434)

Bruno's solution for the condition of the Other Professor—so "wrapped up in
the book"—is to shut the book, an act that awakens the pedagogue, prompt-
ing him to return the volume to its place in a bookshelf. Throughout *Sylvie
and Bruno,* salvation appears to lie in the denial of textuality; the professor
embracing the book is implicitly contrasted with Sylvie and Bruno, who put
their arms around each other in their own garden of "eerie," where professors
cannot read: "You see, it's impossible to read *here,* for all my books are in the
house" (*SB,* p. 448). As opposed to being wrapped up in books and writing
poems that never end, the garden of eerie creates its own autonomous, yet
ever-changing, language. In contrast to the compulsion to measure which the
professors carry into everything they do, Sylvie and Bruno come to recognize
that measurement is entirely arbitrary. Anything, including flora and fauna,
may be used as a linguistic yardstick; but it is a language that always speaks
its self. All of nature is a potential text.

> Peering about in this way, I happened to notice a plant with rounded leaves,
> and with queer little holes cut in the middle of several of them. . . .
>
> Then a little thrill of delight ran through me—for I noticed that the holes were
> all arranged so as to form letters; there were three leaves side by side, with "B,"
> "R," "U," marked on them, and after some search I found two more, which
> contained an "N" and an "O."
>
> (*SB,* p. 458)

The garden of eerie, like the univocally chiming world of Gerard Manley
Hopkins, always "selves" with the vocal and visual fingerprint of its creators,
and the children are the first to recognize its arbitrariness.

Yet, beneath the topical satire on pedagogic methodology is a more
intriguing and disturbing phenomenon: the metaphoric Teutonization of
British cultural life in the late nineteenth century. The interest in Schopenhauer's theories of the will, reflected in the aesthetics of so many fin-de-siècle
aesthetes like Ernest Dowson and popularized by George Bernard Shaw in
Man and Superman; the interest in dark, mythic origins of racial consciousness
in the popular "translations" of William Morris; the stylized militarism of
organizations like the Boy Scouts that came to accompany the Pax Brit-
tanica—all seem to be leaking through the portraits of the various German
professors and their herrs who are attracted to and yet threaten the twilight
of Victorian childhood. That realm is, of course, the competing garden of

Sylvie and her Bruno, whose "oo and me" and careless grammar contrasts so starkly with the exaggeratedly precise gutterals and glottals of the "false" mentors. The quiet admiration for the fruits of German "Junker-idealism" obviously extends through the dance of Eleanor Duse, the *blutbruderschaft* of D. H. Lawrence's apocalyptic world; the homoerotic verse of the Edwardians; Conrad's detached Axel Heyst, who reads incessantly; and even unto the inheritors of *Howard's End,* the Schlegels, who bring culture and civilization to a world muddled by Whig materialism. Underlying this pattern is surely a relationship, not entirely clear, between ideas of aesthetic purity, a unifying cultural fascism, and the cult of the child so visible in the propaganda posters of World War I. Perhaps, for the fin-de-siècle mind, the raising of aesthetics to the level of a religion conversely provided religion with an aesthetic justification. For both, a refinement and a purification—elitist at its base—came to govern an art that would evolve into doctrinaire imagism, as well as the poised, aesthetic Christianity that we see in Pater's child heroes like Emerald Uthwart.[8] The intellectual antecedent of T. S. Eliot and Ezra Pound may well be Outland—with its precise, oracular texts and its ruler and teachers who profess by an arbitrary willing—whose self-revelatory quality serves as its own justification. The Other Professor's poem that never ends may well be a preversion of Pound's "Cantos."

Contrasting with this Teutonic textuality in *Sylvie and Bruno* is another world—constantly reversible rather than incrementally progressive—of charm. But the realm of charm, ruled over by the king-as-beggarman, is decidedly a counterculture, having none of the stability of linguistic order.

> The cloud of dust spread itself out through the air, as if it were alive, forming curious shapes that were forever changing into others.
>
> "It makes letters! It makes words!" Bruno whispered, as he clung half-frightened to Sylvie. "Only I *can't* make them out! Read them, Sylvie!"
>
> "I'll try," Sylvie gravely replied. "Wait a minute—if only I could see that word—"
>
> "I should be very ill!" a discordant voice yelled in our ears.
>
> (*SB,* p. 425)

Textuality is directly linked here with illness, much as it was earlier in the narrator's absorption with textbook cures and in Arthur Forester's use of his library as the retreat from romantic confrontation. As the world of eerie stands opposed to that of commonplace, so the mode of discourse, charms, and rituals induced by talismans, stands opposed to written manuals of instruction and direction. Whereas Alice had been most concerned about how she was to get out of the rabbit-hole and return to home and a linguistic order that, though arbitrary, she might understand, the narrator of the *Sylvie and Bruno* books is most interested in how to continue to dwell in the pre-linguistic universe as long as possible. Hence, the pressure tends to be on the extension rather than the contraction of time.

Indeed, throughout *Sylvie and Bruno* there is a great fear that all discourse will collapse into a self-consciousness in which textuality incessantly feeds upon itself without ever arriving at any point that it might embrace as an origin. People begin to communicate with one another in a language that is almost entirely self-referential. All dialogue seems to have its origins in previous utterance, rather than having any real origin itself. The Earl, Lady Muriel Orme's father, speaks the language of Dickens's Pumblechook, apparently without recognizing it: "A child's first view of life . . . is that it is a period to be spent in accumulating portable property" (*SB,* p. 509). Eric Lindon tells the amazed little Bruno, echoing Keats, that pendulums "are not a joy *for ever*" (*SB,* p. 486). On the picnic with Lady Muriel, Arthur Forester, Eric Lindon, and the Earl, the narrator relates the party's mandatory audience at a lecture on the sight of some ruined castle by an architectural historian, probably a disciple of Ruskin, who speaks about a Gothic revival and the need for indistinctness and imperfection in art. Like the Other Professor's perpetual poem, this threatens to be a lecture "of which no man could foresee the end" (*SB,* p. 475).

The sense to be obtained is one of almost constant déjà vu, a world where everything has already been said by someone, a kingdom, to use the narrator's own words, of "the uncanny . . . echo" (*SB,* p. 478): and hence the recurrent images of entropy in *Sylvie and Bruno,* perhaps akin autobiographically to Dodgson's own chronic feelings of ennui and boredom, born out of his excessive literary projects. This fear of the inevitable exhaustion of all language, all meaningful utterance, is, naturally enough, the most visible parameter of the universe of nonsense to which the man devoted himself. Lady Muriel's early challenge to the existence of the library—the fear that all we experience are revisions of previous knowledge or previous experience—finds its echo in the Earl's fear that "To most of us Life and its pleasures seems like a mine that is nearly worked out" (*SB,* p. 541). A world of no originality, but only reincarnations of the same events and the same utterance, replayed by moving watches forward and backward at will, is easily translatable into a universe patterned on the law of reincarnation, which finds its home in the eastward gaze with which the first volume concludes: the "Vishnu-land" of which Arthur Forester speaks, where a Brahmin logos of reincarnation at least gives the individual the opportunity to be freed from self-consciousness. Only then does Eternity come to be based upon the very ennui that is the cause of all the languorous illnesses of the heart that afflict the characters in *Sylvie and Bruno:* " 'The one idea,' the Earl resumed, 'that has seemed to me to overshadow all the rest, is that of *Eternity*—involving, as it seems to do, the necessary exhaustion of all subjects of human interest' " (*SBC,* p. 642). A condition akin to John Barth's "literature of exhaustion" [9]—the impossibility of saying anything *new*—lurks around the gardens and houses of *Sylvie and Bruno,* and the fatigue of the will that afflicts the narrator, the Earl, and Arthur can only be cured by a different vision, which is salvational at its core.

The realm most afflicted by entropy and linguistic self-consciousness in the late works of Lewis Carroll is the religious. Although the triangulated religious debate between Lady Orme, Arthur Forester, and the absent Eric Lindon that concludes the first volume is complex, it surely hinges upon different notions of the relationship between faith, free will, and language. At the two extremes of religious practice to be avoided for Arthur Forester are the aestheticized religion of the nineties on the one hand and the text-bound muscular Christianity that was its antipode.

For Arthur Forester, Lewis Carroll's necessary knight of the new order in *Sylvie and Bruno,* one nineteenth-century theological misjudgment involves the stylization of the child as an art object in a performance, whereas the other involves a prolongation appropriate only to the childhood need for discipline from well-intentioned adults. What is intriguing here is that both these perversions of the need for faith involve a relationship between prolonging or stylizing the "natural" childhood; Lewis Carroll, the man who combined the careers of curate, don, and author of children's books, obviously regards the impulse of the child and the impulse to faith as being closely related. As the Germanic professors struggle to reduce Bruno's faulty grammar to the arbitrary grammar of established texts, so the "lost" Eric Lindon imagines his fall from religion as being a fall into textuality, as he writes to Lady Muriel:

> When, as a child, I first opened my eyes on a Sunday-morning, a feeling of dismal anticipation, which began at least on the Friday, culminated. I knew what was before me, and my wish, if not my word, was "Would God it were evening!" It was no day of rest, but a day of texts, of catechisms (Watts'), of tracts about converted swearers, godly char-women, and edifying deaths of sinners saved. . . .
>
> The Church-Service was a veritable wilderness of Zin. I wandered in it, pitching the tabernacle of my thoughts on the lining of the square family-pew, the fidgets of my small brothers, and the horror of knowing that, on the Monday, I should have to write out, from memory, jottings of the rambling, disconnected sermon, which might have any text but its own, and to stand or fall by the result. . . .

(SB, p. 531)

IV

The entire burden of the second volume is that of converting the autocratic tyranny of the text—whether used for establishing fictitious constitutions for Outland, falsely restrictive education for children, inadequate medical cures, or the perversion of religious faith—into a world based upon *acts.* Only in that way can the distances, discontinuities, and emotional detachments that characterized the first volume be overcome. *Sylvie and Bruno* presents the reader with an environment where so many of the dwellers believe, to borrow from Bruno himself, that "the world was made for oo to talk in" (*SBC,* p. 552), a place where Arthur Forester "give[s] the whole day to his books" (*SB,* p. 486). *Sylvie and Bruno Concluded* on the other hand is the necessary sequel to the law of the word, the dominance of contracts, the realm of the verbal covenant. *Sylvie and Bruno Concluded* is a sequel to *Sylvie and Bruno* in the same way that the New Testament is a sequel to the Old Testament, with an emphasis upon spirit rather than letter. It may well be a sort of preversion of that Bible for children that Carroll had mentioned in his plans for future projects in the Preface to *Sylvie and Bruno.* The sequel is not a book about exile and wandering, but about the birth of the child into *this* world (not merely the realm of "eerie"), and it has its basis in example rather than in command, edicts, or texts. Little wonder that Dodgson chose December 25, 1893 as the date of its publication. Its landscape is not that of begging and a fallen garden, but rather that of selfless service to the poor followed by Arthur Forester's resurrection, in which both children and adults share—that *concordia discors* that is the necessary sequel to the perspiring agony of illness in exile. The opening chapter of *Sylvie and Bruno Concluded* commences with the narrator still afflicted by the agony of the heart that has now assumed epidemic proportions, insofar as it now afflicts his doctor as well. But the second chapter, "Love's Curfew," attempts to overturn the textual basis for a marriage agreement by making a subtle distinction between an unfulfilled promise—originally made in good faith, but now threatened by changed circumstances—and an intentional deception. Lady Orme feels herself bound to Eric Lindon by a previous betrothal, and feels that breaking off the engagement would be morally wrong. Although relieved by the narrator's argument that in fact she "is entirely free to act as now seems right" (*SBC,* p. 558), Muriel Orme nonetheless wants the narrator to quote a text that would "prove it wrong" (*SBC,* p. 556) to act out of love rather than duty.

Gradually, however, she comes to understand that there are no texts for determining the relative claims of love and duty, that promises may, in fact, involve claims—and hence involve the appropriation of an obligation—but love never does. The distinction is a crucial one. Throughout the first book, learning, moral behavior, affection had been regarded in terms of choices. There is a correct and an incorrect grammar for poor Bruno. Sylvie must choose which amulet she desires—the one inscribed "All will love Sylvie" or the reverse side bearing the epigraph "Sylvie will love all." The choice of the right "key" for unlocking the secrets of the garden or of making the right wish is, of course, the dilemma posed at the outset of so many fairy tales, part of the allegory of right and wrong options. There is a rightful ruler and a group of pretenders to the embattled throne of Outland. One is either an initiate to the charms of "eerie" or must remain forever outside its perennial visitations, the victim of the myth. The first volume is highly symmetrical in just the way that Jean Gattégno has suggested,[10] with its sets of structural and moral correspondences: Muriel corresponding to Sylvie; Mein Herr to the Professor; Arthur to the narrator; Eric to Sibimet (both dispossessed at the conclusion of the second book). But this binary universe, perhaps a reflection of the so-called Christian world of Victorian England, is gradually overturned in *Sylvie and Bruno Concluded* by a recognition of the principle of "sameness within difference": "The whole scene now returned vividly to my memory; and, to make this repetition of it stranger still, there was the same old man, whom I remembered seeing so roughly ordered off, by the Station-Master, to make room for his titled passenger. The same, but 'with a difference': no longer tottering feebly along the platform, but actually seated at Lady Muriel's side, and in conversation with her!" (*SBC,* p. 554). This recognition of sameness within difference is, of course, the process by which metaphor is unveiled, and suggests to the narrator (if not to critics of the *Sylvie and*

Bruno books) the metaphoric nature of a language that is always conditional. Resemblance, repetition, and twinning replace a categorical universe.

The either/or configuration of *Sylvie and Bruno,* with its incessant categorization and positing of moral choices and repressed wishes is overturned by a recognition of the intersubjectivity of different "worlds"; misunderstandings result from the attempt to find correspondences between and among worlds that are unique: " 'Bruno's World!' I pondered. 'Yes, I suppose every child has a world of his own—and every man, too, for the matter of that. I wonder if that's the cause for all the misunderstanding there is in Life?' " (*SBC,* p. 567). Although each world is to a certain extent unique, it is nonetheless potentially inclusive, so long as one avoids the tyranny of regarding language as absolute. The crucial analogy for the second volume is Mein Herr's inversion of the Professor's library in the earlier book: the riddle of Fortunatus's Purse. By combining two handkerchiefs by knots so as to join the four edges of an outer surface to the four edges of a circular opening, Mein Herr creates an "outer" surface entirely continuous with an "inner": "The dear old man beamed upon her, with a jolly smile, looking more exactly like the Professor than ever. 'Don't you see, my child—I should say Miladi? Whatever is *inside* the Purse is *outside* it; and whatever is *outside* it, is *inside* it. So you have all the wealth of the world in that leetle Purse!' " (*SBC,* p. 584). In what could be almost an allegory of Lewis Carroll's career, riddles, puzzles, and aphorisms come to replace (or at least to suggest the limits of) language. Lady Muriel, Arthur Forester, even the narrator must all come to the realization of the lovely moral of Chapter 7: "Unlimited wealth can only be attained by doing things *in the wrong way*" (*SBC,* p. 583), and the Fortunatus Purse—the nineteenth-century equivalent of Borges's labyrinths, which invert the standard relationships between inner and outer—becomes the emblem of a world over an abyss induced by the opacity of language.

> The Earl was listening with a slightly incredulous smile. "Why cannot you explain the process?" he enquired.
>
> Mein Herr was ready with a quite answerable reason. "Because you have no words, in your language, to convey the ideas which are needed. I could explain it in—in—but you would not understand it!"
>
> (*SBC,* p. 584)

There is a necessity to regress beyond all those gaps, commas, and white spaces of discontinuity that continually threaten growth in Lewis Carroll's works; only then does fairy life come to be merged with real life. Only after comprehending the riddle of Fortunatus's Purse can the narrator experience the world of "eerie" without the necessity of dreaming, at the hands of the great Dr. Forester. And Lady Muriel Orme recognizes that Heaven is not a transcendent goal, but an immanent condition. "Lady Muriel clasped her hands, and gazed up into the cloudless sky, with a look which I had often seen in Sylvie's eyes. 'I feel as if it had begun for *me,*' she almost whispered. 'I feel as if *I* were one of the happy children, whom He bid them bring near to Him, though the people would have kept them back' " (*SBC,* p. 580). If *Alice in Wonderland* is about the growth of the child from the innocence of a Fall to the "experience" that is a prerequisite for narrative self-consciousness, the *Sylvie and Bruno* books tend to move in the opposite direction: from the self-consciousness of a heart-weary narrator in search of a cure, which turns out to be a heaven coterminal with a perpetual childhood based, not upon allegorical correspondences, but upon the principle of interchangeability. The nature of language is sufficiently arbitrary to produce the "floating signifier"—which forms the basis of so much poststructuralist thought, and which, in *Sylvie and Bruno Concluded,* finally enables Bruno to "correct" one of his teachers, by ascribing an arbitrary meaning, which is nonetheless linear. Whereas wealth had earlier been a corollary of textuality—the usurpers of Outland had merely printed money to augment the state treasury in a time of economic distress—the message of *Sylvie and Bruno Concluded* is the necessity of living in financial and linguistic poverty.

Chapter 9 of *Sylvie and Bruno Concluded* is entitled (prophetically enough) "The Farewell-Party," and it is in the course of that chapter that the sequel takes shape. The narrator, Carroll's surrogate, has been asked by one of the hosts to bring the two children, Sylvie and Bruno, to the tea. It is perhaps comprehensible only as a parody of all those crazy tea parties that recur as the emblem of life's having become a game. Unlike the memorable afternoon picnic party in 1862 that Dodgson shared with the Liddell daughters—giving rise to a whole world of childhood, at least in literature—at this party, alas, the narrator discovers that he has been abandoned by childhood and the children, and in the space of that abandonment opens an even more important fissure, that which separates langue from parole—revealing the disembodied nature of all speech. " 'I'm very sorry,' I said, 'but really it was impossible to bring them with me.' Here I most certainly *meant* to conclude the sentence: and it was with a feeling of utter amazement, which I cannot adequately describe, that I heard myself *going on speaking" (SBC,* p. 592). He comes to believe that the continuing remark is not his own, that language speaks him instead of him speaking language. And gradually, the idea of a constituted narrator replaces the subjective "I" who had been the narrator of the books, with a sense of a schizoid split in the nature of utterance.

At one extreme is that fear of exhausting all language—involving the ultimate impossibility of all utterance. Lady Muriel comments, nostalgically, that "what people talk of as 'the last new song' always recalls to me some tune I have known *as a child" (SBC,* p. 594; italics mine). Associative memory means that nothing is uniquely original, but also that nothing is ever entirely mine. It is the finite linguistic universe, a world undoubtedly filled with terror for Lewis Carroll, "with every possible pun perpetrated" *(SBC,* p. 594). The threat to the Victorian obsession with locating origins could not be more concretely realized than in this challenge to the very notion of original authorship; instead of saying *"What* book shall I write?" the act of authorship involves only retrieval of a circulating language: *"Which* book shall I write?" *(SBC,* p. 594). Only the mentally ill, whose associative memory is not synthetic, can be original, for they have never been deserted by the symbolic circus animals of their youth: "Lady Muriel gave me an approving smile. 'But *lunatics* would always write new books, surely?' She went on. 'They couldn't write the same books over again.' " (*SBC,* p. 594). A mental primitivity becomes the ontic corollary to chronological primitivity for Carroll, as it does for Yeats, who located fool and child in adjacent phases of the moon.

Of course, this is a continuation of the pattern of necessary inversion: Those on the outside of the asylum find themselves in a prison of entropic repetition and those on the inside are the original artists. Only by inverting subject and object, by understanding the puzzle of Fortunatus's Purse or the secret of the child's amulet—"All Will Love Sylvie" and "Sylvie Will Love All" are not choices, but opposite sides of the same coin—can Outland become Elfland and beggar-exile become king. A world without metaphor involves the tyranny of the text, rule by the fiat of minimilization. On the other hand, a world of infinite puns, where all is metaphoric, is a world of linguistic kinship in which all objects are potentially other objects. All utterance is a version of previous utterance. Discourse breeds only other discourse, as language becomes akin to a Leibnitzian monad in its combination of reflection and self-reflexion. Between these two extremes, Carroll locates the hope for stability in the principle of "sameness within difference," the notion that language is part of a binary set of relationships and proportions. He attempts to achieve the possibility of a transcendent language in Chapter 16 of *Sylvie and Bruno Concluded,* entitled appropriately "Beyond These Voices":

> Now, may not our life a million years hence, have the same relation, to our life now, that the man's life has to the child's? And, just as one might try, all in vain, to express to that child, in the language of bricks and ninepins, the meaning of "politics," so perhaps all those descriptions of Heaven, with its music, and its feasts, and its streets of gold, may be only attempts to describe in *our* words, things for which we *really* have no words at all. Don't you think that, in *your* picture of another life, you are in fact transplanting that child into political life, without making any allowance for his growing up?
>
> (*SBC,* p. 643)

Heaven here is imagined as the limit of metaphor, long before Wallace Stevens was to make the same point in "Sunday Morning." What is most intriguing about the above passage is that Lewis Carroll at last integrates the three themes that have preoccupied him in the *Sylvie and Bruno* books: the relationship of child to man; the relationship of the literal language of necessary texts to metaphoric language; and the relationship of earth to heaven. The writer of children's stories, the linguistic logician, and the curate are all combined: Our life here on earth is to the existence in heaven what the child's summer day is to life itself and what the text (biblical, child's primer, or lecture) is to meaning. Yet, the principle of inversion, of some diachronic likeness within difference, remains: If Lewis Carroll, like Alice, feared the tyrannical boredom of the text sufficiently to diminish its terror by the concentrated attention to drawings and illustrations for both the *Alice* volumes and the *Sylvie and Bruno* volumes, his photographic studies of prepubescent little girls are often dominated by the intrusion of some text, a book rather

(*Top*) Arthur, Amy, Agnes, and Mrs. Hughes; (*bottom*) members of the Dodgson and Murdoch families. (*Courtesy Gernsheim Collection, Humanities Research Center, Univ. of Texas at Austin*)

than a more appropriate doll or toy used by his contemporaries (see the accompanying reproductions of Carroll's photographs of "textualized children"). Children and adults participate in each other's spaces much as do pictures and texts, and the passage from one to another may be imaged as growth or a fall, depending upon perspective.

V

The culminating vision of *Sylvie and Bruno Concluded* is the mission of Dr. Arthur Forester to effect a cure of the strange plague that is sweeping through an impoverished fishing village near Elveston. The weary illness of the heartsick narrator—the psychological manifestation of the spiritual and linguistic exhaustion that is a virtual condition in *Sylvie and Bruno*—has now extended to the physical world. And in order to effect the cure of the kingdom, Arthur Forester must die and be reborn; only in this way can the fatigue of the will, so closely akin to public neurosis, be obliterated. The retreat of the narrator from London to Elveston with which *Sylvie and Bruno* had commenced reaches its culmination when his physician must undergo a similar journey, downward and inward, to death and back again. As the narrator regresses to a symbolic childhood, frequented by the intermittent presence of Sylvie and Bruno, so Arthur Forester immerses himself in financial poverty rather than a kind of chronological poverty, old age. Their joint salvation is brought about by those individuals least resembling them: Eric Lindon, the doctor's rival for the hand of Lady Muriel, and the children, the antithesis of the narrator's aging heart. Only after being saved are we capable of living among those who marry and are given in marriage. As in any journey of salvation to restore health to a blighted kingdom, from the *Canterbury Tales* to *The Waste Land*, rededication through the experience of death and rebirth—the typological continuation of Christ's original healing journey—must be experienced as a public act: in short, as penance.

The verse appended to the Preface to *Sylvie and Bruno*, which serves as a sort of epigraph, are lines taken from "The Rime of the Ancient Mariner":

> Farewell, farewell! but this I tell
> To thee, thou Wedding-Guest!
> He prayeth well, who loveth well
> Both man and bird and beast.
> (*SB*, p. 384)

Theology and love both involve an act of charity—of blessing that which is opposite you, but is, in the largest sense, part of you and sharing the same created universe. The narrator, like all those weary old men who fear death above all, must remain outside the marriage, forbidden access to the New Jerusalem that he has located. Carroll's narrator looks forward, of course, to another narrator of an epic journey to effect a cure upon a blighted kingdom, the ultimate father of all our contemporary *textes du senex:* Tiresias of *The Waste Land*—who must steer us past all the blighted social occasions, cultural detritus, and mechanical repetitions of its inhabitants. Yet even he, tormented as is our narrator of the *Sylvie and Bruno* books, remains outside the garden of peace that passeth all understanding. This narrator—like Tiresias, Coleridge's mariner who stoppeth one of three, the Conchis of *The Magus*, and the solitary narrator of Iris Murdoch's *The Sea, The Sea*—shows us the way out. And as we return for one last glimpse of Elfland and the return of the beggar-king, if not the Fisher King, to see the Germanic Professor obsessed with labeling poor Uggug, who has been transformed into a porcupine, the image of that other doctor of fin-de-siècle Vienna comes to mind. The doctor who taught us, only seven years after the appearance of *Sylvie and Bruno Concluded*, that by inducing a dreamlike state of "eerie" and verbalizing it through a process of associative recall, we could reconstruct the conditions of our neuroses and thereby hope to achieve a cure. In the process, all of us—insofar as we are all potential victims of the same neurotic plague—would be saved by the child in us, so that the regression to "eerie" would involve precisely such a redramatization of the fears and joys of childhood.

NOTES

1. Donald Rackin, "Alice's Journey to the End of the Night," *PMLA*, 81 (1966), 313–26.

2. Jacques Derrida, *Of Grammatology*, trans. Gayatri Spivak (Baltimore: Johns Hopkins Univ. Press, 1974), pp. 6–12. Derrida's distinction between writing and speaking language seems particularly appropriate to Carroll's world, in which narrative subjects are constantly engaged in a process of reconstituting themselves.

3. Jan B. Gordon, "The *Alice* Books and the Metaphors of Victorian Childhood," in *Aspects of Alice*, ed. Robert Phillips (Harmondsworth, England: Penguin, 1974), pp. 127–50. In retrospect, the *Alice* books seem less and less convincing as typical Victorian Bildungsromane. Although the quest motif and dream images are utilized, Alice has no companion-confidant on her journey to discovery.

4. All citations given in text from *Alice in Wonderland (AW)*, *Through the Looking-Glass (TLG)*, *Sylvie and Bruno (SB)*, and *Sylvie and Bruno Concluded (SBC)* are from the one-volume edition, *The Works of Lewis Carroll*, ed. Roger Lancelyn Green (London: Hamlyn, 1965).

5. See Edward Said, *Beginnings: Intention and Method* (New York: Basic Books, 1974). In both the *Alice* and the *Sylvie and Bruno* books, the characters as well as the narrator constantly try to recall the beginning as an acceptable origin for the story—an explanation of how we got here as a clue to identity. There is a certain inevitable sadness accompanying the discovery that the beginning from a specific point is a necessary fiction, as equally arbitrary as all the other events.

6. Bruno Bettelheim, *The Uses of Enchantment: The Meaning and Importance of Fairy Tales* (New York: Alfred A. Knopf, 1975). See especially the section entitled "Fairy Tale Versus Myth," pp. 35–41.

7. This Teutonization of British life apparently extended to other disciplines as well. The brief pause in the tradition of British empiricism provided by the so-called neo-Hegelians, T. H. Green and McTaggart, was accompanied by a sudden tilt toward Germany in British foreign policy during the fin de siècle.

8. Of course, the notion of the eternal child as an emblem in Pater, Wilde, Dowson, and other fin-de-siècle authors is part of the convention whereby life was transformed into art, the suppression of the self in order to escape the ravages of "The World as Will and Idea" that we see in so many dandies. The "aesthetic" side of Schopenhauer's thought, Freud's interest in regression in treating hysteria, and the cult of the naughty child in Beardsley and Wilde would seem to have been mutually reinforcing.

9. John Barth, "The Literature of Exhaustion," *Atlantic*, 220, No. 2 (August 1967), pp. 29–34.

10. Jean Gattégno, *Lewis Carroll: Fragments of a Looking-Glass*, trans. Rosemary Sheed (New York: Crowell, 1976); see also the preceding essay in this volume.

The Mathematical-Political Papers of C. L. Dodgson

FRANCINE ABELES

Lewis Carroll's genius expressed itself in numerous modes: in the *Alice* books, of course, and in his other works of imaginative literature, in his letters, in his photographs, occasionally in his drawings, and at times in his professional work as a mathematical logician. Of course his achievements in these areas have, to varying degrees, been widely recognized and discussed, including in this anthology. What has not been widely recognized is that this extraordinary man's genius is apparent in yet another area of sustained interest and achievement for him, the pamphlets he wrote and published at Oxford over a period of many years—pamphlets on anything about which he had a strong opinion, from lawn tennis tournaments to principles of parliamentary representation. In many ways the pamphlets are singular achievements; indeed, his political pamphlets, especially the ones on elections, contain some of his best and most creative mathematical work.

Between March of 1871 and February of 1885, Charles L. Dodgson wrote a set of papers on committee procedures, elections, and ranking processes that are remarkable both politically and mathematically. The work of the earlier period, 1871–76, was motivated by matters of academic governance at Christ Church, Oxford, while that of the later period, 1881–85, dealt with the more global problem of election reform in the United Kingdom. The two sets of papers, although seemingly disparate, are knit together in extraordinary ways and provide the reader with the opportunity to appreciate Dodgson's diverse talents and to follow his thinking as it developed over these years.

I

As an academic member of a college, Dodgson inevitably became involved in

· 195

matters of selection for studentships and readerships, architectural and build-ing plans, and the like.[1] He wrote the first pamphlet, *A Discussion of the Various Methods of Procedure in Conducting Elections* (1873), in connection with the selec-tion of the first appointee to the Lee's Readership in Physics. It contains his "method of marks," a form of cumulative voting in which each elector can assign any quantity of a previously agreed-on total number of votes to any one candidate or to several. When the number of votes permitted each elector equals the number of seats to be filled, the method is the same as the one first adopted by Earl Grey in 1850 for the legislature of Cape Colony and popu-larized by James G. Marshall, a prominent member of the British movement for proportional representation. When the "method of marks" is used, how-ever, it is susceptible to voter manipulation.

> Suppose that in the opinion of a certain elector, the candidates stand in the order a, b, c, d: then his votes may be represented by giving a the number 3, b 2, c 1, d 0.
>
> Hence all that is necessary is that each elector should make out a list of the candidates, arranging them in order of merit. . . . If the elector cannot arrange all in succession he places two or more in a bracket. . . . The tendency of many electors is to give to the favorite candidate the maximum mark and bracket all the rest . . . in order to reduce their chances as much as possible.[2]

So at the outset of his writing on election procedures, Dodgson states his concern for fairness in ranking and for the selection of the best candidate. Complications in using the "method of marks" forced him to reexamine his approach—which he did in the short 1874 pamphlet *Suggestions as to the Best Method of Taking Votes, Where More Than Two Issues Are to Be Voted On.* Here he proposed the use of a first ballot that he hoped would produce an absolute majority for one candidate. Failing this, he recommended that the candidates be compared in pairs. "This course is suggested in the hope that by it one issue may be discovered, which is preferred by a majority to every other taken separately. . . . But no issue can be considered as the absolute winner, unless it has been put up along with every other."[3] For the first time, Dodgson began to consider pair-comparison methods rather than weighted-ranking systems such as the "method of marks." These proposals were used to decide the completion of the belfry, an issue that he was deeply involved with from its inception in December of 1873 to its resolution in June of 1874. Eight architects had been asked to submit designs for the belfry. By June 1874, the Belfry Committee had reduced the number to four who were acceptable. But the Governing Body of Christ Church was sharply divided over them. Using Dodgson's method in the second pamphlet, the Governing Body finally was able to select one of them even though he did not receive a majority of first preference votes. Both of Dodgson's pamphlets appeared at critical moments in the selection processes. In the Preface of the 1874 pamphlet he wrote: "In the immediate prospect of a meeting of the Governing Body, where matters may be debated of very great importance, on which various and conflicting opinions are known to be held, I venture to offer a few suggestions as to the mode of taking votes." And in the Preface to the first pamphlet, dated December 18, 1873, he wrote, "The following paper has been written and printed in great haste." [4] This was only a week before the meeting he attended for the selection of a Senior Student and Reader. Although one cannot with any certainty ascribe meaning to the appearance of the two articles just before these decisive meetings, it seems likely that his need to establish a rational basis for decision making where he felt there would be none was of the utmost importance to him.

The third and the most remarkable pamphlet of this early period, *A Method of Taking Votes on More Than Two Issues,* was published in February 1876, eight days after a heated debate involving a proposed special arrangement for a professor in which Dodgson was clearly in the vocal minority.

An eminent Oxford University scholar, Max Müller, who held the chair in Comparative Philology wanted to be relieved of his teaching duties so that he could devote his time to research interests. He already had been offered a chair at the University of Vienna when Oxford put forward a plan whereby he would be relieved of both his lecturing responsibilities and half his salary. The decision would be made in Convocation where there was known to be an acute difference of opinion. In a broadsheet that he distributed three days prior to that meeting, Dodgson expressed his concern about holding a minority view.

> . . . from the fear of being left in a small, and therefore conspicuous, minority, it seems likely that many of the dissatisfied will abstain from voting, . . . I propose then if thirty names at least are sent to me, by 4 P.M. on Monday, of Members of convocation prepared to vote against this Decree, to print the names I receive, . . . and to circulate the paper. . . . Such a paper would be an assurance to all wishing to vote against the Decree that they will not be singular in doing so.[5]

The protection of minority opinion that he expressed here as only a concern blossomed into a scheme for proportional representation in his writings of the later period. What he did develop in this third pamphlet is a method of ranking candidates with cyclical majorities. In one of many examples, he poses a situation with fifteen electors and four candidates, *a, b, c, d,* where four electors have ranked them in the order *a d b c;* four as *b c d a;* two as *c d a b;* two as *c d b a;* two as *d a c b,* and one as *d b c a.* Dodgson states that the majorities are cyclical in the order *a b c d a*—where each candidate in turn is preferred to the next one. A cyclical majority occurs when *A* is preferred to *B* and *B* is preferred to *C,* but *C* is preferred to *A.* In the opposite sense, an order is acyclic, or transitive, if when the first two conditions hold, *A* is then preferred to *C.* Dodgson constructed a table of those majorities where the number of votes for a candidate is given as the *numerator* of the fraction in the candidate's *column;* the number against him appears as the denominator.[6]

	a	b	c	d
a	—	7/8	9/6	11/4
b	8/7	—	6/9	11/4
c	6/9	9/6	—	7/8
d	4/11	4/11	8/7	—

For example, 7/8 in column 2 means that *b* is preferred to *a* seven times, while *a* is preferred to *b* eight times. He then discusses how many changes of vote each would need in order to win. For any candidate to win, he must be preferred to every other candidate by a majority of the votes. This is known as the Condorcet principle, referring to the work of the Marquis de Condorcet, an eighteenth-century French social scientist and philosopher. So, for *a* to win, he would need six changes: In the first column 6/9 and 4/11 would both become 8/7. For *b* to win, five changes are needed: In column two, 7/8 and 4/11 must each change to 8/7. Similarly, *c* requires two changes—from 6/9 to 8/7 in *c*'s column—while *d* needs just one change, in the last entry of the fourth column. So even though *a* and *b* have a plurality of first-preference votes, neither should be the winner; *d* should. The cyclical order *a b c d a* is obtained from the table of majorities by drawing the majority preferences as a directed graph.

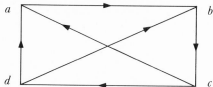

Assuming transitivity, the longest cycle is the path *a b c d a*. Dodgson was genuinely distressed with the effect of cycles on the selection of a winner and wanted to eliminate them. He wrote, "The conclusion I come to is that, in the case of persistent cyclical majorities, there ought to be 'no Election.' " He acknowledged, however, the inevitability of their presence, particularly under open voting and in the course of voter manipulation.

> In any division taken on a pair of issues neither of which you desire, vote against the most popular. There *may* be some one issue which, if all voted according to their real opinion, would beat every other issue when paired against it separately: but, by following this rule, you *may* succeed in getting it beaten *once*, and so prevent it having a clear victory, by introducing a cyclical majority. And this will give, to the issue you desire, a chance it would not otherwise have had.
>
> The advantages of having the preliminary voting taken on paper and not openly are, first, that each elector, not knowing exactly how the others are voting, has less inducement to vote contrary to his real opinion, . . . and cyclical majorities are less likely to occur, . . . and secondly, that if cyclical majorities do *not* occur in this process, they cannot occur in the formal voting except by some one or more of the electors giving votes inconsistent with their written opinions. . . .[7]

Dodgson also proposed two formal steps to eliminate cycles. First, when the candidates have been placed in a maximal cycle, the number of "alterations" of vote, or inversions, each candidate would need to win by a majority must be made known. Then the electors would be allowed to change their votes. Clearly, Dodgson wanted the information exchange to encourage the electors to eliminate the cycle and select the undisputed winner. But in using the inversions, he was really describing a unique ranking of all the candidates based on a probability model that was unknown in his time. This method I have discussed elsewhere and called ranking by inversion, and the model that it anticipated, a maximum-likelihood weak stochastic rank order, was first described by Walter Thompson and Russell Remage, Jr., in 1964.[8]

Dodgson had come quite far in his thinking about selecting the best candidate or issue in a committee process. He had explored different voting schemes—abandoning the Borda type of weighted ranking (i.e., the method of marks) and substituting instead the Condorcet pair-comparison method—and he had settled on a ranking scheme that would work in spite of cyclical majorities.[9] In accomplishing all this, he got involved with other issues that had even broader implications, like minority representation, open voting, and voter manipulation. He had also connected some interesting mathematical ideas like transitivity and a complete ranking that he would explore further in the form of tournaments. Whether the need to supply order to control the emotional outbursts in those heated academic debates was the catalyst that released the creative mathematical-political activity, one cannot actually say. But it is reasonable to suggest that Dodgson was mathematically creative when he was doing mathematics, not for its own sake, but for some other purpose—the whimsy of the *Alice* books, for example, or the academic business of Christ Church. In either case, Dodgson did his best mathematical work in this indirect or hidden way.

II

Perhaps to indicate that the item was not to be taken seriously, *Lawn Tennis Tournaments* was published in 1883 under his pen name, Lewis Carroll. Black considers this short pamphlet to be virtually an isomorphic image of the work on committees and elections.[10] But it is much more than that. By 1876, Dodgson was deeply committed to finding the best way of choosing the winner from a ranked set of candidates in the presence of the inevitable—but, he hoped, minimal—cyclical majorities. In *Lawn Tennis Tournaments,* he extends his view to picking not just the winner but the top three players in a competition. In *A Method of Taking Votes,* he had insisted on pair comparisons of all the issues being voted on. In tournament language, he had worked with a round-robin tournament, the correct setting for ranking all the issues in a list. Dodgson himself establishes the link between voting and playing in the final section of *A Method of Taking Votes.* "This principle of voting [voter manipulation] makes an election more of a game of skill than a real test of the wishes of the electors, . . . I think it desirable that all should know the rule by which this game may be won." [11] The more appropriate tournament for selecting just the first player (the winner) would have been the knockout, or elimination, type. By 1883 he understood this difference. The second section of his pamphlet is entitled "A proof that the present method of assigning prizes is, except in the case of the first prize, entirely unmeaning." What Dodgson succeeded in doing was to present a method—in modern terminology, a triple-elimination tournament—that, although flawed, captured the essence of what was required, at minimum cost. The astonishing part is that the formal analysis of ranking players in a tournament was not yet in existence. This work was initiated by Ernst Zermelo in 1929.[12]

Generally, a tournament is a model of the pair-comparison method. More particularly, a round-robin tournament requires each player to play every other player exactly once, no ties being permitted. For example, for eight players, $\binom{8}{2} = 28$ games are the cost of ranking all of them. For thirty-two players, $\binom{32}{2} = 496$ games are needed, an obvious impracticality. By contrast, a single-elimination (knockout) tournament in which only the winners of a given round advance to the next round requires $8 - 1 = 7$ games for eight players, the winner having won three games in as many rounds with no losses. For thirty-two players, $32 - 1 = 31$ games would have to be played. In a triple-elimination tournament a player is not dropped until he has lost three games. For thirty-two players, $32(3) - \binom{4}{2} = 90$ games are needed. To cut the cost still further, Dodgson recommends that some of the games be virtual rather than actual, i.e., he assumes that the tournament is transitive, so that if player A beats player B and player B beats player C, then player A scores a win against player C without actually playing a game with C.

In Dodgson's tennis tournament, sixty-one games are actual and twenty-nine are virtual, for a total of ninety games. But transitive tournaments are not very likely to occur. A transitive tournament can make the competition dull, while too many cycles can impair its quality. He tried to make his scheme more credible by pairing the players, after the initial random draw, according to the number of superiors each has: I.e., unbeaten players are paired, then those who have lost just one game, etc. Wherever possible, pairing players who have both been beaten by the same player is avoided. As H. A. David points out, the only chance element in the tournament is the initial draw. Afterward, the stronger (by reputation) always defeats the weaker one.[13] This is its flaw. The strengths of the scheme are in reducing the number of games required and in guaranteeing a unique ranking (no ties), banishing that anathema to a proper rank order: cyclical majorities. In a transitive tournament there are no cycles, i.e., no intransitive triples, and there is a unique complete ranking that corresponds to the ranking obtained by the score sequence (of games won). By combining transitivity and triple elimination, Dodgson achieves a proper ranking for the top three players with the least number of games played.[14] In a sense, he has reached a rather elusive goal: He has defined in an ideal way just what a proper ranking is, as opposed to the consensus ranking in the earlier papers on elections and committees, and he's done it at minimal cost. The idealization of the ranking frees it from voter manipulation, of both the strategic-voting and the political-pressure varieties.

More generally, there are two types of preference theories: a prescriptive type that assumes that a rational person must behave in a particular way, which presupposes that his preferences will be transitive, and a descriptive type that recognizes that preferences are more often not transitive. Dodgson's affinity for the prescriptive type is apparent in the justification he offers for his approach.

> Let it not be supposed that, in thus preparing to make these Tournaments a game of pure skill (like chess) instead of a game of mixed skill and chance (like whist), I am altogether eliminating the element of luck, and making it possible to predict the prize-winners. . . . Let us compare the two systems, as to the attractions they hold out to (say) the 5th best player in a Tournament of 32, with 3 prizes. The present system says, "If you play up to your reputation, your chance of a prize is about 1/4th, and even if, by great luck and painstaking, you play 2nd or 3rd best, it never rises above a half." My system says, "It is admitted that, if you play up to your reputation, you will get nothing: but, if you play 2nd or 3rd best, you are certain of the proper prize." [15]

He will use these notions of ideal order at minimal cost again in his game-theoretic development of proportional representation. As Black has pointed out, game theory was not officially invented until 1928.[16] Similarly, the formal analysis of ranking more than the winner in a tournament, but stopping short of a complete ranking, was not actively studied until the 1950s and 1960s.

III

In a sequence of three articles, Black has analyzed the game-theoretic aspect of the theory of proportional representation that Dodgson presented in *The Principles of Parliamentary Representation,* published in November 1884.[17] Black is quick to point out that his interpretation of Dodgson's work as a two-person zero-sum game utilizing a maximin criterion is not immediate from Dodgson's own writing, primarily because of the hidden nature of Dodgson's argument.[18] In the table below, for example, if five members are to be returned, 34 percent of the vote is needed to fill two seats.

Members / district	Seats to fill					
	1	2	3	4	5	6
1	51					
2	34	67				
3	26	51	76			
4	21	41	61	81		
5	17	34	51	67	84	
6	15	29	43	58	72	86

Percentage of the vote needed

How did Dodgson construct the table? The entries are generated by the expression $x > se/(m + 1)$, where x is the number of votes needed for election; s is the number of seats a party wants to fill; m is the number of members (representatives) assigned to the district; and e is the number of voters in that district, each having one vote.[19] So in Dodgson's theory of proportional representation, a political party is entitled to as many seats as it has Droop quotas (the quota $e/(m + 1)$, first advocated by H. R. Droop in the pamphlet *On Methods of Electing Representatives* in 1868.[20] An optimal strategy to fill s seats is to let s candidates stand and to divide the available vote evenly among them. Actually, Dodgson presented a generalized version of the table in his pamphlet, allowing a voter to have more than one vote, but not permitting cumulative voting. A system like this depends on each party having almost complete knowledge of its own voter support and that of its opponent. (The two political parties are the Tories and the Liberals.) More to the point, each party must be able to guarantee a specific distribution of its vote among its candidates. Prior to the Ballot Act of 1872, a political party was able to poll to within 5 percent of its pledged vote with the help of open voting. After an election, printed lists of voters and how each had cast his votes were available. From his diary entries of June 28 and July 8, 1872, we see that Dodgson was very interested in the bill that was to mandate secret voting in conducting the general elections. He attended the debates in both the House of Commons and the House of Lords, the only time he did so. The secret ballot removed some of the social influences on voter behavior. At the same time, it promoted strategic voting by removing accountability. His dilemma was to devise a method that would produce the proper outcome in these new circumstances.

The setting for his ideas has as a backdrop the Reform Acts of 1832, 1867, and 1884. One- and two-member constituencies were the rule—with each elector having as many votes as there were contested seats, but without his being able to give a candidate more than one vote. Voting in general elections took place over several days. Some results of the general elections for the 658-member House of Commons for these years are given in the table below.[21]

Year	Number of constituencies	Number of constituencies returning n members			
		$n = 1$	2	3	4
1830	379	106	270	–	3
1832	401	153	270	7	1
1868	420	196	211	12	1
1880	422	196	211	12	1

It is important to understand the meaning Dodgson gave to unrepresented electors. Although he did not define representation directly, he did provide a definition of the number of electors that are unrepresented. If a political party wants to fill s seats and polls more votes than needed, but not enough to fill $s + 1$ seats, then the number of electors corresponding to the excess number of votes is unrepresented.

The similarity between this theory and the idealization of a proper ranking in *Lawn Tennis Tournaments* is remarkable. In the former, it is as if voter support were the equivalent of representation, while in the latter, player reputation is the guarantee of the game outcome. Support and reputation are, in a sense, prior orders; representation and outcome are the proper results.

IV

Dodgson's concern for minority representation was not just an outgrowth of his own feeling for being in a minority. The Reform Bills of 1832 and 1867 had extended the franchise to merchants and industrial workers, but in a way that did not increase representation fairly. The spectrum ranged from forty-two members of Parliament representing one-quarter of a million voters to forty-three members representing about six and three-quarter million. The disparity affected the larger urban areas of the north most. In 1884, Prime Minister William Gladstone promised a redistribution of seats (passed in June 1885), one of two electoral reforms. The other, the third Reform Act of December 1884, gave the vote to agricultural workers and miners. So again, Dodgson was putting together pamphlets in response to an immediate external need. However, the personal element cannot be discounted, as illustrated by his letters and diary entries during this time.

> *Diary entry:* May 17 (W). 1882. The question came on in the Governing Body Meeting, as to a mode of taking votes for the "Electoral Board." . . . I proposed a scheme, devised while lying awake at night, the principle object of which was to enable a minority to get *one* member in. . . . My scheme was not even seconded. . . . My belief is that the rejected method would be more just, in the interest of *minorities*.[22]

Dodgson's need to impose order where he feared there would be none shows itself in a letter he wrote on "The Purity of Election" to the *St. James's Gazette,* published on May 4, 1881.

> . . . So long as general elections are conducted as at present we shall be liable to oscillations of political power, like those of 1874 and 1880, but of ever-increasing violence—one Parliament wholly at the mercy of one political party, the next wholly at the mercy of the other—while the Government of the hour, joyfully hastening to undo all that its predecessors have done, will wield a majority so immense that the fate of every question will be foredoomed, and debate will be a farce; in one word, we shall be a nation living from hand to mouth, and with no settled principle—an army whose only marching orders will be "Right about face!"[23]

The source of that fear becomes transparently obvious in a letter he wrote on "Parliamentary Elections" that appeared in the *St. James's Gazette* on July 5, 1884.

> The question, how to arrange our constituencies and conduct our Parliamentary elections so as to make the House of Commons, as far as possible, a true index of the state of opinion in the nation it professes to represent, is surely equal in importance to any that the present generation has had to settle. And the leap

in the dark, which we seem about to take in a sudden and vast extension of the franchise, would be robbed of half its terrors could we feel assured that each political party will be duly represented in the next Parliament, so that every side of a question will get a fair hearing.[24]

His remedy is clear. First, determine what "proper" political representation is. Then incorporate it into a fair apportionment scheme, one that does not leave dense population areas shortchanged. Finally, ensure that the procedures are carried out free of contaminating social influences. In his letter on "The Purity of Election," Dodgson proposed that at the end of each day's voting, the votes should be sealed. This proposal was eventually adopted by Parliament, but not until 1917.

The apportionment scheme that he developed has two parts. In the first part, he determines the quota that is due each constituency. He then shows how the number of seats determined by that quota should be alloted to the candidates at the conclusion of the election. We will argue that in that first part he constructed a method similar to one first mentioned in embryonic form by Thomas Jefferson and independently formulated by the Belgian mathematician Victor D'Hondt in 1882, and that in the second part he used an assignment method based on coalition game strategy that developed naturally both from the early work on elections, committees, and ranking and from his thinking about tournaments.

Dodgson's theory of apportionment directly reflects his theory of unrepresented electors. . . . "if 'r' be the number of recorded votes, and 'm' the number of Members to be returned, the quota must be greater than $r/(m + 1)$. For example, if 55,000 votes had to be given, and the District had to return 6 Members the quota needed to return one Member would be just greater than 7,857 and 1/7th, i.e. a member having 7,858 votes, would be returned. . . .[25] The expression, $r/(m + 1)$, is the Droop quota that he used in his theory of proportional representation. The assignment of seats according to quota requires a way to decide how to apportion seats to fractions of that quota. Exact quota, the number of electors divided by the number of seats, was used by Thomas Hare in a pamphlet published in 1859, *The Election of Representatives, Parliamentary and Municipal.* The modified Hare system, in which the Droop quota was used in lieu of exact quota, was very popular among British proportional representationalists. But Dodgson thought about the apportionment problem somewhat differently. He considered a generalized Droop quota $E/(M + D)$, given by the integer just greater than the number of electors E divided by the number of seats M plus the number of districts D in the constituency. We call this Dodgson's quota. He thought that each district should have $e/(m + 1)$ representatives, with one member as a minimum. Just as a district can elect as many members as it has Droop quotas, so an apportionment can assign as many members to a district as it has Dodgson quotas. To establish the uniform quota needed for the apportionment he argued,

Let "e_1" be the number of Electors in District No. 1, "e_2" the number in No. 2, and so on; Let "m_1" be the number of Members assigned to District No. 1, "m_2"

the number assigned to No. 2, and so on; also let "E" be the total number of Electors in the Kingdom, "M" the number of members in the House and "D" the number of Districts. Then we have

$$(m_1 + 1)Q = e_1$$

$$(m_2 + 1)Q = e_2$$

$$. . .$$

$$\therefore (M + D)Q = E, \text{ i.e. } Q = E / M + D$$

$$\therefore m = e\left(\frac{M + D}{E}\right) - 1 \text{ [Dodgson 1884, 10]}.$$

We illustrate this: Consider a country or state with four districts that has twenty-six seats to be assigned and 26,000 electors.

District	Electors	Exact quota	EQ	Droop quota	PQ	Dodgson's quota	DQ
A	9061	9.06	9	9.41	9	9.45	10
B	7179	7.18	7	7.46	7	7.28	7
C	5259	5.26	5	5.46	5	5.07	5
D	4501	4.50	5	4.67	5	4.19	4
	26000	26.00	26	27.00	26	25.99	26

Three quota methods of apportionment

An apportionment based on exact quota is given by $m_i = e_i (M / E)$ for the ith district. If a Droop quota is used, the assignment is given by

$$m_i = e_i \frac{1}{\left\lceil \dfrac{E}{M + 1} \right\rceil}.$$

Basing the apportionment on Dodgson's quota we have

$$m_i = \left(e_i \frac{1}{\left\lceil \dfrac{E}{M + D} \right\rceil}\right) - 1.$$

Ordinary rounding rules, used in the exact quota, EQ, and Droop quota, PQ apportionments if applied to Dodgson's quota would produce 9 seats for District A and a total of one less than the 26 seats to be distributed. That seat is assigned by the size of the remainders to the first district.[26]

Clearly, Dodgson's method deviates from quota in the ordinary sense. He attempted to substitute something other than exact quota or a Droop quota as a basis for apportionment. (Apportionment with the Droop quota ensured that a party with more than half the votes won at least half the seats.) Analyzing his equation, we can write

$$m_i + 1 = Me_i / E + De_i / E$$

The first term on the right is an exact quota for apportioning members by the number of votes. The second term on the right can also be considered an exact quota, but for apportioning *districts* according to the number of voters. Perhaps the term *doubly proportional representation* best describes what Dodgson intended. The district quota measures the adequacy of district size in terms of the number of votes in the district. One indicates ideal size; an entry greater than one shows that a district is too large; an entry less than one, a district too small. The value of the district quota measures the degree of oversize or undersize. Obviously, Dodgson is very much concerned with the state of unfairness of representation, i.e., a range from approximately one representative per 6,000 votes to one member for 157,000 votes. His deep sense of fairness probably motivated his search for a more equitable quota, but it does not explain why he thought that the Droop quota, itself a fair quota, could be reduced still further and still allot the right number of seats.

Another method of apportionment—unfamiliar in England, although described in two pamphlets in 1882 and 1885—had been formulated by D'Hondt working at the University of Ghent.[27] The method is known in modern apportionment literature as the Jefferson or D'Hondt or greatest-divisors method. E. V. Huntington of the Harvard University mathematics faculty gave it its descriptive name. Between 1920 and 1928 he had begun an extensive analysis of apportionment methods using pair-comparison methods and the measurement of the "amount of inequality" between two states. D'Hondt's algorithm for the greatest-divisors method is illustrated below for the data of the previous example.[28]

Divisor	Votes			
1	9061.0 [1]	7179.0 [2]	5259.0 [3]	4501.0 [5]
2	4350.5 [4]	3589.5 [6]	2629.5 [8]	2250.5 [11]
3	3020.3 [7]	2393.0 [9]	1753.0 [14]	1500.3 [16]
4	2265.3 [10]	1794.8 [13]	1314.8 [18]	1125.3 [22]
5	1812.2 [12]	1435.8 [17]	1051.8 [23]	900.2
6	1510.2 [15]	1196.5 [20]	876.5	
7	1294.4 [19]	1025.6 [24]		
8	1132.6 [21]	897.4		
9	1006.8 [25]			
10	906.1 [26]			
11	823.7			

The apportionment is 10, 7, 5, 4: the same as Dodgson's. The greatest divisor is 906.1, the last number of votes that earns a seat. The numerals give the order of assignment of those seats. Dodgson's divisor is 867, too small to be considered a greatest divisor, which for this example could be any number greater than 900.2 and less than or equal to 906.1. Curiously, Dodgson's rounding of his quota was not the ordinary one of rounding to the next integer, but much more generous. In one example he gives $E/(M + D) = 36,000,000/840$, about 43,000 [1884,13]—which suggests that he wanted a larger quota. His method does produce the same apportionment as the recursively obtained greatest divisor in the D'Hondt algorithm, provided that m_i

> 0 for all districts i. Both methods tend to overrepresent large districts and to underrepresent small ones when compared to exact quota. If q_i is exact quota for the ith district, then for large districts,

$$\lfloor q_i \rfloor \leq \lfloor m_i \rfloor \leq \lfloor q_i \rfloor + 1$$

while for small districts,

$$\lfloor q_i \rfloor \leq \lfloor m_i \rfloor + 1 \leq \lfloor q_i \rfloor + 1$$

The apportionment given by greatest divisors is the strictest of the proportional methods for a list system, because if any list wins a seat for a given number of votes (quota), all other lists will win at least the number of seats as the multiple of that quota contained in its vote. It is better than the modified Hare system, which guarantees only that a party polling more than half the votes wins more than half the seats when the number of seats is odd. The significance of the overrepresentation given to large districts in Dodgson's system is that these are the districts where minorities have the greatest possibility for representation by forming coalitions. Dodgson actually envisioned districts with three to five representatives. "The conclusion is that *the* important point is to have as few single-Member, and even as few 2-Member, Districts as possible; but that, when we have got as far as to Districts returning 4 or 5 Members each, it is hardly worthwhile to go further." [29] Recently, Michel Balinski and Peyton Young proved that (among other important characteristics) the method of greatest divisors encourages coalitions in the sense that if two groups form a coalition, the apportionment will allocate to the coalition at least the number of seats that it would allocate to the separate groups.[30] Although he does not comment on it, it seems almost certain that Dodgson understood the strength of his approach for forming coalitions.

V

Dodgson refuted the stand taken by the Proportional Representation Society, which advocated a voter preference order and a transferable vote in the order of preference from a candidate with a surplus to the next preferred. In its place Dodgson suggested two methods, both involving coalitions. He writes in the *Supplement*:

> It is also obvious that it will often happen to a candidate to poll more votes than he needs, and the question arises, how are the spare votes to be utilized? . . .

Let a constituency have to return 3 Members, and let 5 candidates stand, 3 liberals, 1 Independent Liberal and 1 Conservative.

Let 11999 voting-papers be filled up as follows:—

Chamberlain	4	4	2	1	4	—
Gladstone	1	2	1	2	2	—
Goschen	3	3	4	4	1	—
Hartington	2	1	3	3	3	—
Northcote	—	—	—	—	—	1
Nos. of papers	3030	2980	2020	1100	790	2079

... Gladstone, Hartington and Chamberlain ought to be returned, since there are 6010 electors who put Gladstone and Hartington as their first two favorites and, over and above them, 3120 who put Gladstone and Chamberlain as their first two.

. . . .

... May I, in conclusion, point out that the method advocated in my pamphlet (where each elector names one candidate only, and the candidates themselves can, after the numbers are announced, club their votes, so as to bring in others besides those already announced as returned) would be at once perfectly simple and perfectly equitable in its result? [31]

In his first solution to the problem, he considered each of the six voting orders as a player in a weighted majority coalition game. In such a game, a coalition wins if its combined vote contains at least a Droop quota. Clearly player 1 wins (3030 votes) without forming a coalition with player 2 (2980 votes), but the coalition is much more compelling with 6010 votes. If each player is really a segment of a district, the goal is to bring in the three most preferred candidates for the district as a whole. So if players 3 and 4 form a coalition, their 3120 votes will be enough to guarantee their first two choices, Gladstone and Chamberlain. Gladstone and Hartington are the top two choices for the first coalition. So Gladstone, Hartington, and Chamberlain are returned.

Dodgson's preferred approach is to avoid the voters' preference orders altogether, letting the candidates themselves determine the outcome. This approach is very much in the spirit of permitting electors to change votes (to eliminate cyclical majorities), which he had discussed in his 1876 pamphlet. The coalition game too has its roots in the early work on ranking where Dodgson had rejected a plurality of first-preference votes as a basis for choosing a winner, opting instead for a consensus ranking based on inversion. Ranking by inversion cannot be used here, however, because there is, not one, but two essential ingredients for a ranking: the quota and the size of the vote.

In the three pamphlets on elections and committees, the one on tournaments, and the pamphlet plus the supplementary material on general elections, Dodgson showed a grasp on the intuitive level, of ideas that did not begin to be formalized until the 1920s. The work is all the more unusual because of the integrity of its development, with many political, mathematical, and personal interconnections. The suggestion that the work on general elections really consists of two different theories of proportional representation [32] can now be dismissed, and I hope that the reader will come away from this essay with a much deeper appreciation of the abilities of this extraordinary man.

NOTES

1. A fellowship is the modern equivalent of a studentship, while a readership denotes a faculty position below the rank of professor. Dodgson became involved in studentship selection in March 1871, with the printing of a broadsheet on the subject. His diary entries of June 7 and 15 of that year indicate that he retained that interest—one of many that led to the 1873 pamphlet.

2. C. L. Dodgson, *A Discussion of the Various Methods of Procedure in Conducting Elections,* rpt. in Duncan Black's *The Theory of Committees and Elections* (London: Cambridge Univ. Press, 1958), p. 221. All of the pamphlets discussed in this essay are printed in full as an appendix to Black's book.

3. Ibid., pp. 223–24.

4. Ibid., pp. 201, 206.

5. Ibid., p. 210.

6. Ibid., pp. 228–29.

7. Ibid., pp. 230, 233.

8. Francine Abeles, "Ranking by Inversion: A Note on C. L. Dodgson," *Historia Mathematica,* 6 (1979), 310–17.

9. Jean-Charles de Borda was an eighteenth-century military man.

10. Duncan Black, "Lewis Carroll and the Cambridge Mathematical School of P.R.; Arthur Cohen and Edith Denman," *Public Choice,* 8 (1970), 1–28.

11. Black, *Committees and Elections,* pp. 232–33.

12. Dodgson undoubtedly had access to earlier work on the subject of tournaments, e.g., W. A. Whitworth's article in *Messenger of Mathematics* (1878) and possibly M. Reisz's work on round-robin scheduling (1859; in German).

13. In the one example Dodgson offers, there is a single exception, in the third round.

14. In a double-elimination tournament for thirty-two players, $32(2) - \binom{3}{2} = 61$ games are necessary to rank the first two players. Dodgson's scheme permits the ranking of the top three players with the same number of (actual) games needed to rank the top two. His single example has just one player eliminated in two virtual and one actual game; all others require at least two real game losses.

15. C. L. Dodgson, "Lawn Tennis Tournaments [1883], in *The Complete Works of Lewis Carroll* (New York: Vintage [Modern Library], 1976), p. 1210.

16. Black, "Lewis Carroll and the Cambridge Mathematical School," p. 1.

17. Black's 1970 essay, "Lewis Carroll and the Cambridge Mathematical School of P.R.," has already been cited. The other two articles are "The Central Argument in Lewis Carroll's *The Principles of Parliamentary Representation,*" *Papers on Non-Market Decision Making,* 3 (1967), 1–17, and "Lewis Carroll and the Theory of Games," *American Economic Review,* 59 (1969), 206–15.

18. A two-person zero-sum game is one in which one party's gain is the other's loss. A maximin criterion is operative when one party chooses as its strategy the best of the worst outcomes.

19. C. L. Dodgson, *The Principles of Parliamentary Representation* (London: Harrison and Sons, 1884), p. 21.

20. H. R. Droop, *On Methods of Electing Representatives* (London: Macmillan, 1868). The Droop quota is calculated by adding one to the quotient and then disregarding fractions.

21. J. C. Mitchell, "Electoral Strategy under Open Voting: Evidence from England 1832–1880," *Public Choice*, 28 (1976), 33.

22. Black, "Lewis Carroll and the Cambridge Mathematical School," p. 3.

23. Stuart Dodgson Collingwood, *The Life and Letters of Lewis Carroll* (New York: Century, 1899; rpt. Detroit: Gale, 1967), pp. 233–34.

24. Ibid., p. 234.

25. C. L. Dodgson, *The Principles of Parliamentary Representation,* p. 28.

26. The number of seats allocated to the ith district is $[m_i]$ or $[m_i + 1]$, where $[m^i]$ is the *lower quota* or largest integer less than or equal to m_i.

27. The greatest-divisors method had been fully described in 1863 in an obscure pamphlet entitled *Methode, bei jeder Art von Wahlen so wohl der Mehrheit als den Minderheiten die ihrer Stärke entsprechende Zahl von Vertretern zu sichern,* by G. Burnitz and G. Varrentrapp, published in Frankfurt.

28. V. D'Hondt, *La Répresentation Proportionelles des Partis par un Électeur* (Frankfurt, 1886; rpt. Ghent, 1978).

29. Dodgson, *Principles,* p. 26.

30. M. L. Balinski and H. P. Young, "Criteria for Proportional Representation," *Operations Research,* 27 (1979), 80–95.

31. C. L. Dodgson, *The Principles of Parliamentary Representation: Supplement* (Oxford, 1885), pp. 4–5, 7.

32. Black, "Lewis Carroll and the Cambridge Mathematical School," p. 36.

Notes on Contributors

FRANCINE ABELES is Professor of Mathematics and head of the graduate mathematics program at Kean College of New Jersey, and the author of several articles on Dodgson's mathematics. She lives in Manhattan.

ANN MCGARRITY BUKI works at the Institute for Scientific Information in Philadelphia. As a graduate student at Temple University, she published an article entitled "Charlie Chaplin in *Finnegans Wake*" in *A Wake Newsletter.*

MORTON N. COHEN is the editor of the two-volume *Letters of Lewis Carroll,* and the author of numerous essays on Carroll's life and art. He has also written books on H. Rider Haggard and Rudyard Kipling, as well as fiction, and was formerly Professor of English at the City College and Graduate School of the City University of New York.

NINA DEMUROVA is Professor of English and American Literature at Lenin State Pedagogical Institute in Moscow. The author of one book on Lewis Carroll and another on eighteenth- and nineteenth-century children's literature, she is also recognized as a literary translator of distinction; her translations of the *Alice* books into Russian have received wide critical acclaim.

ROBERT DUPREE currently teaches English at the University of Dallas. He is the author of a book on the poetry of Allen Tate, and is completing a study of Lewis Carroll and modern education.

JEAN GATTÉGNO is Professor of English at the University of Paris—VIII. He has published two books on Lewis Carroll, a critical study and a biography, as well as translations of Carroll's work, and a critical study of Charles Dickens.

JAN B. GORDON is a senior lecturer in English literature at Singapore's National University. His previous work on Lewis Carroll includes an essay, "The *Alice* Books and the Metaphors of Victorian Childhood," that appeared in *Aspects of Alice.*

EDWARD GUILIANO, editor of *Lewis Carroll Observed* and author of *Lewis Carroll: An Annotated International Bibliography,* teaches English at the New York Institute of Technology. He is also the editor of *Dickens Annual Studies: Essays on Victorian Fiction,* and is completing a critical edition of Charles Dickens's major novels.

MICHAEL HANCHER teaches English at the University of Minnesota, where he is co-editor of *Centrum*. He has published an essay on Humpty Dumpty's use of language, as well as articles on literary theory, speech-act theory, and Robert Browning.

ROGER B. HENKLE is Professor and Chairman of English at Brown University. He is the editor of *Novel: A Forum on Fiction*, and author of *Comedy and Culture: England 1820–1900* and *Reading the Novel: An Introduction to the Techniques of Interpreting Fiction*.

RICHARD KELLY, Director of Graduate Studies in English at the University of Tennessee, Knoxville, is the author of a critical biography of Lewis Carroll and *Douglas Jerrold*, editor of *The Best of Mr. Punch: The Humorous Writings of Douglas Jerrold*, and co-editor of *Great Cartoonists of 19th Century Punch*.

JANIS LULL has published poetry in numerous magazines and is a doctoral candidate in literary theory at the University of Minnesota.

TERRY OTTEN is Professor and Chairman of English at Wittenberg University, Springfield, Ohio. He is the author of *The Deserted Stage: The Search for Dramatic Form in Nineteenth-Century England* and the forthcoming *After Innocence: Visions of the Fall of Man in Modern Literature*.

DONALD RACKIN is the author of numerous articles on Lewis Carroll, including "Alice's Journey to the End of Night," and editor of *Alice's Adventures in Wonderland: A Critical Handbook*. He has been Professor of English at Temple University since 1962.

JEFFREY STERN is the director of a firm of antiquarian booksellers in York, England. He completed his doctorate at the University of York, and has subsequently edited *Lewis Carroll's Library*.

Index

January 27, 1982, marked the 150th anniversary of the birth of Charles Lutwidge Dodgson—the eccentric, brilliant, paradoxical, proper, and fascinating Victorian clergyman who, as Lewis Carroll, wrote the incomparable *Alice in Wonderland* and *Through the Looking-Glass*. A century and a half later, interest in the man has never been greater, or his work more popular.

This collection of fifteen original essays, written especially for this occasion by distinguished Carrollian authorities from around the world, including Morton Cohen, Roger Henkle, Donald Rackin, Jean Gattégno, and Edward Guiliano, celebrates the many aspects of Carroll's life and art. Not only are there new insights on "the most inexhaustible tale in the world" —the *Alice* books—but also into *The Hunting of the Snark*, the *Sylvie and Bruno* books, and his intriguing but neglected mathematical-political pamphlets. Additional essays explore Carroll's relationships with his contemporaries Ellen Terry and John Tenniel, his influence on James Joyce and